ADVANCE PRAISE

"A fantastic resource that reveals how research informs better teaching practice, presented in the poignant—sometimes mortified—words of real teachers."

Kia Darling-Hammond, PhD

"What does it look like to provide a just and equitable educational experience for all of our students? Through bracing honesty, the authors of this book interrogate their own past practices and share some hard-learned lessons about how to enact justice in the day-to-day work of teaching and learning. This engaging and thought-provoking resource provides real-world strategies for educators and those who train and support educators."

Sola Takahashi
Senior Research Associate
WestEd

"*Mistakes We Have Made: Implications for Social Justice Educators* is an honest and powerful examination of educators' best intentions gone awry and it offers practical advice and suggestions for new and experienced teachers at all levels of classroom experience. The authors' candid and personal vignettes capture the reader immediately and offer opportunities for educators to self-reflect on their own biases, beliefs, and practice. The sound, research-based strategies and resources offered in this text provide solutions for educators to create classrooms grounded in social justice that promote equity for all students. This book is a must-read for anyone in education."

Holli Gonzalez, MBA, MEd
Instructional Specialist, K-8 Science, PLTW & Kern Urban Teacher Residency,
Bakersfield City School District
Adjunct Lecturer, Teacher Education, California State University, Bakersfield

"Practical, timely, but most importantly, this book is written from authentic classroom experiences. *Mistakes We Have Made* is a must-read for new teachers and a refreshing perspective for veteran teachers alike."

Edward González, EdD
Bakersfield City School District Teacher and Community Speaker

MISTAKES WE
HAVE MADE

Published by Myers Education Press, LLC
P.O. Box 424
Gorham, ME 04038

Myers Education Press is an academic publisher specializing in books, e-books, and digital content in the field of education. All of our books are subjected to a rigorous peer review process and produced in compliance with the standards of the Council on Library and Information Resources.

LIBRARY OF CONGRESS CATALOGING-IN-PUBLICATION DATA AVAILABLE FROM LIBRARY OF CONGRESS
13-digit ISBN 978-1-9755-0236-2 (paperback)
13-digit ISBN 978-1-9755-0235-5 (hard cover)
13-digit ISBN 978-1-9755-0237-9 (library networkable e-edition)
13-digit ISBN 978-1-9755-0238-6 (consumer e-edition)

Printed in the United States of America

All first editions printed on acid-free paper that meets the American National Standards Institute Z39-48 standard.

Books published by Myers Education Press may be purchased at special quantity discount rates for groups, workshops, training organizations, and classroom usage. Please call our customer service department at 1-800-232-0223 for details.

Cover design by Sophie Appel.

Visit us on the web at **www.myersedpress.com** to browse our complete list of titles.

MISTAKES WE HAVE MADE

Implications for
Social Justice Educators

BY BRE EVANS-SANTIAGO

Gorham, Maine

Table of Contents

FOREWORD

Lynnette Mawhinney,
University of Illinois at Chicago

MEDIA IS OFTEN saturated with teacher success stories. Films like *Dangerous Minds* or *Freedom Writers* show the wonders of classroom success through true stories of white women situated to be heroes. Teacher films highlight this idea that what works in these particular classrooms will work for all children and classrooms, negating the nuances and complexities of teaching human beings. Even the films featuring teachers of color are over the top. There is Jaime Escalante outfitted in his chef's outfit and using a butcher's knife chopping apples to teach fractions in *Stand and Deliver* or Joe Clark wielding a bat around school in *Lean on Me*. Media depicts teaching as an over the top, almost flawless practice. Yet, teacher education is not far off from these media depictions. Often, teacher educators will discuss their own success stories championing the idea of "if you do this, you too will be successful." It is an easy trap to fall into, as the "warts and all" perspective is harder to reveal.

As a teacher educator, I have also fallen into this trap at times. It is easy for me to share with preservice teachers how I creatively got Tyrone, my 9th grade class clown, to limit class disruptions by giving him time on Fridays to do a 5-minute stand-up routine in class. On the other hand, I do not easily share how I shudder thinking about a conversation I had with Terrell that did not acknowledge the hardships he had in life. This conversation ended up causing unintentional emotional violence and permanently shut down our relationship. Two days later, Terrell left the school, as his uncle shipped him off to a boarding school—or so we are told. I never got to tell Terrell I am sorry. And yet, it is a conversation that haunts me to this day, but one that I learned the most from in my high school teaching career.

Essentially, the reality is that teaching is a career of ups and downs. The mistakes we make and the bumps in the road are what ultimately shape our teacher identity. This is why this edited volume, *Mistakes We Have Made*, fulfills such a critical need in teacher education. Most of the authorship are new teacher education faculty—fresh voices to lead a new wave of teacher education.

All of the authors are vulnerable and wholeheartedly honest in sharing their mistakes as cautionary tales scaffolded with the wisdom of time, distance, and hindsight around becoming a more refined justice-orientated educator. All of the lessons in these pages are founded on the concept of funds of knowledge. Knowing the students, community, and more importantly, knowledge of self, is vital to teacher development and teacher identity. Through the classroom traumas, righteousness, misunderstanding of cultural norms of communication, misguidance on religious values, stripping away of student identity, imprudent gender norming practices, troubled co-teaching relationships, and even wardrobe malfunctions, *Mistakes We Have Made* pushes readers to think deeply and models how to make mistakes meaningful in reshaping justice-oriented pedagogical practices. This book is a work of action with examples of authentic relationships with student success at the core.

Ultimately, *Mistakes We Have Made* takes a "for us, by us" stance and tells readers of mistakes in order for others to not re-create the same mistakes, but also acknowledging that mistakes happens. Mistakes are an important, if not a critical, part to teacher development. So grab a glass of horchata, sit back, and read this book knowing there is a new revolution of honesty happening in teacher education between these pages.

PREFACE

Not everything that is faced can be changed. But nothing can be changed until it is faced.

—JAMES BALDWIN

I BEGAN THIS project with the intent to "do something cool for new teachers." The more I taught in higher education, the more I wanted to write a book that would impact the future: future educators, future students, future educational equity around the country. The preservice teachers and master's-level teachers will be responsible for so many lives as they take on and continue their teaching careers. As I reflected on my current students, I also thought about all the children who have come into my life throughout the years in PreK–8 settings. Many times, I did a disservice to them in some way from my lack of knowledge about several things: family dynamics, professionalism, biases, and so much more. But hindsight is 20/20.

Some of the experiences I thought about from my past included situations in which students were left out or embarrassed because of my inability to include all of them in my classroom. In the past 19 years, I have gathered more and more knowledge of what is needed to ensure that all students, our students, are receiving an equitable education. My knowledge and skills were obtained through teaching and administrative experiences as well as research. I made mistakes, and I learned from them. I made great choices, and I learned from them. I also learned more about my own identity and how my intersectionality and positionality influence this work. I identify as a cisgender, Black, pansexual female, which heightens my awareness of injustices for marginalized populations. I personally understand how it feels to be judged or mistreated because of my identities, both visible and invisible. I am empathetic for children who receive injustices daily, and I cannot go on knowing I did not try to do something.

As I continuously increase my knowledge of culturally sustaining pedagogies while also gaining a deeper understanding of the injustices our minority children face, I appreciate greats such as Dr. James Banks, Dr. Geneva Gay, Dr. Linda Darling-Hammond, Dr. Gloria Ladson-Billings, Dr. Django Paris, Dr. Nel Noddings, Dr. Cris Mayo, and so many more.

Now, in this edited book, I am responding to my responsibility as a professor. I am not a hero or known researcher. I am not a guru or a know-it-all. I just have what other professors have, and that is experience. But, instead of me just telling my story, I created this space to allow other teacher educators to contribute their stories as well. This book provides a platform for teacher educators to be vulnerable and share their narratives. We want social justice educators to know that, first, it is okay to make mistakes, and, second, do not make the same mistakes we have made. While reading this book, readers should be positioned to reflect on themselves, as if looking into a mirror. Becoming self-aware will provide the platform to reexamine and revise one's own thinking to maintain a better balance of social justice instruction. Thereafter, the chapters are set up to have the opportunity to move forward with social justice influenced actions within the classroom. The experiences and implications are given to help each reader look hypothetically through a window. Readers should begin to see what changes need to be made and feel encouraged to do so by the great contributors within this book.

The book is situated into three themes: inclusive classrooms, curriculum implementation, and professionalism. These themes were created with inspiration from my classroom management course that I teach at California State University, Bakersfield. I believe these components are the most important topics to consider in order to make the biggest impact in the lives of students. Lesson plans and management cannot work successfully without understanding the injustices students may face. I believe the themes provide a foundation that allows the space to expand on specific skills, tools, and knowledge needed to teach successfully anywhere.

Within each theme, there are individual chapters written by various authors that reside throughout the country. The various perspectives and experiences come from teacher educators in California, Kansas, Illinois, North Carolina, and Texas. Each chapter is meant to stand on its own but should definitely not go unread. The vulnerability and meticulous research, coupled with strategies and ideas for success in a social justice classroom, is worth the read. Each chapter concludes with action steps and/or reflection questions to ensure that after reading, the book does not "sit on the shelf."

The journey to create this book involved so many people that helped make it happen. A special thanks to each and every author that made this book possible; your professionalism and knowledge of material are greatly appreciated. A special thanks to Dr. Anni Reinking, who has been a part of my writing process for many years. Not only have we personally grown together, but we also have been reliable partners for our scholarship. I am forever appreciative of your insight and listening ear, and I look forward to many more experiences with you. My family will always be at the top of my list for support. My spouse, Mr. Bobbi Evans-Santiago, is my rock and my joy. His undivided attention to my adventures and work endeavors cannot go unnoticed. I love you so much and thank you for being my strength when I am tired. I appreciate you, Michelle Schwartze for endless editing and support; I have learned so much from you. Thank you, Cindy Cotton, for your time and energy toward indexing. My faculty peers at California State University, Bakersfield deserve recognition for their encouragement, and I could not ask for a better work family! My appreciation also goes to my bro-son, Joshua Santiago. Experiencing motherhood with such a special young child has pushed me even further to ensure that every teacher addresses social justice issues and that all kids receive the education they deserve.

To those families and children I did not serve adequately, I apologize. I have learned from my mistakes and therefore am providing this book for the next generations of teachers in hopes that they will learn from our mistakes and become better social justice educators from the start.

Theme One: Inclusive Classrooms

LEARNING TO SEE AND UNLEARN: BUILDING AUTHENTIC RELATIONSHIPS WITH LATINX IMMIGRANT FAMILIES IN SCHOOL AND RESEARCH SETTINGS

Adam Sawyer and Mirna Troncoso Sawyer

IN THIS CHAPTER, we present through the sharing of our real-life stories and processes of change, recommendations for authentic engagement with immigrant Latinx parents as classroom teachers and researchers. From the perspective of Adam's experience as a Spanish bilingual second-/third-grade teacher in East Palo Alto, California, and Mirna's as a health educator and researcher at an elementary school in Arvin, California, we share our foibles and initial missteps—despite the very best of intentions—and the processes of reflection, unlearning, and acquisition of new constructs which led to better future practices. As educators and researchers, we are committed to serving our students and families as agents of change, but as we learned, such transformation does not come about automatically or easily. We begin our chapter with vignettes of these initial failures and how we longed for tools to support our reflection and perspective.

Over time we came to be aware of the biases and unexamined practices we smuggled into this work and how these practices sabotaged the outcomes we had hoped to attain. Ultimately, we were forced to pose the following questions to ourselves: Are we creating opportunities for the engagement of parents that are welcoming and culturally responsive and that value their unique funds of knowledge? Are we as willing to be as transformed by their wisdom and life experiences as they are by ours? What does true partnership with a diverse group of parents really mean? When we represent the experiences of immigrant Latinx families to the broader public are we inclusive of their knowledge? Is our view the same as their view?

Convivencia, Confianza y Respeto[1]: Tinkering Toward Authentic Partnership with Families in East Palo Alto

Adam Sawyer

It was my first Back-to-School Night as a newly minted first-year teacher, yet all I could do was peer enviously over to Ms. Sáez's second-grade classroom next door. Although I had a very polite and quiet group of about five parents touring my class and leafing through their child's work portfolios, in Ms. Sáez's room, parents, grandparents, aunts and uncles, and children of all ages were so abundant that the crowd flowed out the classroom door. One could also hear the gentle sound of cumbia music and smell the aroma of fresh tamales, posole, and enchiladas as it wafted down the corridor. Ms. Sáez herself gracefully wandered through the receptive crowd, welcoming families and inviting them to partake of the bountiful potluck and to enjoy the student work decorating her walls and the folders on each student's desk.

"Wow, what am I doing wrong!" I wondered to myself. "And more important, what is Ms. Sáez doing right?"

This experience of envy continued into our first student conferences. Although more than half my families did not come at their assigned conference time, once again, Ms. Sáez's room was a mildly festive atmosphere of one family after another taking turns to meet with the *maestra* amid the presence of decoration, food, and a clear buzz.

My first year as Spanish bilingual second-grade teacher in East Palo Alto, California, was full of such experiences and perceptions of failure. Although only a short 40 miles from my hometown of Berkeley, California, the predominantly working-class Latinx immigrant community of East Palo Alto was a world apart from the trappings of my middle-class White Jewish upbringing. Sure, I spoke Spanish, but academic vocabulary and the ability to conjugate the imperfect subjunctive were no substitute for the cultural and sociohistorical knowledge one must possess to be a responsive educator to diverse families.

During the 1990s, East Palo Alto was in flux, undergoing a rapid and tense transition. Although having recovered to some degree from the moniker of "Murder Capital of the U.S.," which it had infamously earned in the 1980s, the town was still economically depressed and experiencing palpable racial tension between its shrinking African American and rapidly growing Latinx immigrant communities. Despite being hard to fathom at the time, the presence of such high-tech entities as Sun Microsystems, Yahoo!, and a small start-up known as Google mere minutes from the city foreshadowed a disparate and hyper-gentrified future.

For decades before the present heyday of Silicon Valley, East Palo Alto was known as a tight-knit but economically challenged African American community unceremoniously divided by Highway 101 from the wealth of Palo Alto, home to Stanford University. As in many parts of California, Great Migration Blacks were drawn to East Palo Alto by the lucrative shipyard economy of wartime California. As was the case, however, in other working-class African American communities in the state, such as South Los Angeles and San Francisco's Hunters Point, the postwar economy—and the closing of the shipyards—had left East Palo Alto behind to a cycle of poverty, struggle, and violence.

Also echoing patterns seen throughout the state, the 1980s and 1990s saw massive growth in migration of primarily Mexican Latinx, drawn to East Palo Alto's affordable rents and local service and agricultural work opportunities. This influx of Spanish-speaking newcomers led to visible tensions with the established African American community as the new group members were seen as competitors for scarce housing, jobs, and other resources while dramatically changing the cultural tapestry of the community.

Although the newly Latinx immigrant community in East Palo Alto drew, to some extent, from throughout Mexico and Central America, the largest subgroup by far hailed from the municipality of Apatzingán in the central-west portion of the state of Michoacán, a low-elevation region known as *la tierra caliente* due to its searing climate. As migration observers have long noted, immigrants from a common community of origin—because of the role social networks have always played in immigrant dispersal—often settle in clusters (Cornelius, 1990; Cornelius & Sawyer, 2008; Jensen & Sawyer, 2013; A. Sawyer, 2014).

Although work opportunities were plentiful in the East Palo Alto area for this community of newcomers, for these families and their children, adjusting to the local life was by no means easy. In addition to the everyday challenges of traversing language and culture, East Palo Alto schools were not well equipped to meet the academic needs of these new arrivals. Similar to inner-city school districts throughout the nation, schools in the Ravenswood Unified School District were notoriously underresourced and had long struggled to meet the academic needs and address the cyclical poverty of its long-standing African American community (Kozol, 1991). Now, meeting the cross-cultural and cross-lingual needs of its immigrant newcomers seemed well beyond the capacity of the cash-strapped district. The net result of these seemingly intractable challenges was an understandably demoralized team of administrators and teachers.

For my part, as a 23-year-old, newly minted teacher, I was brimming with energy and idealism. My impeccably behaved and respectful second-graders and their families also helped to motivate me. Although such factors such as interrupted schooling—or no previous schooling whatsoever—led to a wide array of learning needs, the innocence of childhood coupled by the "immigrant optimism" described so famously by Grace Kao and Marta Tienda (1998) made this group and their parents a joy with whom to work. The one thing holding the group back, in my mind, was me. I felt that I lacked the skills not only to raise my students' skills in English and Spanish but also in harnessing the great power of parent engagement.

Although I made sure to stay clear of the teachers' lounge and other spaces where the demoralized culture of our school might prove infectious, Ms. Sáez's success with parent engagement served as a ray of light despite the ways in which it also made me painfully aware of my shortcomings. I began to spend more and more time hanging around with her before and after school and during recess and lunch to see what I might be able to learn.

Alva Sáez was a native of Peru who had immigrated to the United States 10 years prior due to political and economic instability in her homeland. She hailed from a long line of schoolteachers in her native country, a fact that lent her an air of competence and assuredness as a teacher. In observing her work with children, she was firm and almost stern about the comportment of students yet exuded a warmth and whimsical sense of humor with these children—who, despite strict rules of behavior, seemed wonderfully able to be themselves in her care. Her interactions with parents were similarly warm and welcoming, and they, in turn, demonstrated great respect toward her, a trusted and educated confidante. The needs within the immigrant community were abundant, and parents relied on Ms. Sáez for advice on matters ranging from parenting to immigration law to marriage.

One late afternoon after a long day of school, I said to her, "You are amazingly close to your parents; how do you do it?"

"Adam, you could do it too. But you need to stop expecting them to be what they aren't, and adjust your work to what they are."

I asked her to give me an example.

"Okay, so how do you organize your parent–teacher conferences?" she asked.

"I send home the appointment times provided by the school and expect that they will come at that time."

"Adam, do you know how many jobs some of our parents work and what will happen to them if they skip a shift to come to a parent–teacher conference in the middle of the day?"

"Wow, I never thought of it that way. I guess that my mom could always ask for a bit of time off work to come to my parent–teacher conferences."

"And do you really think that anyone in rural Mexico ever has an appointment exactly at 2:15? What you need to do is have one early afternoon and one evening time frame and have people drop by whenever they can without having a specific appointment. If you're busy with a parent, the other parents can wait. But it's been hot, so make sure to leave out some horchata for everyone to enjoy while they wait!"

Although her plan seemed strange and unconventional, I decided to give it a try. I was blown away by the results. Rather than stewing in frustration at parent no-shows and the empty seat across from me at the parent–teacher conference table, I was treated to long lines of parents, grandparents, and children during both the afternoon and evening sessions. Rather than the disgruntled looks I may have expected from families having to wait long periods to speak to me, everyone seemed merry as they enjoyed their horchata and greeted me with a warm "Buenas tardes, maestro!"

All in all, 17 of my 20 families made it to parent–teacher conferences during that week. The meetings themselves were magical. Rather than fulfilling the assumptions many teachers in our school held of parents indifferent to their children's' education, I met a group of parents who saw education as the main pathway to a better future for their children. "Quiero que mis hijos salgan mejor que yo" (I want my children to have a better life than me) was the refrain I heard over and over. As they shared their aspirations and optimism, I also learned about harrowing migration stories—of perilous journeys through deserts with *coyotes*, of detention by Border Patrol, and of constant fear of deportation. I also heard of struggles in the workplace, of insecure positions, of exploitation by employers, and, in the case of many of the mothers, of sexual harassment and even rape. Amid all these struggles, however, remained a determination and a light of hope, mostly channeled through the better lives they imagined for their children.

Exhausted, exhilarated, and inspired all at once, after the week of parent conferences, I was even more determined not only to deliver on the dreams of these families but to also actively, and responsively, engage them in the life of our classroom. First things first, however, was to see about the three families who did not make it to those parent–teacher conferences.

Recalling an article I had skimmed during one of my credentialing courses, "Funds of Knowledge for Teaching in Latino Households," by Norma Gonzalez et al. (1995), I remembered the text advocating for teacher visits to the homes of their students. "Perhaps, this can be the way I finally connect with those parents I've never met," I thought.

Upon recovering the photocopy from an old binder and giving it a read with new eyes, I discerned the real meaning behind the home visits. Alas, the home visit, according to the authors of this classic text, was intended not only to bridge the distance between teachers and Latinx immigrant families but also to learn of the skills, talents, and knowledge bases of these families as a tool for student learning. Rereading this text was revolutionary for me. Although I had been inundated by the scripts of fellow educators and the media about these families being poor, uneducated, unskilled, and unable to provide much in terms of support to their children's education, the "Funds of Knowledge" (Gonzalez et al., 1995) notion turned this dominant deficit paradigm on its head. My thinking turned to how I could utilize the strengths of my classroom parents to catalyze student learning in the class.

In this quest, I decided to give home visits a shot. Instead of these visits simply being a tool to connect with those three families missing from my parent–teacher conferences (which I undertook, with moderate success), they would be an outreach effort to all my classroom households to gain a deeper understanding of the funds of knowledge possessed within these families.

I cannot stress enough how critical an "assets-based" lens was to these home visits. Rather than focusing on the economic vulnerability and humility of these families, I began to see the wealth within each and every one of these households. I learned, for example, of the indigenous roots and practices of families, such as my student Margarita's Yucatecan origins, which led to her mother's subsequent class visit to teach us to count to 10 in Mayan. There were *mariachi*, *norteño*, and Andean musicians among the fathers, which I later leveraged within music classes and school assemblies. Families shared an abundant knowledge base in areas such as cooking, traditional *curandera* medicinal therapies, raising horses, the proper pruning of rose bushes, and many other topics.

Some parents proved to be muses. One night while enjoying *pupusas, posole, and arroz con leche* with Juan and Beatriz Mendoz —a couple with origins from Michoacán, Mexico (him) and Santa Ana, El Salvador (her), whose daughter,

Linda, later went on to study at an Ivy League university—Beatriz began sharing the ways she recalled parents being involved in Latin American schools:

> Los padres de familia, the parents, would divide up in comités. For example, on día de las madres [Mother's Day] and día del maestro [Teacher Appreciation Day], the comíte social [social committee] would take care of decorating the school, organize the potluck, and coordinate the cleanup. The cooperación was beautiful and built convivencia [mutual coexistence], confianza [trust], and respeto [respect] between the school and the families and between the families themselves.

The wheels in my mind began turning. There were several celebrations and school assemblies throughout the year that I had awkwardly fumbled through all by myself. I *needed* the help. Beatriz's emphasis on *confianza* and *convivencia* also stood out to me. The more meaningful time that teachers and parents spent together, the stronger the bonds of trust and mutual respect would be between home and school. If trust and mutual respect were present, my logic continued, then teachers and immigrant parents could work together as *partners* for the academic success of children.

Recalling that Beatriz had attained a *bachillerato* diploma from a college preparatory high school in El Salvador and had completed several community college courses, I asked whether she might be willing to lead an "Academic Committee."

"You know, several of our students struggle with math and we could use extra sets of hands with our science projects. Having volunteer tutors in the class would help me greatly."

"Maestro, with all due respect," she began, "I would be more than happy to support learning in the class as a volunteer whenever I am able. We padres de familia are always happy to help. We also, however, need to have a seat at the table."

"Doña Beatriz, please explain to me what you mean by that," I interjected.

"Well," she continued, "we do not always agree with school policies, and we'd like to have a voice in how and what is taught to our children."

As a first-year teacher just getting used to the idea of having parents be a daily presence in my classroom, the thought of shared governance seemed almost revolutionary. Nevertheless, this notion is well supported in the academic literature on parent engagement. In a classic framework put forth by Joyce Epstein and Karen Salinas (2004) "Partnering With Families and Communities," the authors put forth a six-prong typology for parent engagement. Although such practices as "communicating and volunteering" are given prominent mention, perhaps the most transformational practice advocated for in the framework is "decision making." This value is defined "to mean a process of partnership, of shared views and actions toward shared goals, not just a power struggle between conflicting ideas" (Epstein, 1995, p. 705). It is one thing for such a notion to be included within an academic article but quite another to put such a value to practice. As teachers, we are used to being in charge and in control. Having the self-confidence and courage to let go of that power and control requires a great act of faith and trust. Moreover, accomplishing such collaborative decision-making processes across differences in language, culture, socioeconomic status, power, and rank adds layers of additional complexity.

I resolved to throw caution to the wind. That spring, I established two parent committees in the classroom, the Social Committee and the Academic Committee. The Social Committee became the organizers of all classroom celebrations for U.S., Mexican, and Salvadoran holidays; birthdays; and school assemblies (See Figure 1.1). The Academic Committee (chaired by Beatriz, of course) took charge of academic support for students and families, organized

FIGURE 1.1
ADAM SAWYER WITH PARENT COMMITTEE MEMBERS CIRCA 1998

parent-led show/tell and lessons, and provided critical input on the class curriculum, instructional methods, and homework policies. For each group, I
recruited five representatives from the class families to convene on at least a
bimonthly basis, and I agreed that these committees would not just provide
classroom service but also serve as bodies for shared classroom governance.
Alas, the foundation of authentic partnership with my classroom families had
now been built, and there was no turning back.

Their Culture, My Culture: A Salvation Vest

Mirna Troncoso Sawyer

> *To break bread with someone means more than only eating; it is also about
> fostering a meaningful connection between and among groups of people. As
> Adam Sawyer described his experience with home visits and getting to know
> families through the process of "breaking bread," it is more than only eating.
> However, the diets of cultures and what is eaten can also have implications
> for experiences and education. Here is Mirna Sawyer's story.*

One day I arrived for a second interview with a parent named Sara (pseudonym). I had just started recruiting parents for my PhD dissertation study at
Grimmway Academy, an elementary school in Arvin, California, that actively
seeks to educate and provide tools for healthy eating for low-income immigrant
communities, and I was eager to meet mothers and chat with them about their
food behaviors. My dissertation was a qualitative study of food decisions—or
how people come to eat the food that they do—of Latinx families within the
context of the food environment in the community, school, workplace, and
home. This topic has risen to importance as concern with the high levels of overweight, obesity, and diabetes within the general population, but especially for
the Latinx population. My aim was to expand on what was known about Latinx
food behaviors using a lens that went beyond the dominant acculturation lens.
Essentially, the acculturation lens posits that people change as they adapt to a
new society—that they become more like people from the dominant culture. A
long line of scholars before me had paved the way with articles (Ayala, Baquero,
& Klinger, 2008; Batis, Hernandez-Barrera, Barquera, Rivera, & Popkin, 2011;

Lara, Gamboa, Kahramanian, Morales, & Hayes Bautista, 2005; Mazur, Marquis, & Jensen, 2003) about how Latinos eat differently if their acculturation (the transfer of customs and values from one culture to another) level is higher or lower. But a fundamental problem with many studies was how acculturation was defined and how it was measured. In other words, the marker of how adapted you are to the new society might be whether you speak more Spanish or English. One inherent problem is that many Latinos maintain both a Latino and an American identity. Given this scenario, the acculturation lens assumes a mutual exclusivity not always matched by reality. I sought—through the gathering of stories from these parents—other, more useful explanatory frameworks for understanding food choices among this population.

Fast-forward to my meeting with Sara. I met Sara at the school on a previous occasion, and we had talked about her family's dinner routine. She had attended a parent cooking class at the Grimmway Academy that I had also assisted as a participant observer. Upon arriving at her house, I asked if she had planned to make beets like she had learned to make at the cooking class. She responded that once in a while, she did try making the meals again but not often because they did not really fit in with the dishes she would normally make. It seemed that the topics of the cooking classes were interesting but not easy to incorporate. Here was my first clue that both the school and I were eager to engage parents but that we did not necessarily utilize methods that truly connected to their daily practices and lives.

During my interview with Sara, I was eager to get to the topic I had come to learn about, so I quickly shifted our conversation to how she had learned how to cook. What came next hit me like a ton of bricks. She began talking about her childhood spent migrating to and from to the United States for seasonal harvest. She would leave school for periods to harvest in the United States and then go back to Mexico. She had a hard time in school because she would miss so much material, she said. I experienced cognitive dissonance because I had not fathomed meeting or talking to someone who actually had been a migrant farmworker or imagined that it might be relevant to understanding food decisions.

Initially, I did not know how to process this. As the offspring of Mexican immigrants, I was familiar with the stories of my parents, uncles, aunts, and even grandparents who had attained no more than a sixth-grade educational level. Many of them had attained no more than a second- or third-grade educational level. My paternal grandfather was born in Anaheim, California, but moved to Mexico as a child, so his educational level mirrored that of Mexicans. He was even paid through the Bracero Program, a diplomatic agreement between the United States and Mexico that ran from 1942 until 1964 and that allowed laborers to come to the United States during World War II with a minimum wage. *Braceros*, as they were called, filled the labor pool while many American men left to wage war in Europe and the Pacific. My grandfather would leave my grandmother and mother, aunts, and uncle in Mexico for long periods to work in the United States. But I had not heard stories of migrant farmer children firsthand.

I was also familiar with the concept of transnationalism. As Robert Courtney Smith (2006) wrote in *Mexican New York*, transnational life emerges from attempts by migrants and their children to live meaningful lives, to gain respect and recognition, within the larger processes of migration from Mexico, on one hand, and assimilation in the United States, on the other. And, as I carefully took notes about how Sara learned to cook and what she cooked regularly, I understood that I was only reaching the surface level with her. Witnessing Sara tell her story, all the while smiling and talking with quiet dignity, was humbling. Most of the stories about farmworkers I heard growing up were about perilous and wretched conditions. Like many other Mexican Americans, I was aware of the United Farm Workers (UFW) and Cesar Chavez's triumphs. But what was one story compared to the many others heard on the news daily or in such novels as *The Grapes of Wrath* (Steinbeck, 1939)? So much had happened in her life, and she was about to share it with me.

Arvin, California, according to the 2010 Census, is home to 19,000 people (U.S. Census, 2019). During my experience conducting field research in Arvin, I quickly learned that many of the Mexican immigrants I spoke to came from the state of Guanajuato, where both my mother and father have roots. In fact, almost anyone who was Spanish-speaking was from Guanajuato. Being an immigrant meant that these women had left one life in Mexico and had come to the United States to make another. I reflected on Abraham Maslow's (1998) hierarchy of needs theory, which reminds us that human beings need to take care of their basic physiological needs before they can address psychological or self-fulfillment needs. Ultimately, as I was interested in the psychology behind food decisions. I began to realize that all the stories I would learn would

be necessary for a true understanding of my topic. How can we truly understand what it means to be first and foremost concerned with one's physiological
needs if we have not experienced the scintillating vulnerability of not having
resources to eat, of not having legal documentation that allows us to be safe?
Perhaps I decided it is through these stories that the Other is no longer the
other. As Ladson-Billings (1998) has argued the primary reason that stories
and counterstories are used in critical race theory is that they add context to
the "objectivity" of positivist perspectives.

Sara's story also pushed me to think about who I was and what I thought
I knew about any of the "Mexicans" I was meeting. I was familiar with Tomas
Jimenez's (2010) work *Replenished Ethnicity* in which he argues that Mexican
American identity and assimilation are shaped by continuous ethnic replen-
ishment due to ongoing flows of immigrants to the United States from Mexico.
Because the context of what it means to be Mexican or Mexican American is always shifting, as a Mexican American teacher, health educator, and researcher,
I was often surprised. The clothing or accents my participants donned were by
no means clear indicators of where they came from or how long they had been
here. In fact, these did not tell me any of the things I was expecting. More than
once I started the conversation in Spanish thinking the person I was recruiting
for an interview was an immigrant only to find they were U.S.-born and vice
versa. I needed to work on being reflexive.

Reflexivity is the conscious use of reflection to analyze our personal biases, views, and motivations to become more self-aware in our interactions
with others (Xerri, 2018). Reflection in practice can be used to improve professional work. For teachers, their practice can be enhanced by reflection on
understanding the process of knowledge construction, both the way we think
about knowledge and knowing (Hofer, 2017). After each interview, I spent time
writing notes about my thoughts and assumptions so that I would later be able
to incorporate them with my field notes. This process helped me face the internal thoughts I was having.

I later interviewed Donna, who invited me over to her house to conduct
an interview while she prepared enchiladas (a classic Mexican dish of chili-
fried tortillas filled with cheese and onion). I was there to understand how she
decided what to make for dinner. And, as I talked with her and sampled her
delicious enchiladas, many different things were going on in her household

that made me feel adrift in the sea. One child needed to read a book to someone, so I volunteered. Her husband and other children came and went—they sat and ate—meanwhile, Donna provided her explanation for why nutrition among second-generation Mexican Americans has declined. She talked about how despite her efforts to maintain a daily family dinner routine, her children still have been Americanized. American fast food, she said, is cheap and readily available. And she shared her own experience in learning to cook, which was so different from her daughter's. The most salient factor was that she stopped going to school in sixth grade and that her only job at that point was to learn to be a homemaker whereas, in the United States, her daughter was required by law to complete high school.

My first reaction to Donna's explanation was that people were not adapting to the new reality. But after considering that what we know and what we believe are mutually constructed and reinforced by society, it dawned on me that Latino immigrants are in a unique cultural conundrum. How can you maintain your cultural practices in a new society where the structures that once supported your ways are no longer there? A social constructivist paradigm, with its premise that knowledge is formed through discussions within groups of people, draws from the work of Vygotsky (1930). Vygotsky's social constructivism holds that knowledge is constructed when people in a given setting talk and share stories of experiences among themselves (Nyika & Murray-Orr, 2017). So through discussions with Donna, I gained respect and compassion for the ways in which immigrants are challenged to maintain their cultural ways. As health educators, teachers, or researchers, we might focus on the absence of a behavior and be irritated by it. Spending time in the home and milieu of our students and parents is essential for a better understanding of how we can support those with whom we work.

Perhaps my cultural background had been the salvation vest that helped me believe that I could reach a population that was absent from the literature. That is, sometimes my culture felt burdensome, as a salvation vest might, yet it gave me the confidence to know that I would not drown but survive eventually. So, when I connected with my participants, so much was unclear and foreign, with symbols misfiring, but between us, we held our Guanajuato connection. Later, I would learn that stories and counterstories are used in critical race theory because by sharing experiences of marginalization, isolation, and othering (McCoy & Rodricks, 2015), we learn how families negotiate these circumstances. As I spent time with my participants, I also dug deeper into my own family's stories of cultural change—the things that had been lost and the things that remained. And later when *"flautas, albondigas, enchiladas, tacos, posole, menudo, lentejas, coctel de camaron"* (Sawyer, Duran, & Wallace, 2019) were featured prominently in an article I published, I felt that I had provided a counterstory. I was not necessarily providing an alternative explanation, but I was providing context and rich detail to elaborate how and what families were eating and why they organized their lives in such a way to do that. Doing so was important for me because up to that point, I really had not read about the foods I grew up eating in the articles I read on nutrition and the food decisions of Latinos. Not only did my participants become real because I had written about them—in my eyes—but I had also become real. And ultimately, as I have described throughout this vignette, stories help us connect with and remind us of our humanity. Our humanity is at the heart of having tolerance for one another, being just and kind, and having gratitude for the ways in which all people have something to contribute to our society.

Conclusion

In this chapter, we have shared two vignettes—one from Adam's experience as a second-/third-grade teacher in East Palo Alto, California, and one from Mirna's role as a health educator and researcher at an elementary school in Arvin, California—that illuminate our efforts to build authentic relationships with Latinx immigrant families. While our professional roles and positionality in relation to the immigrant Latinx community were disparate, our stories yield important common threads. In both cases, shedding unexamined dominant scripts and practices to see our work and the community itself with new eyes was necessary. With this new lens, we were able to see the perspectives and lived experiences of these families as valuable assets and to attain greater levels of depth and trust in our relationships with them. In the process, we gained a heightened sense of awareness and were reminded of the importance of being reflexive in our practice as educators and researchers.

As teachers and researchers engaging with diverse families, a good rule of thumb is to assess whether a practice we are conducting is working, and if it is not, why? The reflection questions that follow will help you think about the current engagement practices. You may want to partner with a colleague as you consider these questions.

Reflection Questions

1. *What kinds of opportunities for the engagement of parents are you using? In what ways are these opportunities you are using welcoming? In what ways can you make these opportunities more welcoming? In what ways are these opportunities you are using culturally responsive? In what ways are these opportunities valuing families' unique funds of knowledge? In what ways can you make these opportunities more valuable?*

2. *How are you shaped by the wisdom and life experiences of the families and children you work with? Discuss one example.*

3. *Are you currently partnering with diverse parents for school activities? If not, how might that be possible?*

4. *In what ways is your research or practice inclusive of the knowledge of the families and students you work with?*

5. *Are parents excited to participate in your research/classroom activities? Why is that? If not, do you know why?*

6. *What are your biggest obstacles to your research/classroom practice with this community? And how can you learn from those obstacles?*

Note

1. Within Mexico and other parts of the Spanish-speaking world, the term *convivencia* possesses connotations that go well above and beyond the literal English

translation of "coexistence." In the presence of convivencia, actors bond, mutually accommodate, and expansively accept one another in profound and meaningful ways necessary for the instilling of confianza (trust) and respeto (mutual respect).

References

Ayala, G. X., Baquero, B., & Klinger, S. (2008). A systematic review of the relationship between acculturation and diet among Latinos in the United States: Implications for future research. *Journal of the American Dietetic Association, 108*, 1330–1344.

Batis, C., Hernandez-Barrera, L., Barquera, S., Rivera, J. A., & Popkin, B. (2011). Food acculturation drives dietary differences among Mexicans, Mexican Americans, and non-Hispanic Whites. *The Journal of Nutrition, 141*, 1898–1901.

Cornelius, W. C. (1990). *Labor migration to the United States: Development outcomes and alternatives in Mexican sending communities* (Working Paper No. 38). Washington, DC: U.S. Commission for the Study of International Migration and Cooperative Economic Development.

Cornelius, W. C., & Sawyer, A. (2008, March 25). *Does migration impact educational mobility? Evidence from a Oaxacan sending community and its U.S. satellites.* Paper presented at the 2008 Annual Meeting of the American Educational Association, New York, NY.

Epstein, J. (1995). School/family/community partnerships: Caring for the children we share. *Phi Delta Kappan, 76*, 701–712.

Epstein, J., & Salinas, K. (2004). Partnering with families and communities. *Educational Leadership, 61*(8), 12–18.

Gonzalez, N., Moll, L. C., Floyd Tenery, M., Rivera, A., Rendon, P., Gonzalez, R., & Amanti, C. (1995). Funds of knowledge for teaching in Latino households. *Urban Education, 29*, 443–470.

Hofer, B. K. (2017). Shaping the epistemology of teacher practice through reflection and reflexivity, *Educational Psychologist, 52*, 299–306. doi:10.1080/00461520.2017.1355247

Jensen, B. T., & Sawyer, A. (Eds.). (2013). *Regarding Educación: Mexican-American schooling, immigration and binational improvement.* New York, NY: Teachers College Press.

Jimenez, T. (2010). *Replenished ethnicity. Mexican Americans, immigration, and identity.* Berkeley: University of California Press.

Kao, G., & Tienda, M. (1995). Optimism and achievement: The educational performance of immigrant youth. *Social Science Quarterly, 76*(1), 1–19.

Kozol, J. (1991). *Savage inequalities: Children in America's schools.* New York, NY: Crown Publishing.

Ladson-Billings, G. (1998). Just what is critical race theory and what's it doing in a nice field like education? *Qualitative Studies in Education, 11*(1), 7–24.

Lara, M., Gamboa, M., Kahramanian, M. I., Morales, L. S., & Hayes Bautista, D. E. (2005). Acculturation and Latino health in the United States: A review of the literature. *Annual Review of Public Health, 26,* 367–397.

Maslow, A. H. (1998). *Toward a psychology of being.* New York, NY: J. Wiley & Sons.

Mazur, R. E., Marquis, G. S., & Jensen, H. H. (2003). Diet and food insufficiency among Hispanic youths: Acculturation and socioeconomic factors in the third National Health and Nutrition Examination Survey. *The American Journal of Clinical Nutrition, 78,* 1120–1127.

McCoy, D. L., & Rodricks, D. J. (2015). Critical race theory. *ASHE Higher Education Report, 41*(3), 1–117. https://doi-org.libproxy.csun.edu/10.1002/aehe.20021

Nyika, L., & Murray-Orr, A. (2017). Critical race theory–social constructivist bricolage: A health-promoting schools research methodology. *Health Education Journal, 76,* 432–441.

Sawyer, A. (2014). Is money enough? The effect of migrant remittances on parent educational aspirations and youth educational attainment in southern Mexico. *International Migration Review, 50,* 231-266.

Sawyer, M. T., Duran, N., & Wallace, S. P. (2019). Exploring food decision processes of Latino families in California's Central Valley. *Californian Journal of Health Promotion, 1*(17), 31–34.

Smith, R.C. (2006). *Mexican New York: Translational Worlds of New Immigrants.* Berkeley: University of California Press.

Steinbeck, J. (1939). *The Grapes of Wrath.* New York City, NY: Viking Books.

U.S. Census. (2019). Arvin City, California. Retrieved from www.census.gov/quickfacts/arvincitycalifornia

Vygotsky, (1930). *Mind and society.* Boston, MA: Harvard University Press.

Xerri, X. (2018). Two methodological challenges for teacher-researchers: Reflexivity and trustworthiness. *The Clearing House: A Journal of Educational Strategies, Issues and Ideas, 91*(1), 37–41, doi:10.1080/00098655.2017.1371549

CHAPTER TWO

Engaging Students Through Universal Design for Learning

Jay C. Percell

Some of my former high school teacher colleagues and I had the opportunity to attend the 10-year reunion of one class of our former students. It was quite an honor. The members of this class had invited several of their most influential teachers to be present at their reunion festivities to celebrate and reconnect with them 10 years later. Truly, it was one of the more gratifying and vindicating experiences of my career, and selfishly, it proved to be just as much of a reunion for my colleagues and me as it was for our former students.

Nevertheless, it was a wonderful evening, with familiar face after familiar face gushing and recounting wonderful and meaningful moments from the past—moments of learning that had endured for a decade, all of which were born out of our former classrooms. It was very moving and the type of emotional reward that I hope every single teacher experiences at some point in his or her career. Yet during the overflow of positive reminiscing, moving from circle to circle of former students and colleagues, I noticed one of my former students, Brandon Williams (pseudonym), who was rather standoffish toward me. His disconnect seemed out of place, one, because of the overwhelmingly positive responses all around and, two, because Brandon had been in my class for 2 years and he would have undoubtedly recalled our experience together.

The evening proceeded, and after a change of venue to a second establishment, I crossed paths with Brandon in a circle of his friends once again. Possibly aided by some evening libations, Brandon finally chose to speak to me. "You know what, man?" he said to me. "Do you want to know the truth?"

"Yes," I replied earnestly. Finally, the truth, I thought.

"The truth is I hated your class," he said, "every single day of it."

Ouch. Scathing criticism to be sure, but being so contrary to the positivity I had been hearing from others all evening, it was almost welcome. I only had one question.

"Why, Brandon?" I asked.

"Because you made me write sentences every day, over and over again, and I hated it."

Upon hearing these words, it was as if a time warp opened in my memory and I was whisked back 10 years. I remembered Brandon, then, struggling to construct sentences, his grammatical structure lacking and his penmanship abysmal. And what he was saying was true. I remembered forcing him to redo and rewrite sentence after sentence, paragraph after paragraph. In fact, the reason Brandon had been with me for 2 years was that he had failed my class the first time, and he had barely passed the second. Thinking back, I was shocked at how inflexible I had once been as a classroom teacher.

A Framework to Overcome Barriers

In that moment, how drastically I had failed Brandon as his teacher was clear, and it was a powerful lesson for me, albeit 10 years too late. The exchange motivated me to return to my preservice teacher candidates and implore them not to make the same mistakes I had. "Do as I say, not as I did," I wanted to tell them. I renewed my mission to fill future teachers' toolboxes with strategies to connect with future Brandons out there and engage students presently to foster a lasting love of learning.

One framework that I offer them that could have truly benefited my instruction is the Universal Design for Learning (UDL) framework. Conceived by David Rose, Ann Myer, and the Center for Applied Special Technologies (CAST), UDL is an instructional design framework to represent ideas, content, and production in the classroom to accommodate a diverse array of learners (Meyer, Rose, & Gordon, 2014). UDL is a framework that seeks to overcome barriers to learning by presenting content in multiple ways and through multiple means to engage a wide array of learners. UDL is governed by three main principles: multiple means of representation, multiple means of engagement, and multiple means of action and expression. Taken together, these principles work to provide students a measure of choice regarding the ways in which they demonstrate their understanding. Instruction designed according to UDL engages students of every ability and schema, allowing them an element of control and power over their learning, all while appealing to their individual interests and strengths.

Multiple Means of Representation

The first principle in the UDL framework is *multiple means of representation*. With a foundation based on neuroscience research, this principle represents the *what* of the learning process (CAST, 2018). So often, teachers can inadvertently fall into a trap of representing their content to students in just one way. Perhaps it is because that is the way they understand it best or, more likely, that is the way in which it was taught to them. However, all learners are not the same, and UDL provides a framework for teachers to diversify how concepts are represented in their classrooms.

My fallback example for my teacher candidates is often an objective from physical education: kicking a soccer ball with the inside part of the foot. When I ask how they will represent this concept, their immediate response is typical: demonstrate—I will demonstrate kicking the soccer ball with the inside part of the foot. "Perfect," I tell them. "Now, how else will you represent the concept?" Perhaps they show a video compilation of professional soccer players kicking the ball with the inside part of their foot. Making use of multimedia tools is an excellent way to represent concepts as multiple means. Or perhaps they invite members of the girls' soccer team to come to class and demonstrate kicking the ball with the inside part of the foot. Although still demonstration, inviting content-area experts, such as the girls' soccer team, is also a way to foster multiple means of engagement (Anderson, 2017). Concepts presented from someone other than the teacher, especially content-area experts—such as the girls' soccer team—can appeal to students in a fresh way that is different from hearing the same teacher-based instruction.

Outside of physical education, I challenge candidates across all disciplines to imagine how they would represent big ideas in multiple ways. Imagine a miniature me standing on your shoulder, I tell them, and each time you present a concept, hear my voice saying, "Great! Now, how else will you represent this?"

Once they get the hang of it, my candidates are often able to capitalize on representing their content through multiple means. The trick is to avoid remaining solely in this first principle and drilling down into the *what* of learning at the expense of the other two principles, the *why* and the *how* of learning.

Multiple Means of Action and Expression

The second principle of UDL is multiple *means of action and expression*, the *how* of learning (CAST, 2018). Instructional designs incorporating this principle offer students options for how they demonstrate their knowledge of a certain subject matter. Oftentimes, teachers may provide a list of choices for ways in which students may complete a project, or they may be allowed to select their own. Offering students opportunities to choose their products is another way to engage them in the learning process and illicit student buy-in. Building student choice into class instruction may take the form of projects, assignments, or daily class activities.

One assignment I give my teacher candidates is to try to design a project for their students to complete that is structured as a "dinner menu." Elements of the project may be broken down into categories: appetizers, entrees, desserts, and sides, with a list of several items to choose from in each category. In this way, students' final projects will be individually tailored to their interests. In addition to specific assignments or projects, whole units or projects can be designed using UDL to allow students a measure of choice as to how they present information.

Nevertheless, just as some teachers may occasionally find themselves in a rut regarding the *what* of learning, focusing too narrowly on the *how* of learning is equally dangerous. Particularly in subjects that prioritize procedural fluency, students may come away with a strong sense of *how* to solve a problem or accomplish a task without actually knowing *what* they are doing. The three UDL principles operate best when taken together rather than in isolation from one to another (Mizerny, 2019).

Multiple Means of Engagement

Finally, *multiple means of engagement*, the *why* of learning, is the third and final UDL principle (CAST, 2018). This principle is one that students and teachers both crave—the knowledge that the work they are engaged in has valuable, lasting benefits and does not solely exist in a vacuum. Instructionally, this could take the form of collaborative assignments—not the age-old "group work" students loathe, mind you, but course work that is shared and collaboratively generative. It could be assignments that are student-driven and student-led. It could be instruction delivered from guest speakers or from virtual tours. Any range of instructional elements could fall into the category of engagement, as long as they provide students with a sense of curiosity, wonder, and purpose. Essentially, to establish that students are fully comprehending the *why* of their learning is to never hear them ask, "Why are we doing this?"

Challenges to Incorporating UDL

As simple as the three UDL principles may seem, they do not necessarily come without some inherent challenges. In addition to being intentional about the design of instruction from the outset, other challenges to incorporating UDL are confusing it with differentiated instruction and being willing to shift the locus of control in the classroom from the teacher to the students.

UDL Versus DI

Differentiated instruction (DI) is a well-known and credible framework to adapt learning to students' individual needs (Tomlinson, 1999). As it has been promoted so widely, I often hear teachers and/or teacher candidates defaulting to DI models when attempting to accommodate for diverse learning needs among students. The DI framework attempts to account for each individual difference and requires the teacher to interface with each learner in unique ways. Although admirable and sometimes effective, differentiating for such a diverse array of individual students' needs can be a daunting task for teachers and, ultimately, remains a teacher-centered approach.

Instead, teachers may choose to rely on UDL, whereby they will be designing instruction to meet the needs of a wide range of diverse learners from the outset in a more comprehensive and holistic manner. Although the two frameworks, DI and UDL, do have some overlap, there are also some distinctive differences. Novak (2017) draws a clear analogy of a dinner party to establish these differences. Essentially, UDL is a pre-instructional design strategy that is student-centered in its allotment for student choice based on their preferred learning styles, backgrounds, and interests.

Shifting the Locus of Control

Another challenge to incorporating UDL is the shifting of the locus of control in the classroom. In an inherently student-centered framework such as UDL, some measure of control over the learning and potentially the class direction will be given over to the students. Although empowering for the students, this can also be uncomfortable for teachers—especially teachers who have been trained to maintain strict control of the classroom environment or those who view themselves as the ultimate authority in the classroom. Teachers who embrace such educational philosophies will have to make some compromises to employ the UDL framework. It necessitates teachers who are comfortable in their role as a guide in the learning process as opposed to the fountain of knowledge or control.

Conclusion

UDL is built on a foundation of research, and the framework continues to make inroads into mainstream school curriculum throughout the country. Teachers who choose to take up the mantle of UDL and begin to design their instruction to incorporate the three guiding principles—multiple means of representation, multiple means of action and expression, and multiple means of engagement—can create powerful learning environments where students are afforded the opportunity to dissolve barriers to their learning. Incorporating UDL requires an intentionality in lesson design and a willingness to allow students to take ownership of their learning. Teachers must be flexible and adaptable, as well as nuanced enough to act as a copilots through the curriculum while the students do the driving, unlike how I conducted myself as an emergent teacher.

> *My experience at the class reunion allowed me to vividly recall my teaching infancy, particularly my interactions with Brandon. I suppose I had fallen prey to the adage that relentlessly rigid instruction was intended for the students' own good, that they would need those skills—grammar and spelling and penmanship—"later on in life" when they would "get a job someday."*
>
> *I asked Brandon, "What are you doing now?"*
>
> *"I am a film editor for an advertising and marketing agency."*
>
> *"Do you like film editing?"*
>
> *"Yes, I love it."*
>
> *"Do you ever have to write sentences or narrative essays?" I asked.*
>
> *"No," he said.*
>
> *I was pensive and quiet for a few moments, imagining all the ways I should have approached a student such as Brandon. I wish I had known strategies I should have implemented back then, such as UDL, to remove barriers to Brandon's learning and instead focus on his interests and strengths.*

"What if I had allowed you to represent your understanding through a documentary or a short film clip rather than making you write out sentences over and over?" I asked. "Would you have liked that better?"

"Yes," he said. "I would have loved that."

"I'm sorry, Brandon. I feel like I failed you. If only I knew then what I know now, maybe I could have been the teacher that you needed me to be."

Reflection Questions

Teachers may find it useful to reflect on the following questions when considering adopting a UDL framework prior to beginning a lesson, a unit, or a semester:

1. *How can I design instruction to represent ideas and content in multiple ways?*

2. *How can I create assignments and projects that allow students a measure of choice when it comes to demonstrating what they know and can do?*

3. *How might I lean on resources and materials found outside of the classroom to peak students' sense of wonder and engagement?*

4. *How can I shift the locus of control in the classroom from myself to the individual students? And how do I feel about doing so?*

References

Anderson, C. (2017). Engaging graduate students with guest experts: Following principles for universal design for learning (UDL). In P. Resta & S. Smith (Eds.), *Proceedings of Society for Information Technology & Teacher Education International Conference* (pp. 2223–2224). Austin, TX: Association for the Advancement of Computing in Education. Retrieved from https://www.learntechlib.org/primary/p/177514/

Center of Applied Special Technologies. (2018). Universal Design for Learning guidelines (Version 2.2). Retrieved from http://udlguidelines.cast.org

eLearning Infographics. (2019, February 4). Infographic: What is UDL? Retrieved from https://elearninginfographics.com/what-is-udl-universal-design-learning-infographic/

Meyer, A., Rose, D., & Gordon, D. (2014). *Universal Design for Learning*. Wakefield, MA: CAST Professional Publishing.

Mizerny, C. (2019, February 22). Learning for all with UDL in the classroom. Retrieved from https://www.middleweb.com/39684/learning-for-all-with-udl-in-the-classroom/

Novak, K. (2017, February 1). UDL vs DI: The dinner party analogy. Retrieved from https://www.novakeducation.com/udl-vs-di-dinner-party-analogy/

Tomlinson, C. A. (1999). *The differentiated classroom: responding to the needs of all learners*. Alexandria, VA: Association for Supervision and Curriculum Development.

CHAPTER THREE

UNDERSTANDING AND ADDRESSING BEHAVIOR: FROM SCREAMING TO CRYING TO TANTRUMS TO VIOLENCE

Anni K. Reinking

Remember, a "child/student is not bad, but a child/student may make choices that could be improved."

Teaching, Year 4

While stabbing me in the arm with a pencil, Annisa was yelling, "MS. MAYFIELD. WHY DID HE TAKE MY PENCIL? I HATE HIM! I WANT HIM TO DIE!"

As I was trying to get the pencil out of Annisa's hand, a little stream of blood ran down my forearm from the pencil puncture. Calmly, but agitated, I firmly stated, "Annisa, I did not take it. We will talk to Jordan about personal items. But right now I need you to please hand me the pencil so we can all be safe."

"No!"

By this point, we were in a staring contest. I was sitting in my desk chair, unable to get up because Annisa was standing over me in my personal space. Her legs were touching my knees. I was stuck. Annisa was at my eye level.

Beyond frustrated, I yelled, "GIVE ME THE PENCIL ANNISA. I AM DONE!" I lost my cool.

A little shocked that I yelled at her, Annisa froze and then became more agitated. I could see the change in her eyes; they turned to what I would describe as "tunnels" focusing directly on me. She stabbed me again and again in the forearm until I could control her little arm. By this point, I had no other options; as I restrained her pencil-bearing hand using the training I had previously received, I called for the office to come take her out of my class.

A few minutes later, the counselor showed up at my door. Annisa had run to the other side of the room and dug her feet in. She was not going to go willingly.

Teaching, Year 3

"Ms. Mayfield, I don't have to listen to you. You are just some White lady trying to tell me what to do," Jaquain stated calmly one Monday morning. His voice was not loud or agitated, and he said this statement with a factual, nonchalant demeanor. He was actually one of my favorite kindergarten students this year and had the most challenging behaviors in the classroom.

Puzzled, I said, "Oh, okay. Well, in this classroom, I like to keep you safe."

Not letting up, Jaquain continued. "My momma said White ladies only want to take your man and snitch. So you a snitch."

Confused, I looked at Jaquain. "Okay." I knew I was not going to make any movement in this conversation at 7:30 a.m.

He walked to his desk and began eating his breakfast.

Teaching, Year 2

"I am not dealing with this today. I am calling Mr. Juan." I picked up the classroom phone and called the social worker to come down to the classroom. It was nap time, and Emily was doing her usual antics. She was running, screaming, and throwing books, toys, anything she could get her hands on. I had already moved all my kids out of the room and into the conjoining room for what remained of their nap time. In my mind, I was nervous as I thought about my present condition. I was 8 months' pregnant, and I was not about to get hurt by a 5-year-old girl displaying challenging behaviors, assumed to be stemming from her mother's pregnancy and new boyfriend.

Teaching, Year 1

Seemingly calm, I said, "Julian, it is time to sit down and eat your breakfast."

"NO!" he screamed in my face.

I was a first-year teacher. Julian was a child I dreaded interacting with every day. After screaming at me, he began running around the classroom. I started chasing him from the math area to the library area, and then I finally caught him when he rounded the corner into the block area. I was thinking, "You are not going to get the best of me. You will behave."

Once I got ahold of Julian's upper arms, right above his elbows, I said, "Julian, no. Sit down! We are not doing this." I was not calm. I was yelling. I could feel my face getting red. My blood pressure was pumping in my ears. I was mad! I was using my restraint training to restrain the crying, kicking, and spitting child I was not sitting with on the carpet. And then I felt it. My flesh was being ripped apart. My forearm was throbbing. Julian had just bitten my arm, and blood was streaming down my arm. I had teeth marks— teeth marks—and they lasted for weeks.

These are just a few stories from my first 4 years of teaching. These are not the "worst" incidents, but they provide a good picture of what a first-year teacher, or even a veteran teacher, could experience.

Regardless of how hard it may have felt in the moment, or how hard it may sound reading it now, I stayed in the teaching field for another 3 years. I had many more experiences I could add to this list, all of which focused on behavior. Since leaving the classroom, however, I have focused much of my research on classroom management/engagement, developmentally appropriate behavior management/engagement, and understanding the underlying issues of challenging behaviors. Now, 5 years since I was a full-time classroom teacher, and 4 years in higher education, I have more insight, more patience, and helpful tips for teachers.

> Remember: "He or she is not giving *you* a hard time. He or she is *having* a hard time."

This quote is a quote to reflect on. When a child or student displays challenging behaviors, oftentimes something else is going on that is resulting in the behavior. Due to children's brain development and language acquisition, it is oftentimes very difficult for students to say, "I am angry; here is why." Rather, they display their emotions and the feelings they have in their bodies through challenging behaviors. Asking yourself, "What is the 'why' behind this behavior?" is always good because there is most likely is a disconnection between the feeling and the ability to verbally express feelings.

Understanding Student Behavior

Student behavior can be impacted by many factors: trauma, community violence, family and community interactions, and exposure to learning/reading, along with many more internal and external factors. Regardless of the early experiences in a child's life, understanding that the foundations of behavior, both challenging and nonchallenging, all begin in the brain, is important.

The brain has been researched for generations; however, in the last decade, more and more research has led to a better understanding of how the brain in children works and how it develops. Specifically, the prefrontal cortex is the part of the brain that educators are "working" on constructing through the whole educational trajectory. What should be noted is that researchers have determined that the prefrontal cortex does not fully develop until the early to mid 20s. Therefore, the children in elementary classrooms, and even in middle and high school classrooms, are very far away from having a fully developed brain. Educators, this is important to remember! If you are interested in learning more information, check out this article about your <u>child's brain</u>[1] at Integrated Learning Strategies (2019).

What happens in the prefrontal cortex? Everything, including impulse control, problem solving, making connections, focusing and organizing, and ignoring external distractions. Therefore, how, when, and what teachers communicate to students are extremely important because solid connections within the brain structure are developing. When analyzing teacher–student interactions during heightened behavioral issues, there are questions to ask: Is the teacher staying calm? Is the teacher displaying mutual respect? Is the teacher providing a reason for actions and learning in the classroom (logical consequences)? All these factors, plus more, have an impact on the connections made in the child's brain.

Furthermore, students' communication and interaction experiences are key to the development and success of academic and social achievement. Although educators cannot directly control the language children hear or interact with at home, the language that teachers use in the classroom can have an impact on a child's life. When engaging with students in classrooms and school buildings, having a plan focused on positive interactions, along with considering preventative measures, is important. But does only planning prevention strategies reach the root of the issue? No. Before developing a prevention plan, understanding the "why" of behavior is important. Ask yourself these questions when attempting to understand a child's or student's behavior:

> Why does a student behave the way he or she does?
> What has occurred in the student's life to impact his or her behavior?

---

1   See Integrated Learning Strategies Learning Corner in the Online Sources section at the end of the chapter.

What are the outlying factors that impact the student's behavior?
Do you know the "whole" child and understand the interactions
he or she engages in outside of school?

Trauma

One factor which has been seen more frequently researched in recent years is the impact of trauma on the brain. Brain development in infancy and early childhood lays the foundation for all future development. Neural pathways form at great speed and depend on the repetition of experiences. Experiences teach the brain what to expect and how to respond. When experiences are traumatic, the pathways getting the most use are those that respond to trauma; *this reduces the information of other pathways needed for adaptive behavior.* Trauma in early childhood and elementary grades can result in disrupted attachment, cognitive delays, and impaired emotional regulation. Also, the overdevelopment of certain pathways and the underdevelopment of other progressions can lead to impairment later in life (Perry, Pollard, Blakley, Baker & Vigilante, 1995). For example, when a child experiences trauma for a majority of his or her life, the overdeveloped adrenal (fight-or-flight) instinct occurs with the underdeveloped capacity for coping "appropriately." This also impacts sleeping, eating, thinking, and behavior. Therefore, for educators, understanding where students are coming from and the experiences the children are enduring, and entering each situation with a listening ear, a compassionate mind-set, and an eye toward the overall child are imperative.

The term trauma[2] has various definitions; however, it is, essentially, "a deeply distressing or disturbing experience" (SAMHSA-HRSA, n.d.). It can be an experience that happens once (e.g., a tornado or a house fire) or an enduring event (e.g., community violence or poverty). Trauma impacts not only the "here and now," but it also has the potential to have a lifelong impact because of the variety of situational factors.

What is important to remember, however, is that trauma is unique to individual experiences and based on perceptions of each experience. For

---

2   See SAMSHA-HRSA Center for Integrated Health Solutions in the Online Sources at the end of the chapter.

example, a child who is often hit or physically harmed by an adult will have a different response to an adult touching him or her compared to a child who is never physically harmed by an adult. This example became real a few years ago when I witnessed an interaction between a coach and a student on my son's baseball team.

The child in this interaction was in the foster care system as a result of his father breaking his arm by throwing him down the stairs. This child, as a result, had a very high startle response around adult men. One day, the male coach, not knowing the child's background, was trying to teach him something about hitting and catching and pretended to hit him with a bat. The boy ran away screaming and crying. The adult coach was caught off-guard because that response was not typical. The adult coach had completed the same activity with other boys on the team and they did not react that way. The boy's trauma and past experiences impacted his response and, hopefully, was a reflective learning experience for the coach.

Many times, trauma is associated with what is known as ACEs (adverse childhood experiences). To find out more, there is a great Facebook page[3] that posts often regarding trauma and the brain, or check out the ACE questionnaire.[4]

Challenging Behaviors

Challenging behaviors are defined as a culturally abnormal behavior that is so intense that personal safety or environmental safety (others' safety) is in jeopardy. If you would like to find out more information about challenging behaviors for children ages 0 to 3, this article[5] at Zero to Three (2019) is a great resource.

Challenging behaviors include the following:

- Causing injury to self or others
- Causing damage to the physical environment

---

3   See Connect the Dots to ACEs in the Online Sources section at the end of the chapter.
4   See National Council of Juvenile and Family Court Judges in the Online Sources section at the end of the chapter.
5   See Zero to Three in the Online Sources section at the end of the chapter.

- Interfering with learning new skills
- Socially isolating a student
- Acting inappropriate for the age or cultural background of the student
- Acting in a way that challenges educators' or family members' attempts to manage

As educators, challenging behaviors can take many forms but fall into the general challenging behaviors listed earlier. Now what? Understanding the form and function of the behavior is important before diving into the prevention plan.

Identifying the forms and functions of challenging behaviors begin with the process of asking questions. What is the form (the what) of that behavior? What does the behavior look like? What is the function (the why) of that behavior? Why does this student do this behavior? What does the student "get from" doing the behavior?

The form of challenging behavior is defined by the child/student's action. Examples listed in Table 3.1.

TABLE 3.1
FORMS OF CHALLENGING BEHAVIOR

Form of Behavior				
Aggression	**Tantrum**	**Non-Compliance**	**Social Withdrawal**	**Self-Injury/ Repetitive Behavior**
Hitting Scratching Kicking Biting Throwing things Pinching Threatening	Screaming Crying Whining Cussing	Refuses to respond to a request Passive when a request is made	Primarily plays alone Doesn't respond to peers' attempts to play	Scratching self Biting self Hitting self Rocking back and forth Spinning objects

The function of challenging behavior is defined by the child/student's goal or purpose of engaging in the challenging behavior. There are three main functions of challenging behaviors:

1. Obtaining something

      a. Attention of an adult or peer

      b. Activity, toy, food, material, one-on-one time

  2. Escaping Something

      a. Attention of an adult or peer

      b. Activity, toy, food, materials

  3. Self-Stimulation

When thinking about the function of behaviors, not placing the "obtain" or "escape" in a positive or negative box is important. For example, a teacher may feel that taking a child out of circle time is a "negative" consequence, but the child may see it as one-on-one time with an individual teacher or as escaping something he or she does not like—circle time.

So is the behavior challenging? Yes or no? (This can also differ due to perceptions, personalities, and experiences of individual teachers). What are the form and function of the behavior? What is the underlying cause of the challenging behavior? Get to know the students. Understand what is happening in the lives of the students. Recognize that some students have not developed the coping strategies to express emotions in socially acceptable ways. Also, remember that students can have bad days just like all of us.

FIGURE 3.1
FLOW CHART FOR ADDRESSING CHALLENGING BEHAVIORS

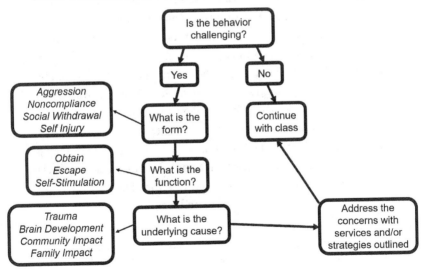

Strategies for Working With Students
With Challenging Behaviors

Working with students who have challenging behaviors can be exhausting, both physically and emotionally. However, there are strategies that, if completed consistently, have the potential to effect change in your classroom.

Strategy 1: Classroom Environment

Beginning the school year and school day with a positive foundation is essential to the overall classroom community. One strategy for reaching this goal is through the implementation of morning meetings. During morning meetings, every student hears his or her name in the classroom environment or school building said by a peer or teacher. The structure of a morning meeting is part of the Responsive Classroom[6] (2019) management system. There are four parts to a morning meeting, and every part is essential for creating a welcoming, safe, and caring environment for students to feel safe during difficult conversations, misbehaviors, and various other interactions:

1. Greeting: As part of the greeting, every student hears his or her name in the classroom or school environment, interacts with eye contact, and builds a sense of community. When students feel safe with the educators/administrators and students, risks and learning can occur at a higher level.
2. Share: The share is a part of the morning meeting that can be completed in several ways. However, it is a time when students can share about their lives, others can ask questions, and a sense of community and family is built.
3. Game/Activity: Again, various games can be played during this time. However, the goal is to build a sense of camaraderie and friendship (More games and activities can be found here[7] at the Minnesota Literacy Council, 2019).

---

6   See Responsive Classroom in the Online Sources section at the end of the chapter.
7   See Minnesota Literacy Council in the Online Sources section at the end of the chapter.

4. Message: This is when the teacher shares information about the day as a way to be transparent and open.

After developing a solid social structure, evaluating the environment and social design is also important. How many students are working together throughout the day? Do you have enough supplies when there is an activity? Are you modeling and teaching socially appropriate behavior or just telling students to "be respectful?" (The difference between modeling and teaching is important. Modeling is when the teacher demonstrates the new idea. Teaching is when the teacher is engaging the students in learning through engagement, through what we do, you do.)

Additionally, recognize that children may demonstrate challenging behaviors during teacher-led activities that they find difficult, uninteresting, or overwhelming. Therefore, make sure that much of the day includes student-voice and student-led activities. Teachers can use their knowledge of children's preferred activities and materials to embed activities that may be more challenging (e.g., if a child love trains but does not like using any writing materials, provide pictures of trains for the child to color at the writing center). Additionally, including students in the day-to-day schedule of the classroom develops a sense of ownership and accountability. Some examples include the following:

- Assign classroom jobs or responsibilities to help children/students feel a sense of belonging.
- Make sure that every child/student has the opportunity to be a leader and a helper.
- Make sure that every child/student has frequent opportunities to answer questions, make choices, or offer comments in a verbal or nonverbal way.

Strategy 2: Logical Consequences

The goal for classrooms should be one of mutual respect that leads to the idea of behavior management systems that encourage and support students' brain development, specifically through logical consequences. In this section, logical consequences and why engaging in the behavior management system of logical consequences builds the foundation of mutual respect, as compared to a behavior management system of punishment and social embarrassment, are discussed.

Logical consequences, as compared to behavior charts, punishments, or time-outs, help develop the prefrontal cortex and the tasks developed in the prefrontal cortex. Logical consequences should be the goal of classroom management systems because when a student has a disciplinary action that directly relates to the misbehavior, the prefrontal cortex builds deeper connections for cause and effect.

So what is a logical consequence? "Punishment that fits the crime." Essentially, if a student misbehaves, the consequence should logically connect. What you will notice, however, is that not every "misbehavior" is bad or intentional. However, there is still a "consequence" to the action. Table 3.2 provides examples.

TABLE 3.2
LOGICAL CONSEQUENCES

Misbehavior	Logical Consequence
A student continues to break his/her or their pencil.	Provide the student with a golf pencil that cannot be broken.
A student draws on a desk/wall/locker.	Provide the student with the materials to clean up the item.
A student knocks over a tray that another student is carrying.	The student helps pick up the tray.
A student waves scissors around.	The student cannot use scissors the rest of the day. (Make sure to provide a time when the student can show you that he/she or they know how to appropriately behave.)
A student touches another student when lining up.	The student stands next to the teacher.
Student is not engaged in an activity that is needed for mastery.	Ask the student, "What do you think will help you do better with ___?"

The most important thing to remember when implementing logical consequences is to use the statement structure "I see that *you* made the *choice* to _____. Therefore, you will need to make a different choice. Do you want to choose _____ or _____?" This sentence structure places the ownership and decision in the hands of the child. One important idea to remember, however, is that the choices provided need to be choices you, as the teacher, can live with. If a child chooses one of your choices, let him or her complete that choice.

Incorporating logical consequences and choices (no more than two that the teacher can live with) into classrooms develops a link between the misbehavior and the consequence, which, in turn, helps the prefrontal cortex develop. The idea of choice, by stating to the student, "It is your choice," when a logical consequence is given, develops a sense of autonomy.

When engaging in logical consequences, remembering the following guidelines is important:

1. Ask the student to help choose (put the consequence in the form of a choice).
2. Make sure the consequence is logically connected to the misbehavior.
3. Only give choices you can live with as the educator or administrator.
4. Keep your tone of voice firm and calm.
5. Give the choice one time, then act to enforce the consequence. (Do not get into a power struggle.)
6. Expect testing, but be consistent (this also helps with brain development).
7. Allow the student to try again (do not hold a grudge).

Logical consequences can be difficult at times; however, with reflection and consistency, a change in student behavior will be recognized.

Reflection Questions

1. *As a teacher, how can you support the needs children display through their behavior and words after gaining knowledge on how the brain functions?*

2. *Refer to the vignettes at the beginning of the chapter. If you were the teacher in those situations, what strategies would you use after reading this chapter?*

3. *Which strategy are you going to try first? Why?*

4. *What are the forms and functions of the challenging behavior in your classroom? How do you know?*

Online Sources

Connect the Dots to ACEs: https://www.facebook.com/cherylleahsmyth/
Integrated Learning Strategies Learning Corner: https://ilslearningcorner.com/2016-03-brain-hierarchy-when-your-childs-lower-brain-levels-are-weak-they-cant-learn/
Minnesota Literacy Council: https://mnliteracy.org/sites/default/files/gamesactivities book_o.pdf.
National Council of Juvenile and Family Court Judges: https://www.ncjfcj.org/sites/default/files/Finding%20Your%20ACE%20Score.pdf
Responsive Classroom: https://www.responsiveclassroom.org/
SAMSHA-HRSA Center for Integrated Health Solutions: https://www.integration.samhsa.gov/clinical-practice/trauma
Zero to Three: https://www.zerotothree.org/espanol/challenging-behaviors

References

Integrated Learning Strategies (2019). *Brain hierarchy: When your child's lower brain levels are weak, they can't learn.* Retrieved from https://ilslearningcorner.com/2016-03-brain-hierarchy-when-your-childs-lower-brain-levels-are-weak-they-cant-learn/

Minnesota Literacy Council. (2019). *Morning meeting games and activities.* Retrieved from https://mnliteracy.org/sites/default/files/gamesactivitiesbook_0.pdf

Perry, B., Pollard, R., Blakley, T., Baker, W., & Vigilante, D. (1995). Childhood trauma, the neurobiology of adaptation, and "use-dependent" development of the brain: How "states" become "traits." *Infant Mental Health Journal, 16*(4), 271-291. doi:10.1002/1097- 0355(199524)16:43.0.CO;2-B

Responsive Classroom. (2019). Retrieved from https://www.responsiveclassroom.org/

SAMHSA-HRSA. (n.d.). *Trauma.* Retrieved from https://www.integration.samhsa.gov/clinical-practice/trauma

Zero to Three. (2019). *Challenging behaviors.* Retrieved from https://www.zerotothree.org/espanol/challenging-behaviors

CHAPTER FOUR

REACHING ALL LEARNERS WITH MULTICULTURAL CONNECTIONS

Sara Schwerdtfeger

I began my first teaching job when I was 22 years old. I was hired to teach in a school that was a sixth-grade center, meaning the entire building contained only sixth graders. Yes, we had 375 sixth graders in one building. For me, this was a huge group of students. I was born and raised in a small central Kansas town where my graduating class contained only 24 students. My first teaching job had more students in one building than in my entire home school district.

After the first 3 months of my first year, we were scheduled to hold par-ent–teacher conferences. The first set of parent–teacher conferences in my building was made up of student-led conferences. This type of conference requires students to attend the conference with their parents, and the student takes the lead during the conference to describe the experiences of class so far. Weeks of preparation went into planning for the student-led conferences in my sixth-grade classroom. Students worked for several class sessions to prepare several pages for their parents explaining new projects completed, grades, effort, personal learning, and goals set for the next semester. I had it

perfectly timed (or so I thought) for students to talk through all their infor-
mation in about 15 minutes with 5 minutes left for questions from parents.

The day of parent–teacher conferences arrived. I was as nervous as all the
students for conferences! At 6:00 p.m., my first parent arrived. As I intro-
duced myself to the parent, I quickly learned that the person was not a parent
but the translator assigned to my room for the evening. As a new teacher, I
knew that many of my students spoke Spanish at home, but I did not make
the connection that, obviously, their parents would speak Spanish too. As we
began the conferences, the translator tried her best to translate for both the
parents and myself. I found many times the parents would be explaining a
story or asking me a very detailed question, and when the translator spoke
in English to me, she would say something very brief, such as "They want to
know if Juan is doing his homework." Clearly, the parents wanted to share
much more with me, but in the interest of time and understanding, I only
received the CliffsNotes version of the information.

This was an eye-opening experience for me and truly affected the course of my
teaching career. The very next semester, I began to take coursework to earn
my English as a Second Language endorsement. I also began to take Span-
ish-language classes because most of my students spoke Spanish at home, to
help support my students. My teaching career expanded and grew in ways I
never thought possible through learning about multicultural education and
studying a new language.

Multicultural Connections in Elementary Education

Elementary students are eager and willing to learn new things all the time.
These amazing and constantly growing young minds take their cues from the
adults in their lives. Elementary classrooms are becoming more diverse (Reys,
Lindquist, Lambdin, & Smith, 2015). According to Reyes et al. (2015), data from
the National Center for Educational Statistics summarize the typical American
classroom of 25 students approximately as follows:

- 11 students are members of a minority group
- 4 students speak a language other than English at home

- 10 students qualify for free or reduced-price lunch
- 6 students live in poverty
- 4 students with disabilities receive special services, a little more than half of whom spend more than 80% of their school day in a regular classroom

Reflecting on the fact that your experience as a teacher in education may (and probably will) be different from your experience in education as a student, identifying ways to reach all the students in your classroom is important. Preservice teachers must be able to teach all students when they enter the teaching profession. In this chapter, making multicultural connections as a preservice teacher; in elementary social students and civics education; in elementary mathematics; and in elementary science, technology, engineering, and mathematics (STEM) as well as making multicultural community connections, are explored.

Multicultural Connections as an Elementary Preservice Teacher

As preservice teachers begin their journey in understanding education in elementary schools, life experiences tie into their repertoire of knowledge. Most likely, preservice teachers will teach in a school or city different from the one they attended as a child. The life experiences prior to teaching will tie into the knowledge they have as teachers. Preservice teachers bring a vast set of knowledge, skills, and dispositions to the student teaching experience (Lyman, Foyle, Morehead, Schwerdtfeger & Lyman, 2017). Using the time during the university experience to grow and expand one's knowledge of education is extremely important. Exploring options while still at the university will help enrich the teaching experience for the preservice teacher as well as for the future students they will serve.

One of the many options that preservice teachers may have available to them is the student teaching experience. According to Engel (2017), the student teaching-abroad experience for undergraduate students has dramatically increased in the last three decades. At Emporia State University in Emporia,

Kansas, preservice teachers are offered several different student-teaching options. After successfully completing 12 weeks of student teaching, as required by the Kansas State Department of Education, preservice teachers may take part in one of four additional 4-week student-teaching placements in varied and diverse settings, including the following (Hill, Lickteig, & Schwerdtfeger, 2019):

- Parochial or private school placements: Private schools or parochial schools are not typically traditional student-teaching placements and can host student teachers during this 4-week option.
- Areas of high-vacancy placements: Schools that have a teacher shortage or are designated as a high-vacancy school can host student teachers during this 4-week option.
- National Teacher Hall of Fame placements: Teachers who have earned the high honor of being inducted into the National Teacher Hall of Fame have the option to host student teachers during this 4-week teaching option.
- International placements: Partnership schools in Paraguay, Indonesia, Finland, Denmark, and Germany are eligible to host student teachers during this 4-week option.

Participating in additional student-teaching experiences will expand the preservice teachers' understanding of other cultures and diverse settings different from the traditional student-teaching semester. By challenging preservice teachers' ethnocentric and monocultural perspectives, these short- or long-term student teaching experiences broaden "intercultural competence in a way that directly fosters culturally responsive teaching practices" (Moss, Barry, & MacCleoud, 2018, p. 199).

According to Lynch (2015), there are six ways to begin to incorporate real multicultural learning in the classroom:

- Multiculturalism: The first way is to define *multiculturalism*. In this context, *multicultural education* is defined as "a progressive approach for transforming education based on educational equality and social justice" (Lynch, 2015, p.1).

- Value real-life experience of diversity: Another way is to value real-life experience of diversity over the textbook version. Examining student groups in your classroom using concrete experience, reflective observation, and active experimentation is more powerful than reading about similar students in textbooks.
- Learning styles: The third way is to learn about your students' learning styles. Academic strengths can be discovered by helping students find ways they are motivated to learn.
- Encourage pride of heritage: The fourth way is to encourage students to be proud of their heritage. Helping students continue developing their first language, learning about family history, and studying their own culture are all ways to accomplish this.
- Examine personal biases: The fifth way is to be aware of your personal biases. Educators must examine their own cultural beliefs, ideas, and bias. Preservice teachers can begin this process during their education courses and continue to widen their circle of understanding.
- Authentic assignments to celebrate multiculturalism: The last way is to create meaningful assignments that celebrate multiculturalism. Writing assignments, interviews, traditions, incorporating parents, and visiting neighborhoods are all authentic ways to involve students in authentic assignments.

Multicultural Connections in Elementary Social Studies and Civics Education

A benefit of teaching in an elementary school is that teachers are able to be with their class most of the day. The elementary teacher is a generalist who specializes in science, math, English language arts, and social studies, as well as social-emotional learning in their classrooms. One way teachers can begin to incorporate multicultural lessons into their classroom is through social studies and civics education.

Social studies curriculum seeks to impart both historical and geographical knowledge and understanding of ethics and values inherent in a democratic society (Chamot & O'Malley, 2009). This can be represented to students in your classrooms through literature that is easy to relate to as elementary students. Using chapter books as read-alouds to the class or as a unit of study is a great way to incorporate educational justice with the elementary students. Students are transported to another culture, another time, or another way of life through literature to make connections and develop an understanding that there are other ways to live besides their experience so far.

An example of using literature to make multicultural connections is to use the book *Esperanza Rising* (2000) as a unit of study. This amazing piece of children's literature is a historical novel set in Mexico and California during the 1940s. Esperanza is a girl who lives on a large ranch in Mexico with her very wealthy family. After a family tragedy, Esperanza and her mom find themselves traveling as migrant workers to California. The chapters in the book are labeled as the crop seasons, such as "Las Uvas, Los Higos, y Las Cebollas." The author paints a realistic picture of life during that time while transforming the understanding of the migrant workers' plight.

Table 4.1 includes several books that could be used in elementary classrooms to make multicultural connections with students in your classroom.

Multicultural Connections With
Elementary Mathematics Education

Another content area that elementary teachers must know and understand is teaching mathematics to elementary students. Van de Walle, Karp, and Bay-Williams (2016) describe "teaching for equity is much more than providing students with an equal opportunity to learn mathematics. Teaching for equity attempts to attain equal outcomes for all students by being sensitive to individual differences" pg. 104. Multicultural mathematical literature is literature that contains mathematics demonstrated in various ways across many different cultures. This concept will help students identify mathematics as a universal language spoken by all cultures across the globe (Iliev, N, & D'Angelo, F, 2014).

Culturally responsive instruction is for all students. Several areas must be considered as an elementary teacher builds lessons for their students. Four main

TABLE 4.1
CHILDREN'S LITERATURE WITH MULTICULTURAL CONNECTIONS
THROUGH SOCIAL STUDIES AND CIVICS EDUCATION

Book Title	Author and Date	Literature Summary
Chu Ju's House	Gloria Whelan, 2004	Historical novel that shares the experiences of a 14-year-old girl in China after the Cultural Revolution
Homeless Bird	Gloria Whelan, 2000	Historical novel that explores the story of a girl from India as she experiences an arranged marriage at the age of 13
Esperanza Rising	Pam Munoz Ryan, 2000	Historical novel that describes the life of a young girl from Mexico as she travels to the United States in search of work with her family
The Sandwich Swap	Queen Rania of Jordan Al-Abdulla, 2010	Nonfiction story that demonstrates that true friendship is stronger than the differences among us
Last Stop on Market Street	Matt de la Pena, 2015	Fictional story about an African American boy and his grandmother and their experiences as they live in a big city
Grandfather's Journey	Allen Say, 1993	Fictional story about a Japanese American man as he recounts his grandfather's journey from Japan to the United States and back to Japan

Whelan, G. (2000). *Homeless bird.* New York, NY: HarperCollins Publishers.
Whelan, G. (2004). *Chu Ju's house.* New York, NY: HarperCollins Publishers.
Munoz Ryan, P. (2000) *Esperanza rising.* New York, NY: Scholastic.
Al-Abdulla, R. & DiPucchio, K. (2010) *The sandwich swap.* New York, NY: Disney-Hyperion.
De la Pena, M. (2015). *Last stop on market street.* New York, NY: Penguin Group.
Say, A. (1993). Grandfather's journey. New York, NY: Houghton Mifflin Company.

strategies for differentiation address the needs of linguistically and culturally diverse students in our classroom (Van de Walle et al., 2016):

- Focus on important mathematics
- Make content relevant

- Incorporate students' identities
- Ensure shared power

In addition, Boaler (2016) identifies six ways to make math more equitable and inclusive for all students. Teachers should offer all students high-level content, work to change ideas about who can achieve in mathematics, encourage students to think deeply about mathematics, teach students to work together, give girls and students of color additional encouragement to learn math and science, and eliminate (or at least change the nature of) homework (Boaler, 2016). Using both sets of these strategies, elementary teachers can begin to employ ideas and lessons to ensure equitable learning of multicultural students in their classroom. Table 4.2 lists children's literature that has a mathematics focus through a multicultural lens.

Multicultural Connections With Elementary STEM Education

Another more recent area of study for elementary teachers is the content area of integrating STEM. One of the ways that you can easily incorporate multiculturalism into your elementary classroom is to integrate it as a theme of study into projects you are already teaching. Stereotypes, biases, and misconceptions about STEM and STEM in elementary schools must be addressed so the trends can be intentionally reversed (Hoffer, 2016).

Here are several examples of innovative STEM projects for your science classroom that can incorporate a multicultural connection. Many students (and teachers) think science is just something in a textbook. Incorporating hands-on, authentic work for students will encourage all elementary students to see themselves as successful in the STEM fields.

- Innovation in science: Design and implement a long-term classroom project by having students identify a social entrepreneurship project in the school or community. Students will talk with community partners or school stakeholders to find a way to fill a need in the school or community. This could be something

TABLE 4.2
CHILDREN'S MATHEMATICS LITERATURE
WITH MULTICULTURAL CONNECTIONS

Book Title	Author and Date	Literature Summary
My Granny Went to Market	Stella Blackstone, 1995	A multicultural counting book
One Grain of Rice	Demi, 1997	An Indian folktale about the power of doubling
Grandfather Counts	Andrea Cheng, 2000	Intergenerational story about a grandfather and a granddaughter from China
Two Ways to Count to Ten: A Liberian Folktale	Rudy Dee, 2010	Liberian folktale about strength and leadership
Count on Pablo	Barbara deRubertis, 2006	Pablo helps his *Abuelo* count and wash items for the market
Feast for Ten	Cathryn Falwell, 1993	Counting book with an African American family preparing dinner
Ten Mice for Tet	Pegi Deitz Shea & Cynthia Weill, 2003	Counting book on the topic of the Vietnamese New Year
The Librarian Who Measured the Earth	Kathryn Lasky, 1994	Tells the story of the ancient Greek philosopher Eratosthenes and how he measured the circumference of the Earth

Blackstone, S. (1995). *My granny went to market.* Cambridge, MA: Barefoot Books.
Demi. (1997). *One grain of rice.* New York, NY: Scholastic.
Cheng, A. (2000). *Grandfather counts.* New York, NY: Lee and Low Books.
Dee. R. (1988). *Two ways to count to ten.* New York, NY: Henry Holt and Company, LLC.
deRubertis, B. (2006). *Count on Pablo.* Minneapolis, MN: Kane Press.
Falwell, C. (1993). *Feast for Ten.* New York, NY: Houghton Mifflin Company.
Shea, P., & Weill, C. (2003). *Ten mice for Tet.* San Francisco, CA: Chronicle Books LLC.
Lasky, K. (1994). *The librarian who measured the Earth.* Hong Kong: South China Printing Company.

such as starting a school/community garden, helping the local food bank, improving a way of life for a group of students, raising money for food for students or animal shelters, and so on.

Any of these topics should be tied in with the current science or math curriculum as well as social-emotional learning or character education in your school.

- After reading and learning about typhoons, hurricanes, tornados, or any other weather in an area that your students have lived, students can design storm shelters that will withstand wind or water. Students can also improve on the current recipe for clay by creating their own clay using flour, salt, oil, and water. Students should be allowed to raise money to purchase these items and budget their projects (Reagan, 2016).

- After reading Dr. Seuss's *The Lorax*, students can be challenged to create a commercial or a public service announcement to help save any wildlife or plant life in their area. This could also be expanded for students to study a country or other area where endangered animals or plants live. Use technology to record the videos and help students write a campaign to show the videos to other classes in the school or community (Reagan, 2016).

- After studying many different holidays from around the world, students should design and build a confetti launcher to help everyone celebrate their selected holiday. The class can create objectives for the success of the launcher and engineer the design of launcher. Students can use recycled materials and budget the project. The science concepts of force, trajectory, and the laws of motion can be included (Reagan, 2016).

- After students study the use of fossil fuels and the diminishing amount of fossil fuels, have students design and build a model vehicle that runs on an alternative energy source. Students will record each design they develop and document the changes and revisions (Hoffer, 2016).

Multicultural Community Connections

One of the most helpful and underutilized resources for promoting multiculturalism in your classroom and schools is right in the backyard of the school. Your community has a wealth of, possibly untapped, resources available for you to use.

During my first years of teaching, one of my most memorable students was Salim. Salim arrived in our classroom in the middle of the school year as a student that had recently immigrated to the United States. His first experience in a school in the United States was in my classroom. I really wanted to get started on the right foot with him and his family. So the first thing that I did was to schedule a meeting with him and his parents. They were so excited to be included in our school and were eager to learn about the United States as much as we were eager to learn about their country. A beautiful partnership developed, and the entire family was a large part of our classroom that year.

Another example of a time when I learned about cultural differences was when Raji was in my sixth-grade class. Raji was typically a quiet student that mostly worked hard in school. He had a very funny personality and loved to have other students' attention as he had students laugh at him during class. As the semester progressed, Raji stopped turning in work and began to create "funny" assignments instead of actual assignments. I knew Raji's father was an assistant professor at our local university, and he had already approached me earlier in the year about the expected success of his son in my class. Therefore, as assignments stopped coming in from Raji, I contacted his father. We had a great conversation on the phone as I shared some of the things happening in the classroom. We decided on Raji staying for after-school homework help with me for a couple days a week.

One day, Raji was not sure if he could stay after school but could not get in touch with his father at work. So he called his mom at home and asked me to ask her if he could stay after school for help. His mother said that would be fine, and then Raji and his mom discussed how he would get home after homework help. About 45 minutes after that phone call took place, Raji's dad was walking into our classroom. He asked me to step in the hallway and proceeded to let me know that in his culture, his wife is not allowed to make decisions for his children. If Raji ever needed to stay after school, we were to notify him and let him know.

The following is a list of resources and descriptions of connections that may be available to you in your community. This list can certainly be added to for you and your community. Use it as a starting point to begin to make connections to people in your community.

- Parents: Involving parents in your classroom is a must. Depending on what culture and area the parents are from, they may or may not think the school is a welcoming place for them. Reaching out to family members with authentic ways for them to work with the school is a great first step. Honoring the choice of parents to not be involved is also essential.
- Local library: There are many untapped resources at your local library. Uncover the treasures of books, community resources, outreach specialists, and free community programs.
- Local ethnic restaurants and markets: In my community, we have amazing restaurants that reflect the diversity and ethnic makeup of the students in our schools. Food is an excellent way to connect with others and to demonstrate different fruits and vegetables that are grown in other parts of the world.
- Local businesses: Many local businesses are owned and operated by community members that were born and raised outside your community. Connecting with business owners helps your students see other avenues by which they can support their local community.
- University and speaking partners: One of the amazing programs we have available at our local university is the Speaking Partners program. A community member can volunteer to be partnered up with an international student for a semester to meet weekly for the student to practice English-speaking

skills. However, so much more is learned through this partnership. The community member gets a one-on-one experience with an international student while the international student makes local connections. Typically, lifelong friendships are born during this process. Most universities have similar programs for outreach with local stakeholders and diverse students.

- High schools/elementary schools: Depending on which school you are in, making connections with other students across your district may be the easiest way to start a multicultural connection. An activity would be to find another classroom that has a different ethnic makeup than your classroom and become digital partners with them. Skype or Zoom or Google Hangouts all offer free video-chatting software for you to connect with other classrooms in your community or across the world.

Reflection Questions and Activities

1. *When student teaching, ask permission to participate in parent–teacher conferences. Take note of similarities and differences between the students and the parents, the questions parents ask the teachers, and the interactions between students and parents and parents and teachers. How do the parents in your class differ from your parents? Continue examining your personal beliefs about students and learning as you continue your journey in education.*

2. *Discover the rich, authentic community connections that can be made in your city. Contact your local library, university, and/or restaurants to inquire about partnerships that can be made. Parents will be an integral part of these connections. Parent volunteers in your class can help you begin making these connections. How can the students in your school/classroom feel accepted and validated by your local community partners?*

3. *Reflect on your current curriculum used in your school. Think about your math textbook, English language arts textbook, science textbook, social studies textbook, authentic texts, children's literature, and so on. Does your curriculum represent all students in your school or focus only on the majority of your students? Will all students in your school be able to make connections with the characters in the stories you share? Are women, minorities, and students with disabilities represented in your curriculum and children's literature? How will you ensure as a teacher that your students will be well represented through your lessons and academic content?*

References

Boaler, J. (2016). *Mathematical mindsets: unleashing students' potential through creative math, inspiring messages and innovative teaching.* San Francisco, CA: Jossey-Bass.

Chamot, A., & O'Malley, J. (2009). *The CALLA handbook.* Boston, MA: Pearson Education.

Engel, L. C. (2017, October). *Underrepresented students in US study abroad: Investigating impacts* (IIE Research and Policy Brief Issue No. 1). Retrieved from https://www.iie.org/Research-and-Insights/Publications/Underrepresented-Students-and-Study-Abroad

Hill, T., Lickteig, A., & Schwerdtfeger, S. (in press, 2020). Field-based experiences in teacher preparation: From private schools to Paraguay. *School-University Partnerships.*

Hoffer, W. (2016). *Cultivating STEM identities.* Portsmouth, NH: Heinemann.

Iliev, N, & D'Angelo, F. (2014). Teaching mathematics through multicultural literature. *Teaching Children Mathematics, 20*(7), 453–457.

Lynch, M. (2015). *6 ways to implement a real multicultural change in the classroom.* Retrieved from https://www.theedadvocate.org/6-ways-to-implement-a-real-multicultural-education-in-the-classroom/

Morehead, M., Lyman, L., Foyle, H., Schwerdtfeger, S., & Lyman, A. (2017). *Working with student teachers: Getting and giving the best.* Lanham, MD: Rowman & Littlefield.

Moss, D. M., Barry, C. A., & MacCleoud, H. (2018). Promoting intercultural learning through an international teaching internship program. In T. Huber & P.

S. Roberson (Eds.), *Inquiries into literacy learning and cultural competencies in a world of borders* (pp. 199–217). Charlotte, NC: Information Age Publishing.

Reagan, M. (2016). *STEM infusing the elementary classroom.* Thousand Oaks, CA: Corwin.

Reyes, R., Lindquist, M., Lambdin, D., & Smith, N. (2014). *Helping children learn mathematics.* Hoboken, NJ: Wiley.

Ryan, P. M. (2000). *Esperanza rising.* New York, NY: Scholastic, Inc.

Suess, Dr. (1971). *The Lorax.* New York, NY: Random House.

Van De Walle, J., Karp, K., & Bay-Williams, J. (2016). *Elementary and middle school mathematics: Teaching developmentally.* Boston, MA: Pearson.

CHAPTER FIVE

UNDERSTANDING AND EMBRACING AFRICAN AMERICAN VERNACULAR ENGLISH

David Sandles

Admittedly, during my first year of teaching, I adopted an age-old practice that emulated my colleagues. I endeavored to make every attempt to "standardize" the language of my Black students. Now, certainly, as educators, we have a duty to prepare our students for college and career possibilities, and one way we do that is by ensuring students possess the requisite speaking skills for conveying lucid, grammatically correct thoughts. What I did, however, was tantamount to educational malpractice. I would sit passively and watch my colleagues belittle Black students by saying things such as, "No, you don't use that language here. Use that language in the streets. Here, we speak properly." Admonishments such as this served as a model for me. Unfortunately, these admonishments also became a refrain for me.

I will never forget one particular exchange with a "well-intentioned" colleague who confided the following: "You know, if we don't help them, they will never learn how to speak English correctly. Their parents don't know how to speak well, so where else will they learn if we don't force them to speak the right way?" My colleague continued: "Don't let them use words like ain't, *yeah, and* aight." *I remember that statement vividly, as it was the day after Halloween during my first year of teaching. I was struck by that statement. I took it to heart. In fact, I became as much of a staunch proponent of "proper speech" for students as that colleague, especially for my Black students, who, my colleague intimated, needed to be saved more so than the other students. For the next couple of years, I disallowed the use of certain words in my classroom. I even had a bank of forbidden words taped to my whiteboard for constant reference. Complete with words such as* ain't, aight, yeah, *and* prolly *(an analog for probably), this word bank represented an attempt to constrain student expression under the auspices of education.*

Fastidious to a fault, I would correct every verbal solecism on the part of my students. I would stop them midsentence to prevent the word ain't *from escaping their lips, or I would ask them to restate an entire sentence, paragraph or stanza if a verboten word was used either in speech or writing. In retrospect, I was far more destructive than helpful. In fact, an analysis of my colleague's earlier words and the actions taken in my classroom represent a linguistically imperialist mindset that makes me shudder. When I reflect on her words "if we don't force them to speak the right way," I bristle. In this context, the word force evokes images of people being stripped of their native inclinations in favor of practices someone else deems more pragmatic or productive. Regretfully, practices of this kind are spread throughout the annals of history and leave people feeling aimless and discomfited.*

Thankfully, I decided to adopt an alternative ideology concerning language use in my classroom. Instead of chiding those who used double negatives in sentences, for example, I began to embrace the speech patterns as distinctive and culturally pertinent to those using the language. For me, the change came as a result of consultation with a sagacious, well-meaning colleague who challenged my thinking in a manner that proved cathartic. Simply, my colleague asked, "Why do you do that?" With that query, I was forced to defend my fossilized practice of forcing students into a linguistic box. With each offer of evidence, my colleague parried the explanation and demanded stronger justification. Despite each impassioned effort at absolution, my colleague would not let me off the hook. I was forced to reconcile my reality with the new information confronting me. Very shortly after this conversation, I resolved to learn more about the speech patterns of many Black Americans. Although my research is ongoing, my learning to this point changed the way I interacted with students and, presumably, increased the self-efficacy of the students I have since encountered.

The History of African American Vernacular English

Ask teachers about their pet peeves and, invariably, many will lament their frustrations with students' speech patterns in the classroom. Some will describe in elaborate detail the challenges and exasperation of hearing students use taboo words such as *yeah* or *ain't* in school. For me as a teacher, those were significant problems. These verbal challenges forcefully raise the hackles of dedicated teachers everywhere. Upon closer analysis, however, another brand of speech deeply vexes teachers and evokes images of indolent, sloppy thinking on the part of students. Arguably, this brand of speech originated out of American slavery and the subsequent milieu that spawned Jim Crow segregation across the United States (Carpenter, 2009).

Characterized by letter omissions, alternate pronunciations, and unconventional emphasis on certain syllables, these speech patterns are sometimes known as Black English or Ebonics or are derisively labeled broken English. Although many prefer the term Black to describe people of African descent, in academia, the accepted moniker for these rich, unique speech patterns is African American Vernacular English (AAVE). There are several views regarding the origin of AAVE. Some contend that AAVE is a by-product of the Great Migration, during which thousands of Black Americans moved from the rural South to large metropolitan areas of the North in the early and mid-20th century (Harris & Schroeder, 2013). Many speculate that during this trek, Black people brought their linguistic innovations to the northern states and, commingling with the denizens there, brought about a new, distinct language known as a pidgin language (Turner & Ives, 2013). Pidgins are the consequence of multiple language groups combining in situations in which communication is necessary (Wigglesworth, Billington, & Loakes, 2013). Many pidgins grew as a consequence of European colonization, when distinct language groups fused because of forced contact; usually, groups commingled because they were forced to labor together (Wigglesworth et al., 2013). For example, during American slavery, Africans from various linguistic backgrounds were forcibly made to labor for slaveholders. Because these distinct language groups were in proximity, intergroup communication became vital. Consequently, new, hybridized forms of the previous languages emerged. After prolonged contact between language groups, language rules often form, and subsequent generations begin to speak the new language, which classifies the language as a creole (Wigglesworth et al., 2013).

Another view is that AAVE results from cognitive inferiority possessed by people of African descent (Kendi, 2017). This perspective is born from the racist idea that Africans are comparably less intellectual than their White counterparts and are therefore incapable of thinking at higher levels. According to Kendi (2017), these ideas trace back to the earliest days of American society and permeate all sectors of contemporary society. Similarly, Baugh (1999) found that the racist perspective offers those seeking to demonize AAVE speakers a sensible explanation as to why Standard American English (SAE) is not utilized by AAVE speakers.

A final perspective is that AAVE is a language derived from American English. Under this theory, AAVE is a dialect of English and emerged from English through the inaccurate interpretations of Blacks enslaved during the early stages of United States history (Baugh, 1999). This view is affixed to a deficit perspective orientation, as many believe that Blacks can simply cease with being lazy and easily learn to assimilate SAE into their existing schemata (Harris & Schroeder, 2013). The deficit perspective often factors in social class, racial differences, and agency with language to forge mental models concerning a person's overall capacity and aptitude. In short, partly because of the negative perceptions of AAVE, many ask, "Why can they not just learn how to speak correctly?"

Irrespective of its origin, AAVE is often mischaracterized as a language spoken by indolent Blacks lacking ambition. As a teacher, I would regularly hear exchanges between staff members supporting this harmful narrative. Further perpetuating this trope, many non-Black Americans often resort to using elements of AAVE to represent their credibility in certain circles and to demonstrate an acquaintance with Black culture (Smokoski, 2016). For instance, in the popular media, non-Blacks can be heard uttering words such as *finna* (about to), *shawty* (usually referring to a female love interest), and *playa* (usually referring to a male with several sexual conquests). This brand of cultural misappropriation is common and detrimental, as it mocks the speech patterns legitimately and authentically spoken by scores of Black Americans (Ticco, 2015). Conversely, within the classroom, many students are forbidden from speaking their home language and are forced to communicate in a manner that is oftentimes unfamiliar and associated with Whiteness. To some, speaking proper (White) shows a large degree of assimilation. Whereas many Black youths desperately desire to retain their street credibility, education insists that they speak properly. According to Ogbu (2004), the *acting White* hypothesis is an actual phenomenon and states that some Black students develop opposition to conducting themselves in a manner that appears to be White. Furthermore, due to the historical racial oppression perpetuated against Black Americans and the fact that European Americans typically set the political, linguistic, economic, and other societal standards, the racial hegemony of SAE makes voluntary acquiescence to SAE exceedingly difficult for Black children (Baugh, 1999).

Although some seek to appropriate AAVE for ulterior purposes, the Clinton administration sought to strike down its use in public classrooms across the country by issuing the following statements: "Black English is a form of slang that does not belong in the classroom" and "'Elevating Black English to the status of a language is not the way to raise standards of achievement in our schools and for our students" (Bennet, 1996, p. 1). Richard W. Riley, President Clinton's secretary of education, declared that Black English was a "nonstandard form of English" (Bennet, 1996, p. 1) and that it should not be utilized in the classroom. Accompanying the Clinton administration's ideas about AAVE are notions of it essentially being comprised of slang or broken English. The overarching consideration should not be whether AAVE is a "nonstandard form of English" but, rather, whether it possesses a structure worth studying to improve student outcomes (Ticco, 2015).

Although AAVE is an essential aspect of the total Black linguistic tapestry, it is not monolithic and all-encompassing. In fact, AAVE represents only a part of the African American English (AAE) structure, especially with respect to the phonological and regional distinctions that can influence a language. In other words, AAVE is not spoken by all Black people. For a greater perspective, African American English (AAE) refers to the speech used by Blacks in general, including those from all socioeconomic classes. It should be noted, however, that AAVE relates specifically to the vernacular form primarily utilized by Black Americans identified as members of the working class, the lower class, and the underclass. In addition, some individuals speak AAVE continuously and without exception, while others gauge the situation and audience to determine if they should switch between SAE and AAVE (Harris & Schroeder, 2013). Known as code-switching, this phenomenon is the relatively seamless alternation between one language/dialect and another (Fisher & Lapp, 2013). People who can successfully code-switch are often referred to as bidialectical. Utilizing code-switching, ideally, students should be able to make the necessary language adjustments between their home and school environments. In reality, however, many students cannot manage this language shift. In fact, Black students in classrooms all over the country utilize this brand of speech and regularly deal with academic difficulties borne from misapprehension and frustration by their teachers (Smitherman, 2000). In misguided attempts to curb the academic challenges of Black students, unenlightened educational leaders misconstrue and attempt to eradicate the use of patent syntactic, lexical, and semantic nuances endemic of AAVE.

Characteristics of AAVE

As an AAVE speaker and a longtime classroom teacher, I intimately understand the nuances of AAVE and how it is perceived within educational confines. I understand that many feel it is not a legitimate language and that it lacks linguistic structure and form. Despite these contentions, AAVE is quite structured and rule-governed. According to Delpit (1997), characterizations of AAVE as "slang," "mutant," "lazy," "defective," "ungrammatical," or "broken English" are incorrect and demeaning (p. 8). Many grammatical and phonological aspects of AAVE distinguish it from SAE, and over the last several decades, numerous scientific studies have demonstrated those distinctions and the grammatical and syntactical viability of AAVE (Charity, Scarborough, & Griffin, 2004). The studies show that AAVE is governed by rules and predictable patterns just as other languages are.

Although AAVE is regularly derided and diminished, in popular culture, elements of AAVE are pervasive and have penetrated the language patterns of many non-Blacks. However, many maintain that the linguistic misappropriation of AAVE's speech patterns is especially egregious when done by educated people under the auspices of sophistication and cultural admiration. Smokoski (2016) found that in such situations, socially acceptable utterances such as the following predominate: "I don't cur [care]" and "We be goin' dere errday [every day]." Although customary, speech dalliances such as these minimize the actual linguistic patterns of scores of people around the world. The use of appropriated AAVE words in movies, television, and books has the effect of mocking the language. According to Hill (1995), a similar misappropriation takes place with the Spanish language. Hill (1995, p. 10) calls the phenomenon *Mock Spanish* and specifically identifies terms such as "Hasta la vista, baby," "Let's go get a cerveza," or "No problemo" as some of the more odious examples. Similarly, in AAVE, the linguistic misappropriations and amusing forays into the lives of Black people mock the overall experience of the people.

An overview of some regular characteristics of AAVE is presented in Table 5.1. Although there are numerous distinctions between SAE and AAVE, some of the benchmark distinctions are offered for perspective; however, this list is not meant to be comprehensive. Rather, it is intended to provide a basic lexicon for those seeking to develop a working knowledge of AAVE.

TABLE 5.1
CHARACTERISTICS OF AAVE

The past tense indicated by (*–ed*) is regularly omitted.	"I live there for two years"
The absence of copula is a regular feature.	"Why he doin' that?"
The word *been* is a common feature used to demonstrate an action completed long ago.	"They been took off."
The verb *be* regularly replaces the SAE adverb inclusion.	"We be drivin' to the store."
Ain't often serves as a negative signifier.	"He ain't got it" or "Why we ain't get picked?"
Third-person singular *–s* is absent.	"She think she look cool."

In AAVE, the conventional aspects of language (semantics, syntax, morphology, pragmatics, and phonology) are sometimes structurally altered in ways that bring about confusion in many classroom teachers, whose language is often standardized (Rickford & King, 2016). Often, when students enter classrooms speaking with nonstandard vernacular, teachers immediately want to correct or "fix" the speech. This tendency frequently causes consternation in many educators and mighty frustrations in students. One particular AAVE trait that causes particular consternation in educators everywhere is negative concord.

Negative concord is the use of multiple words (morphemes) in a single sentence denoting a negative or opposite meaning (Mufwene, Rickford, Bailey & Baugh, 1998). A representative example is shown in the following sentence: "It *ain't never* been another fighter like me. *Ain't never* been *no nothing* like me." Offered by boxing great and civil rights activist Muhammad Ali, this quote uses numerous negatives within a single sentence to forcefully convey the point that Ali considers himself unique (Tischler, 2015). In Ali's sentence "Ain't never been no nothing like me," the words *ain't, never, no,* and *nothing* serve as the negative markers. As noted by Mufwene et al. (1998), in AAVE, negatives are often used near the front of sentences to establish the negative tone of the sentence. The examples in Table 5.2 illustrate that point.

TABLE 5.2
NEGATIVE CONCORD IN AAVE

Double and triple negatives are regularly used	"We don't got no money." "Don't nobody want no ___."
Ain't is often used as a negative marker.	"Ain't he comin'?"

According to Martin and Wolfram (1998), there are definitive negative markers in AAVE, meaning signature words serve as the main modifier in the case of double (or triple) negatives. Martin and Wolfram (1998) maintain that *ain't, can't,* and *nobody* are common negative markers in AAVE. Additionally, Martin and Wolfram contend that although AAVE speakers regularly use multiple negative markers within a sentence, SAE uses a single negative word, often accompanied by a negative polarity item (NPI) such as *any, ever, a bit,* and so on. See Table 5.3 for an example.

TABLE 5.3
NEGATIVE POLARITY ITEMS (NPI)

I don't want *any* food. (The word *any* serves as the NPI).
She didn't want *a bit* of the food. (The word *any* serves as the NPI).

In each of the sentences in Table 5.3, the NPI prevents the sentence from containing "double negatives," a verboten notion in SAE. For many speakers of AAVE, however, double negatives afford users an accurate expression of feelings and thoughts. In fact, many researchers believe negative concord and other conspicuous features of AAVE most readily surface when speakers become more expressive (e.g., angry, embarrassed, or frustrated).

Another common feature of AAVE is the "nonstandard" emphasis on certain syllables of everyday English words, usually the initial syllable. Referred to as phonological nuances, examples include *PO-lice, HO-tel,* and *DE-troit* (Smitherman, 2000). Although concentrations such as these are common in AAVE, in SAE, the same words have the emphasis placed on the final syllable, giving pronunciations such as *po-LICE, ho-TEL,* and *de-TROIT.* These phonological nuances of AAVE are often a basis for implicit bias against students and instructional misapprehension on the part of students (Wheeler, Cartwright, & Swords, 2012).

Characteristics such as the preceding are regular features of AAVE and provide a basic context for understanding the structure of the language form. Armed with this foundational information, learners can consider the purpose and details of acquiring a working knowledge of AAVE.

The Rationale for Studying AAVE

Numerous facts justify the study of AAVE. On the surface, learners should desire to learn about the language form because early AAVE speakers contributed African-originated words to the American English lexicon, including *gumbo, yam,* and *banjo.* Ideally, this information would pique curiosity about additional contributions made by AAVE to the mainstream English lexicon. More practically, however, an understanding of AAVE is essential to aid scores of students who struggle with SAE acquisition and converting between the two language forms. Teachers, in particular, should endeavor to learn more about the speech patterns utilized by AAVE speakers.

In hindsight, as a classroom teacher, I would have definitely been better positioned to help my students had I known more about AAVE's grammatical nuances. With this knowledge, I could have assisted students more deftly in understanding the similarities and distinctions between AAVE and SAE. I also believe chronicling and analyzing the development of the language form could have enriched my history lessons and offered AAVE-speaking students greater validity and pride in their culture. Despite these lost opportunities, I remain emboldened that I can influence scores of educators, through writings such as this, to not only embrace and encourage the use of AAVE but to also understand, contextually, how and when to code-switch.

As a consequence of constant code-switching, many AAVE speakers, according to Seidenberg (2013), have lower literacy skills than their school-age contemporaries. There are numerous possible reasons for this occurrence; however, chief among those reasons is that AAVE speakers are more likely than their counterparts to live in poverty and be constantly exposed to the unconventional, nonstandard language patterns often spoken by Black families around the world (Jencks & Phillips, 2011). To assist AAVE speakers and create legitimate college and career pathways for students, educators should intimately acquaint themselves with the nuances of AAVE to become more culturally sensitive to the experiences and instructional needs of these students.

Additionally, although many students simply vacillate between AAVE and SAE, according to Dillard (1972), the preponderance of Black students are unable to effectively alternate between the two. I noticed this quite regularly. In my experience, many of my AAVE-speaking students could effectively speak either AAVE or SAE, but overwhelmingly, most students could not successfully navigate both. In fact, Dillard (1973) estimated that approximately 80% of Black people exclusively speak AAVE and are incapable of meaningfully accessing SAE. In short, Dillard (1973) posits that 80% of Black people lack the bidialectalism needed for favorable academic and social outcomes. If Dillard's (1973) estimates are proximate, scores of students require specific techniques for bridging AAVE and SAE so that they can successfully navigate the confines of not only academia but also society in general. For example, the acquisition of skills like the previously mentioned code-switching affords students opportunities to participate in their home environs and society events with equal facility and relative comfort.

Furthermore, the language that AAVE speakers use in the classroom is depreciated because of its lack of orthodoxy and misalignment with the teachers' language (Champion, Cobb-Roberts, & Bland-Stewart, 2012). Linguists and language scholars maintain that, collectively, educators must undergo a conceptual shift to employ practices that value what multilingual speakers bring. However, many classrooms around the United States continue to utilize harmful, monolingual ideologies. When teachers fail to understand and acknowledge the differences between AAVE speakers and their speech, they create conditions that can influence the performance and desire of students to perform optimally. Whether or not in school contexts, language use and literacy practices include syntax, lexicon, and semantics. These discussions also implicitly involve references to power and influence, as they include the important information about people, namely, their connections with people, places, and periods throughout history (Turner & Ives, 2013).

Language Registers

An effective teacher should never attempt to destroy a student's language, particularly one that children use fluently. Thinking back on my early teaching years, inadvertently, I did just that. I attempted to destroy the richness and the power of my students' native speech patterns. Fundamentally, a teacher should add to the student's speech a dialect for SAE to be utilized at times depending on the circumstance. Taking this additive approach leaves children with their native dialect intact and fosters an acknowledgment of students' family and friends. To take this approach, however, teachers should be acquainted with language registers.

"A language register is a linguistic repertoire that is associated, culture-internally, with particular social practices and with persons who engage in such practices" (Agha, 2004, p. 24). With that, language registers can also be seen as linguistic parameters within which people operate in social, private, and intimate settings. The discussion of language registers is important because, often, students are not explicitly taught distinctions among the kinds of language used and the accompanying perceptions people hold of the speaker(s). With a basic understanding of language registers, teachers can begin the process by purposefully planning lessons that utilize, rather than destroy, students' native speech. Table 5.4 illustrates the registers of language.

TABLE 5.4
LANGUAGE REGISTERS

Register	Explanation
Formal	The standard sentence syntax and word choice of work and school; has complete sentences and specific word choices
Frozen	Language that is always the same, for example, the Lord's Prayer, wedding vows, etc.
Consultative	Formal register when used in conversation; discourse pattern not quite as direct as formal register
Casual	Language between friends characterized by a 400- to 800-word vocabulary; general, and not specific, word choice
Intimate	Language between lovers or twins; language of sexual harassment

It should also be noted that SAE, or the formal register, is not qualitatively superior to AAVE, and it should not be exalted as such. Unfortunately, to this point, society has not developed respect and appreciation for nonstandard forms of English; therefore, educators are obligated to imbue students with a healthy sense of their linguistic gifts through instruction and encouragement. This instruction must also include acknowledgment of the familial cohesion possessed by native speakers, but it must also help students acquire the linguistic capital needed to access institutions of power in society (i.e., formal register).

Recommendations for Educators

According to Gee (1999), language is a vehicle for three things: saying, doing, and being. Put differently, for readers to fully understand a writer's ideas, the reader must have more than just the writer's words to contextualize the meaning. Using this tenet of Gee's (1999) discourse theory, that educators immerse themselves into the words, the psyches, and even the milieu of Black authors to deeply appreciate their meaning is imperative. For instance, when reading the rap lyrics of Tupac Shakur, one must understand what he is saying (inform), what he is doing (act), and what he is (be) to truly comprehend his work. Similarly, educators should also immerse themselves into the culture to assist their AAVE-speaking students to bring about successful acquisition of what Gee (1999) calls secondary discourse.

To Gee (1999), primary discourse is that which a person learns from family and the surrounding community. Secondary discourse is language one must learn to become literate in certain settings. Specifically, secondary discourses include those a person might acquire to successfully navigate school and/or church, play video games, or interact with government agencies. Using Gee's (1999) theory, that teachers help students assimilate secondary discourse using varying methods is important.

1. Above all, affirm AAVE; don't ridicule or disparage it. Violating this suggestion is a surefire way to lose some students. Seek to understand the structure of the dialect and its history; then guide students toward secondary discourse acquisition.

2. Explicitly teach code-switching. This important technique provides students with instruction in the successful navigation of a range of social environments, and it enables students to build agency in unfamiliar, uncomfortable circumstances.

3. Briefly teach students the history of AAVE. Children should learn the history of their language. As a way of affirming the language of Black students (and other speakers of AAVE), a legitimate study of the history and linguistic nuances of AAVE can help students make connections with the material.

4. Teach the language registers. Help students understand which register they use at any given time; encourage and model the changes between formal and informal registers.

5. Use scripted AAVE sentences as teaching tools to support conversion into SAE. Use sentence frames. Commonly used in classrooms around the world, this invaluable method is used

to visually represent conventional English. Similarly, AAVE sentences should also be displayed so students can begin to appreciate the structure of the language and make the conversions between both brands of discourse. By extension, teachers should use sentence frames to demonstrate the syntax and overall structure of AAVE.

Additionally, Delpit (1997) found that educators must be knowledgeable of AAVE features to demonstrate corresponding rule-governed aspects between AAVE and SAE. Using code-switching as a technique to appropriately and skillfully alternate between AAVE and SAE could be an immeasurably important tool for teachers to use, as it values students' home language and creates a bridge between the two language styles. Although AAVE speakers have models for written SAE, they often do not have models for written AAVE. Principally, AAVE is an oral linguistic system, and students have minimal experience interacting with it in print. Therefore, scripted and spoken versions of AAVE speech patterns should be utilized by educators to help students understand its structural nuances and to bridge it with SAE.

Moreover, teachers should regularly reflect on their own language learning experiences, specifically recalling how they felt when their language was corrected. Next, teachers should question how they felt during the experience. This level of reflection has the potential to create empathy toward students and offers teachers a chance to unpack some of their feelings concerning language instruction.

Reflection Questions and Activities

1. *Think about a time when someone in your classroom/home used one of the "forbidden" words (ain't, yeah, etc.). What reaction did that person receive? Was it warranted? Explain.*

2. *Admitting bias is difficult. Reflect on your thoughts when you hear people speak AAVE. If any, what judgments do you make about*

their speech? How can you incorporate a greater appreciation for AAVE and other distinct speech patterns into your classroom?

3. *Think about some of your different classroom experiences. Have you ever been reluctant to speak aloud in class? If so, was your apprehension in any way attributed to difficulty with language? What are two techniques teachers can employ to assist students attempting to acquire SAE?*

References

Agha, A. (2004). *Registers of language. A companion to linguistic anthropology,* 23–45. Malden, MA: Blackwell.

Bennet, J. (1996, December 25). Administration rejects Black English as a second language. *The New York Times.*

Baugh, J. (1999). *Out of the mouths of slaves: African American language and educational malpractice.* Austin, TX: University of Texas Press.

Carpenter, Jennifer. (2009). Voices of Jim Crow: Early urban African American English in the segregated south. [Doctoral dissertation Duke University]

Champion, T. B., Cobb-Roberts, D., & Bland-Stewart, L. (2012). Future educators' perceptions of African American Vernacular English (AAVE). *Online Journal of Education Research, 1*(5), 80–89.

Charity, A. H., Scarborough, H. S., & Griffin, D. M. (2004). Familiarity with school English in African American children and its relation to early reading achievement. *Child Development, 75,* 1340–1356.

Delpit, L. (1997). Ebonics and culturally responsive instruction. *Rethinking Schools,* 12(1), 6-7.

Dillard, J. L. (1973). *Black English: Its history and usage in the United States* (pp. 77-8). New York: Vintage Books.

Fisher, D., & Lapp, D. (2013). Learning to talk like the test: Guiding speakers of African American Vernacular English. *Journal of Adolescent & Adult Literacy, 56,* 634–648.

Gee, J. (1999). *Introduction to discourse analysis: Theory and method.* London: Routledge.

Harris, Y. R., & Schroeder, V. M. (2013). Language deficits or differences: What we know about African American Vernacular English in the 21st century. *International Education Studies, 6,* 194–204.

Hill, J. (2007). Mock Spanish: A site for the indexical reproduction of racism in American English. *Race, ethnicity, and gender: Selected readings*, 270–284.

Jencks, C., & Phillips, M. (Eds.). (2011). *The Black-White test score gap*. Washington, DC: Brookings Institution Press.

Kendi, I. X. (2017). *Stamped from the beginning: The definitive history of racist ideas in America*. New York: Random House.

Martin, S., & Wolfram, W. (1998). The sentence in African-American vernacular English. In S. S. Mufwene, G. Bailey, J. R. Rickford, & J. Baugh (Eds.), *African-American English: Structure, history, and use* (pp. 11–36). New York: Psychology Press.

Mufwene, S. S., Bailey, G., Rickford, J. R., & Baugh, J. (Eds.). (1998). *African-American English: Structure, history, and use*. New York: Psychology Press.

Ogbu, J. U. (2004). Collective identity and the burden of "acting White" in Black history, community, and education. *The Urban Review, 36*(1), 1–34.

Rickford, J. R., & King, S. (2016). Language and linguistics on trial: Hearing Rachel Jeantel (and other vernacular speakers) in the courtroom and beyond. *Language, 92*, 948–988.

Smitherman, G. (2000). *Black talk: Words and phrases from the hood to the amen corner*. Boston: Houghton Mifflin Harcourt.

Seidenberg, M. S. (2013). The science of reading and its educational implications. *Language Learning and Development, 9*, 331–360. doi:10.1080/15475441.2013.812017.

Smokoski, H. L. (2016). Voicing the other: mock AAVE on social media. City University of New York, New York, NY.

Ticco, J. E. (2015). *Using African American Vernacular English and hip hop nation language to teach Standard American English: Creating a bidialectal classroom* [unpublished doctoral dissertation]. State University of New York at Fredonia.

Tischler, B. (2015). *Muhammad Ali: A man of many voices*. New York, NY: Routledge.

Turner, K. N., & Ives, D. (2013). Social justice approaches to African American language and literacy practices: Guest editors' introduction. *Equity & Excellence in Education, 46*, 285–299.

Wheeler, R., Cartwright, K. B., & Swords, R. (2012). Factoring AAVE into reading assessment and instruction. *The Reading Teacher, 65*, 416–425.

Wigglesworth, G., Billington, R., & Loakes, D. (2013). Creole speakers and standard language education. *Language and Linguistics Compass, 7*, 388–397.

CHAPTER SIX

ARE YOU A BOY OR A GIRL? STUDENT IDENTITY

Anni K. Reinking and Bre Evans-Santiago

Elementary School

"Okay, this is girls' week. So, girls, you get to go first in line and get to pick the gym activities," Ms. Peets yelled over the loud second-grade class in the gym.

This discourse—"Girls line up first" or "boys on this side and girls on the other side" or "boys versus girls today"—was a normal occurrence in Ms. Peets's physical education class as well as other classrooms with several teachers in the school building. Aware of the school culture, a substitute teacher walked into the gym one bright morning. The lesson plans read that it was girls' week and outlined what that meant. After reading the plans, the substitute teacher began the day with the first class, a class of third graders.

"Good morning, boys and girls. I hear that it is girls' week, so girls line up over here, and boys line up over here." After she made that statement, the students went to their respective lines. However, the substitute saw a child,

with a short buzz haircut, wearing long cargo shorts and baseball T-shirt standing in the girls' line.

Assuming this child was a "boy" and trying to be funny, the substitute said, "Now, you can't do that to me. You are a boy; go stand in that line." An awkward silence filled the room as they followed the teacher's directions and the student did not move. "I said go to that line; you are not a girl. You are in third grade; you should know whether you are a boy or a girl." The student just stared back at the teacher defiantly. One brave student raised a hand and said, "Excuse me, Miss, but that is Etta; she is a girl."

Middle School

A sixth-grade class always lined up in the same format—boys on the right and girls on the left. They would enter and exit the room, with girls going first and boys going last. They learned how to hold the door for the ladies and to control their laughter and to respect space as the ladies walked in. The class seating arrangement alternated boy–girl as much as possible to avoid behavioral issues. The students were used to this procedure by sixth grade, as it had been instilled as a habit of mind. One biologically identified male in the class, David, enjoyed sitting with the girl next to him. They would compare colored pens, and the girl would ask him to write or decorate her folders or artwork because she loved David's writing.

This sixth-grade class was very active with jumping rope during the first semester. All the girls plus David would go out and play double Dutch. The boys were usually on the grass field playing soccer. This was the daily routine—boys over here and girls over there. Everyone was "programmed" to act and think this way, but David was different.

David did not fit the "assigned" gender role expectations. He would rather play jump rope and write beautifully in notebooks. As sixth graders, it was noticed, and students began to act based on their judgments. David never told the teacher of any of the incidents, but the girls who played with him outside did. They said that the boys were teasing him and calling him a "fag" and saying, "Go put on your pretty dress." The teacher was very upset about this. She spoke with the whole class and said if she heard about the behavior continuing, there would be negative consequences. The kids feared her motherly tone, so they stopped, or were more secretive about what they said, and that was that. The teacher lacked resources and support to continue a deeper conversation, so she used her motherly tone to threaten negative consequences to try to protect David. When asked about the situation, she said, "I wish I could help David more. This is awful, and I don't know how to make it better."

Due to the fact that the United States census continues to exempt lesbian, gay, bisexual, transgender, and queer (LGBTQ) demographic data, it is estimated that 4.5% of the U.S. population identify as LGBT, which equates to "roughly 11, 343, 000 people," with Washington, D.C.; Oregon; Nevada; Massachusetts; and California having the highest populations (Williams Institute, 2019a, 2019b). According to the Williams Institute (2019a), 29% of the LGBT population have children. These data indicate that teachers either will have students who identify on the LGBTQ spectrum or are children of LGBTQ parents sometime in their teaching careers. All students and families have the right to be represented and recognized in schools, including LGBTQ students and families. As teachers, the obligation to ensure this happens is necessary and urgent for decreasing the number of students depressed and attempting suicide at young ages. LGBTQ inclusivity combats oppression and marginalization, while it reiterates the importance of individuality and family acceptance.

Whether the situation is in an elementary or middle school environment, students' gender identity[1] (Human Rights Campaign, 2019) and gender expression are areas where teachers must learn to be more inclusive with words and activities. Children begin to develop their gender identity by the age of four (Healthychildren.org, 2019) through their mannerisms, dress, hair, and other social behaviors. Throughout the United States, binary identities have been a guiding factor when managing and instructing students (Chappell, Ketchum, & Richardson, 2018). Identity directly connects with the moniker LGBTQ,

---

1   See Human Rights Campaign in the Online Sources at the end of the chapter.

and the letters that follow the LGB reference <u>gender identity</u>[2] (Planned Parenthood, 2019). Sexual orientation is a label given to identify common non-heteronormative relationships or sexual preference. Most recently the term *Queer* has been known to represent either sexual or gender identity, and the "+" often seen at the end of the acronym can represent a plethora of both gender and sexual identities. Because identities are fluid, several terms are emerging to support individuals who identify with something other than the LGBT or Q. Therefore, when gender identity is discussed, it falls under the LGBTQ umbrella. In this chapter, we discuss not only gender identity but also family identity based on sexuality.

Curricula

Nationwide, students who had exposure to curricula that promoted and honored difference, such as LGBTQ identities, refrained from using negative slang that is harmful to the LGBTQ community much less than those students who lack exposure to curricula do (Kosciw, Greytak, Zongrone, Clark, & Truong, 2017). Title IX is an education equality amendment that prohibits discrimination in various entities, including sexual and gender identity (Chappell et al., 2018). Because of this federal law, several states and public school districts are working toward the inclusion of LGBTQ events and individuals within a mandated curriculum. The principal deputy assistant attorney general, Vanita Gupta, stated, "Every child deserves to attend school in a safe, supportive environment that allows them to thrive and grow" (U.S. Department of Justice, 2016). This statement supports the idea that the educational system in the United States is striving to help students and teachers incorporate multicultural topics and practices into classrooms. However, deep historical persistence regarding LGBTQ discrimination in the United States remains (Graves, 2007; Johnson, 2019), and only <u>20 states</u>[3] (Freedom for All Americans, 2018) have antidiscrimination laws protecting this vulnerable population.

Because of this concern, the integration of LGBTQ themes in elementary classrooms has been studied. For example, Flores (2014) found,

2   See Planned Parenthood in the Online Sources at the end of the chapter.
3   See Freedom for All Americans in the Online Sources section at the end of the chapter.

> Teachers do not implement gay themes in their multicultural education that includes lesbian, gay, bisexual, and transgender (LGBT) themes and gay-themed children's literature . . . because of fear of criticism from parents and administrators, lack of professional training, and their own negative attitudes. (p. 114)

This statement of LGBTQ topics under the umbrella of multicultural education is supported by the work of Banks (1999) that provides a topical list of multicultural topics, such as socioeconomics, race, culture, sexuality, family demographics, and religion. Flores (2014) identified fear and knowledge deficits as obstacles to addressing LGBTQ topics. This is understandable since less than 20 years ago, some parents believed LGBTQ educators should not be allowed to teach in public schools (Bishop, Caraway, & Stader, 2010).

For educators, addressing LGBTQ themes can be a difficult process (Flores, 2014). Flores recounts situations with colleagues that resulted in verbal abuse and/or harassment from parents when LGBTQ themes were brought up in the classroom. Nonetheless, understanding, reflecting on, and being aware of their own beliefs while also creating an environment for students to feel accepted and welcomed is important for teachers. Understanding that Title IX gives students at all grade levels the freedom to an education without discrimination of sex, a growth mind-set must be established to develop the knowledge and resources for gender and family inclusion within the classroom. Teachers should embrace the need to actively end oppression, to engage all students, and to continually reexamine educational practices that may negatively affect students.

One strategy to engage students is through reexamining the classroom books and ensuring they represent all types of students in an age-appropriate way. The following are seven key areas, outlined by Husband (2015), for age-appropriate books in classrooms:

1. Check for offensive attitudes and/or stereotypical representations.
2. Check to make sure the historical events in the text are accurate.
3. Check to make sure the book is of good literary quality.

4. Check to make sure the book does not oversimplify highly complicated events in history.
5. Check to make sure the book uses clear and appropriate language to describe LGBTQ+ families and children.
6. Check to make sure the book does not romanticize issues of power.
7. Check to make sure the book reflects a diversity of experiences of a particular (the LGBTQ+) community. Additionally, a list of books can be found at _Huffpost_[4] (2019).

Another difficult aspect of implementing an LGBTQ+-inclusive curriculum is teachers who report, "I do not agree with that lifestyle so how can I include it in my classroom?" Regardless of personal beliefs, inclusion is the ethical underpinning of being an educator. Why? Because hidden curricula can create an environment where not all students feel welcome in a classroom. Ignoring or not addressing gender and sexual identity in K–12 schools is a form of hidden curricula. A hidden curriculum refers to the unwritten, unofficial, and often unintended lessons, values, and perspectives students learn in schools (Jackson, 1968). Hidden curricula have the potential to be both detrimental and favorable to students' knowledge set. In school settings, a hidden curriculum is a common daily occurrence as children learn from the crossing guards, bus drivers, yard supervisors, students, teachers, administrators, and staff. What students hear and see or do not hear and see around them influences their assumptions and learnings. They are learning far more from their environment and social cues than from what text was read during a day. An example of a hidden curriculum is discussed later.

Family Identity

When addressing family identity in schools, students might feel left out. Hidden curricula may suggest that some families are considered more

---

4   See _Huffpost_ in the Online Sources section at the end of the chapter.

important than others. More often than not, heteronormative practices are promoted with school activities. The following includes examples to reflect on.

> *"Okay, boys and girls, today we are going to start our family books. Everyone has the same book, so we are going to go through and see what we can add to each page."*

> *Ms. Sarah and Ms. Alexis guided the preschool students writing their "All About Me" books. Ms. Sarah continued: "Okay, on page 1, we have a page where you are going to draw yourself, then your mom, your dad, then your brothers and sisters if you have any, and any pets you may have. Finally, you are going to add your grandparents or aunts and uncles if you would like to." The students were listening closely to Ms. Sarah, Ms. Alexis sat in the back of the room. During the lesson, Ms. Alexis began to think about the students in her class who had only one parent or had two moms and no dads. How were they going to fill out the book? The family book project was supposed to be fun, but maybe it would be hard for some of the students.*

> *After reflecting on this experience, Ms. Alexis took it on herself to change the wording on some of the book's pages because each page was not representative of each student's family. She knew not everyone in the classroom had a mom, a dad, a grandma, a grandpa, and/or other family members represented in the family book.*

Muffins With Mom and Donuts With Dad: A Blog Reflection

Anni K. Reinking

Is Muffins with Mom and Donuts with Dad a Midwest tradition? Is it a tradition as schools are planning events to include families more? Regardless of why this event began, the message (hidden message) promotes heteronormative family types.

In 2010, I (Anni) became a single parent and wondered, "What is my son going to do on Donuts with Dad" day? I knew my dad would go with him, but the event still did not sit right with me. I began to discuss the event with colleagues (I was working in a school building that had these two events). What do students do who have two moms? Who maybe have a mom and not a dad? Who are wards of the state? Some child is going to be left out, and how is that inclusion?

A conversation I often heard as a teacher was "Hey, we missed you today at Muffins with Mom," or "Why didn't you come to Donuts with Dad today? It was great food." How is a child supposed to respond? "I don't have a dad." "I don't have a mom; I have two dads."

How can we prevent this line of questioning? Or prevent the noninclusive events? Stop planning the events with a focus on moms and dads. Think outside the box: Breakfast with Bigs or Eggs with Everyone or Donuts with Dudes.

This is a great strategy for including everyone, regardless of family dynamics. A few years ago, there was a news story of a single mom who wanted to take her daughter to the Daddy–Daughter dance (another event to reflectively think about). This mother thought it would be fun to dress up like a man (drawn on beard and suit). However, when they arrived at the door to enter the event, they were refused entrance. Why?

There are many examples of hidden curricula when addressing family identity. In the events described earlier, parents are considered binary, with a mom and a dad, and students "need" a father and/or mother to be included in special celebratory events (Evans-Santiago & Lin, 2016). An example of this hidden curriculum in a classroom became apparent for one little girl when she was not allowed to make a family tree with two mothers (Kosciw & Diaz, 2008). The teachers questioned her and essentially told her that she had to have a father. The little girl may have felt that her family is wrong based on her teacher's message.

Additionally, the use of language also resonates within a hidden curriculum in relation to LGBTQ students and families. When students or teachers are allowed to say "homo" or "that's gay," a culture of bullying based on one's sexuality becomes the hidden curriculum in the school environment (Kosciw & Diaz, 2008). Students are learning that "gay" is bad and that it means dumb or stupid. Instead, a positive hidden curriculum can be applied. Visual representations around the classroom, of all types of people, including LGBTQ persons, have the potential to teach all students, regardless of their gender identity or sexuality, that successful people are diverse. Hosting inclusive events teaches students that every type of family is accepted. At times, a negative hidden curriculum is difficult to identify, but with active reflection and open communication between and among educators, parents, and students, a culture of respect and safety is possible.

Strategies for Family Identity Inclusivity

When children feel unsafe or depressed through verbal or physical harassment, or as a result of hidden curricula, attempts of self-harm or suicide are evident. Students who identify as or are perceived to be LGBTQ are among groups with the highest suicide rates[5] (stopbullying.gov, 2017), and children younger than 13 commit suicide[6] (Hanna, 2017) almost once a week. Evans and Hurrell (2016) established five themes when researching self-harm and schools:

1. Self-harm is often rendered invisible or not addressed within educational settings.
2. Self-harm is viewed as a "bad behavior" because it goes beyond the institutional (school) rules; therefore, adequate support is denied.
3. Schools' informal management strategy of escalating incidents of self-harm to external "experts" serves to contribute to non-help-seeking behavior among students who desire confidential support from teachers.
4. Anxiety and stress associated with school performance may escalate self-harm and suicide.

---

5   See Stopbullying.gov in the Online Sources section at the end of the chapter.
6   See CNN in the Online Sources section at the end of the chapter.

5. Bullying within the school context can contribute to self-harm, while some young people may engage in these practices as initiation into a social group.

When addressing bullying and suicide, teachers need professional development opportunities to learn how to create a safe, inclusive environment. This can be done by integrating LGBTQ role models and historical and relevant contributions within the curricula (Chappell et al., 2018). Evans-Santiago and Lin (2016) focused research on including LGBTQ families in lower elementary grades. They suggest that teachers need to take the inquiry approach with all families, ultimately resulting in an inclusive, rather than exclusive, classroom. An inquiry approach asks that for "students (or families) to explore academic content by posing, investigating, and answering questions . . . this approach puts students' questions at the center of the curriculum" (Center for Inspired Teaching, 2008, p. 1). Using the inquiry approach, teachers develop a classroom environment that is student-centered and family-centered, which supports the ideas summarized by Gorski (2010).

Additionally, teachers can engage in storytelling and incorporate multicultural books, including books focused on LGBTQ topics. Although minimal, on its website, Welcoming Schools (2019) provides a list of LGBTQ books,[7] which is a great start for both elementary and middle school teachers. Administrators can also act by "hav[ing] anti-bullying policies and include LGBTQ language within said policies" (Evans-Santiago & Lin, 2016, p. 58).

Although events such as Donuts with Dads do occur in schools, in research and conversations with educators, a lack of awareness around the notion of hidden curricula persists in schools. When teachers and administrators are blind to the hidden curricula of school environments, fear becomes a factor in the school culture. Families may be fearful that they will not be accepted if they do not fit the heterosexual family lifestyle portrayed by hidden curricula. In today's society, heteronormativity is not as strong among younger generations because of the media's attempts to normalize LGBTQ communities, but older generations have experienced it more and therefore may still hide or feel uncomfortable due to society's past norms. Teachers also may express the fear

---

7   See Welcoming Schools in the Online Sources section at the end of the chapter.

of the unknown. Questions might arise, such as "Will my students accept this lesson?" or "What sorts of repercussions might occur as a result of this lesson?"

Asking professional learning communities or administration what others are doing and what can be done to combat the heteronormative hidden curricula can help ease the fear. Taking the initiative to support all students in your class should be the ultimate goal. If teachers are not reflective and educated and begin to widen their view of what a family is in American schools, the fear of pushback will result in detrimental effects on students' well-being. Overall, communication with all involved parties, including families and school personnel, is essential. Learning the dynamics of each student's family requires discussion and inquiry, so providing those opportunities to confer is beneficial. Although fear may be a felt emotion when addressing LGBTQ topics in the classroom, the goal of creating inclusive schools should be one's intent.

To create a confident and welcoming school culture, it is important for the school staff to fully embrace Gorski's (2010) six commonly shared ideas:

1. Every student in an education setting must have an equal opportunity to reach [their] maximum potential.
2. School buildings must prepare students to participate in the ever-changing multicultural society.
3. Students have the responsibility to learn how to interact and embrace changing demographics—[with the] teacher effectively preparing and facilitating learning.
4. Students must be active in ending the oppression.
5. Education must be student-centered and inclusive for all.
6. Educators and advocates for educational equity need to re-examine how educational practices affect student learning.

Educators need to ensure every student has an equal opportunity to reach his or her maximum potential through the implementation of inclusive multicultural education (Gorski, 2010). Educators need to ensure that students are provided with resources that promote success. Additionally, they should question and reimagine events and activities already in place that potentially ostracize families and students.

As national and school demographics continue to change, teachers are tasked with the goal of creating student-centered environments that encourage students to question and engage in activities that end oppressive situations rather than solidify them. Often, students enter classrooms nervous and fearful of a new environment. Teachers attempt to make the classroom inviting in a variety of ways, but most of the time, the LGBTQ community is left out of this welcoming environment. Posters of families or influential people, literature, or phrases on the walls lack LGBTQ inclusivity. Educators who are able to reflect, change fear mentalities, and question the implementation of hidden curricula will have a positive impact on the lives of students. Students will see themselves or their families represented, they will be able to learn about their curiosities that are becoming present in media, and they will see that their classroom is a place of support and comfort.

Children spend more than 30 hours a week in classrooms with teachers who prune and build their young minds. Children's lives are delicate, and their social-emotional skills are developing. To address students' insecurities, bullying, and suicide rates, educators, administrators, and parents need to actively engage in ways in ways that diminish a fearful response when discussing multicultural topics. Administrators and educators need to be knowledgeable of and taught useful, effective multicultural curriculum implementation techniques. Sample lessons and resources can be found on the Teaching Tolerance[8] (Teaching Tolerance, 2019) and GLSEN[9] (GLSEN, 2019) websites. Educators are in a position to incorporate ideas, activities, and topics as a way to positively change school cultures resulting in beneficial experiences for a multitude of students and families.

Reflection Questions and Activities

1. *Review your school discrimination policies. Is LGBTQ+ inclusive language present?*

---

8   See Teaching Tolerance in the Online Sources section at the end of the chapter.
9   See GLSEN in the Online Sources section at the end of the chapter.

2. *Complete a small book review of at least three to five books that include LGBTQ+ families and/or individuals. After reviewing the books, do you feel that they would be okay in your classroom library? Why or why not?*

3. *Compare and contrast your ideas or plans that include various cultures. Is the LGBTQ+ community left out? If so, how might you change this?*

Online Sources

CNN: https://www.cnn.com/2017/08/14/health/child-suicides/index.html

Freedom for All Americans: https://www.freedomforallamericans.org/states/

GLSEN: https://www.glsen.org/

Huffpost: https://www.huffpost.com/entry/lgbtq-kids-books-pride-month_n_5b1023bce4b0fcd6a834bbdb

Human Rights Campaign: https://www.hrc.org/resources/sexual-orientation-and-gender-identity-terminology-and-definitions

Planned Parenthood: https://www.plannedparenthood.org/learn/sexual-orientation-gender/gender-gender-identity

Stopbullying.gov: https://www.stopbullying.gov/at-risk/effects/index.html

Teaching Tolerance: https://www.tolerance.org/

Welcoming Schools: http://www.welcomingschools.org/pages/great-diverse-middle-grade-books-on-family-bullying-bias-and-gender/

References

Banks, J. A. (1999). *An introduction to multicultural education* (2nd ed.). Boston, MA: Allyn & Bacon.

Bishop, H. N., Caraway, C., & Stader, D. L. (2010). A case for legal protection for sexual minority educators. *The Clearing House, 83*(3), 84–88. doi:10.1080/00098651003655878

Center for Inspired Teaching. (2008). *Inspired issue brief: Inquiry-based teaching.* Retrieved from https://inspiredteaching.org/wp-content/uploads/impact-research-briefs-inquiry-based-teaching.pdf

Chappell, S. V., Ketchum, K. E., & Richardson, L. (2018). *Gender diversity and LGBTQ Inclusion in K–12 schools: A guide to supporting students, changing lives.* New York, NY: Routledge.

Evans, R., & Hurrell, C. (2016). The role of schools in children and young people's self-harm and suicide: Systematic review and meta-ethnography of qualitative research. *BMC Public Health, 16*(1) 1–16.

Evans-Santiago, B., & Lin, M. (2016). Preschool through Grade 3. Inclusion with sensitivity: Teaching children with LGBTQ families. *Young Children, 21*(2), 56–63.

Flores, G. (2014). Teachers working cooperatively with parents and caregivers when implementing LGBT themes in the elementary classroom. *American Journal of Sexuality Education, 9,* 114–120.

Freedom for All Americans. (2018). *LGBTQ Americans aren't fully protected from discrimination in 30 states.* Retrieved from https://www.freedomforallamericans.org

GLSEN. (2019). Retrieved from https://www.glsen.org/

Gorski, P. C. (2010). *Multicultural reform: Stages of multicultural curriculum transformation.* Retrieved from http://www.edchange.org/multicultural/curriculum/steps.html

Graves, K. (2007). Doing the public's business: Florida's purge of gay and lesbian teachers, 1959–1964. *Educational Studies, 41*(1), 7–32. doi:10.1080/00131940701308197

Hanna, J. (2017, August 14). *Suicides under age 13: One every 5 days.* Retrieved from https://www.cnn.com/2017/08/14/health/child-suicides/index.html

Healthychildren.org. (2019). *Gender identity development in children.* Retrieved from https://www.healthychildren.org/English/ages-stages/gradeschool/Pages Gender-Identity-and-Gender-Confusion-In-Children.aspx

Huffpost. (2019). *17 LGBTQ books to read to your kid in honor of pride.* Retrieved from https://www.huffpost.com/entry/lgbtq-kids-books-pride-month_n_5b1023b ce4b0fcd6a834bbdb?guccounter=1

Humans Rights Campaign. (2019). *Explore: Transgender.* Retrieved from https://www.hrc.org/explore/topic/transgender/3438.htm

Husband, T. (2015, February, 9). Moving beyond Black and White: Recommendations for using multicultural children's literature in early childhood classrooms [Blog post]. Retrieved from https://eceteachertalk.wordpress.com/2015/02/09/moving-beyond-black-and-white-recommendations-for-using-multicultural-childrens-literature-in-early-childhood-classrooms/

Jackson, P. W. (1968). *Life in classrooms.* New York, NY: Holt, Reinhart & Winston.

Johnson, M. (2019, July 16). ACLU to represent LGBTQ student group in lawsuit over Williamston schools' gender identity policies. *Lansing State Journal.* Retrieved from https://www.lansingstatejournal.com/story/news/2019/07/16/lgbtq-student-group-joins-lawsuit-over-williamston-schools-policies/1738249001/

Kosciw, J. G., Greytak, E. A., Zongrone, A. D., Clark, C. M., & Truong, N. L. (2017). *National school climate survey.* Washington, DC: GLSEN

Planned Parenthood. (2019). *Sexual orientation and gender.* Retrieved from https://www.plannedparenthood.org/learn/sexual-orientation-gender

Stopbullying.gov. (2017). *Effects of bullying.* Retrieved from https://www.stopbullying.gov/at-risk/effects/index.html

U.S. Department of Justice. (2016). *U.S. Departments of Education and Justice release joint guidance to help schools ensure the civil rights of transgender students.* Retrieve from https://www.ed.gov/news/press-releases/us-departments-education-and-justice-release-joint-guidance-help-schools-ensure-civil-rights-transgender-students

Welcoming Schools. (2019). *Great LGBTQ inclusive picture & middle grade books.* Retrieved from http://www.welcomingschools.org/pages/great-diverse-middle-grade-books-on-family-bullying-bias-and-gender/

Teaching Tolerance. (2019). Retrieved from https://www.tolerance.org/

Williams Institute. (2019a). *Adult LGBT population in the US.* Retrieved from https://williamsinstitute.law.ucla.edu/research/lgbt-adults-in-the-us/

Williams Institute. (2019b). *LGBT demographic data interactive.* Retrieved from https://williamsinstitute.law.ucla.edu/visualization/lgbt-stats/?topic=LGBT#about-the-data

Theme Two: Curriculum Implementation

CHAPTER SEVEN

CHRISTMAS FOR EVERYONE?

Bre Evans-Santiago

It was my first year of teaching, and because it was my very own classroom, I loved making it visibly appealing and keeping everything fresh and exciting. As the holidays approached, goosebumps often covered my arms with anticipation of the sparkling lights and warm Christmas spirits. I wanted to decorate the classroom and fill it with cheer so that my students would feel what I felt. The classroom was a beautiful Christmas sight!

Our reading group table was covered with a festive red tablecloth edged with fluffy white cotton. There was even a tiny fiberoptic light-up Christmas tree that shimmered with various colors. The windows were covered with artificial snow and festive decals, and when the students walked in every morning, Christmas music was playing softly in the background. As a Scholastic Book Order fanatic, I had accumulated an ample amount of points toward book purchases, which I used to buy books for all 34 students in my class. Not only did I buy each student a book, but I also signed each book and wrote a sweet note in beautiful writing with glittery colored pens. "You are a hardworking student, Troy, and I hope you have a great Christmas. Love, Ms. Evans." After I signed each book, I wrapped it in Christmas wrapping paper and placed the books around the tiny tree. Seeing the tree and table full of presents for each of the children, I giggled with anticipation, counting the days to see them open their presents and read my thoughtful notes.

Christmas break arrived, and I called each student up to receive their gifts while enjoying treats at our Christmas party. As more and more students opened their gifts, I noticed Lana did not open her present; it just sat on her desk untouched. I then asked her, "Lana, don't you want to open your present?" As she stared at me with glossy eyes and remained silent, I began to think, "She must want to put it under her tree." My heart melted. I thought not only did I provide fun activities and a festive time for my kids, but I was also giving something to her that she may not have! I could not have been prouder. So I left the present on her desk, gave her a kind pat on her back, and went back to the festivities in the classroom.

At dismissal, Lana came up to me after everyone had left and handed me the unopened gift. Quite shocked and almost offended, I asked, "Why are you giving the gift back? Don't you want it for your Christmas?" She then replied in the softest, meekest voice I have ever heard, "Please, Ms. Evans. I am not allowed to have this present." I did not understand, and I wanted to make sure she had a present for her Christmas tree. "No, Lana, it's okay, I want you to have it." She again tried to give it back to me. I was now very confused, my concern growing. "Lana, this gift is from my heart and I could afford it, so you do not need to worry." Lana shook her head. "Ms. Evans, I am a Jehovah's Witness, and we don't celebrate holidays."

My heart sank! I was so enthralled in the holiday celebrations and what I loved about Christmas that I never noticed her lack of participation or that her quiet spirit was purposeful. My biases also played a role. I had always assumed that Mexicans and Mexican Americans were all Catholic. Therefore, I assumed all my Mexican and Mexican American students were Catholic and celebrated Christmas. I had good intentions when I created the Christmas environment at school. At that moment, embarrassed and regretful, I had to think fast so that Lana was not isolated. I said softly, "Lana, if I unwrap it for you, could you take a gift that doesn't represent any holiday?" She responded, "Yes." So I unwrapped the gift and handed her the book. Her smile lit up her face; she gave me the biggest hug and skipped out of the classroom, carrying her special book home.

Christianity is a traditionally dominant religion in the United States (Berry, 2011). Therefore, a majority of U.S. citizens seem to be comfortable with the traditions associated with holidays connected with that heritage. Stores play Christmas music, small towns and businesses are lit up with twinkling lights, and many schools have special Christmas programs filled with singing and dancing to traditional holiday music. Without intending to harm, teachers guide students to think about Christmas in everything from Santa visits to Elf on the Shelf in schools and classrooms. However, with reflection, teachers can be creating a detrimental atmosphere for students (National Association for the Education of Young Children, 2017; Teaching Tolerance, 2013). As teachers, it is our job to ensure that everyone in our classroom feels respected as a contributor to the class environment.

Remembering that some families who are not Christian celebrate Christmas and that, conversely, some families who are Christian do not celebrate Christmas is important. Teachers will have new students with various religious affiliations and cultural backgrounds (Abo-Zena, 2012). This will result in a diverse population with varied traditions, cultures, and religious/nonreligious mind-sets. Throughout their time in school, religious minority students[1] (Newport, 2017) may hide, remain silent, or get bullied because they are not Christian. For instance, since the 9/11 attacks, Muslims have been discriminated against in schools at all levels (Abo-Zena, 2012). Recently in Arizona, a Muslim student was told by their teacher, "I can't wait until Trump is elected. He's going to deport all you Muslims" (Ochieng, 2017). Also, the publicly displayed executive order toward Muslim immigration into the United States heightened anti-Muslim rhetoric and behavior in schools (Hossain, 2017). Jewish children celebrate High Holidays[2] (chabad.org, 2019) and, at times, will miss school for celebrations and wear certain clothing items that other children may not understand (Kronenfeld, 2017). In a recent study, 23% of more than 800 Jewish participants reported school bullying (Institute for Social Policy and Understanding, 2017). These two groups in particular have visual identities that inform those around them of their religion. Because of this, implicit biases[3] (Kirwan Institute for the Study of Race and Ethnicity, 2016) or a variety of microaggressions[4] ("Microaggression," 2019) are more apt to occur with religious minority students.

Holidays are naturally a part of the school culture, but the way we celebrate and acknowledge them needs attention. Celebrating holidays in schools is complex because of the First Amendment's "separation of church and state"

---

1   See Gallup in the Online Sources section at the end of the chapter.
2   See Chabad.org in the Online Sources section at the end of the chapter.
3   See Kirwin Institute in the Online Sources section at the end of the chapter.
4   See Merriam-Webster—Microaggression in the Online Sources section at the end of the chapter.

clause intertwined with individualized district policies (Berry, 2011). Many of the assumed secular holidays celebrated in school come from various religious contexts. Therefore, as a reflective and informed teacher, researching the history behind the holidays celebrated and implemented in schools would be beneficial. Do they include all? Do they exclude others?

There are also economic considerations when including holidays. Poverty can greatly affect decisions made around the holidays because of stresses to have large family dinners, paying for childcare when schools are out, gifts, and much more. Smaller holidays throughout the year that are celebrated at school might cause extra stress at home because the families feel obligated to have their children participate in dressing up, bringing gifts or items for crafts, or having special fundraisers. When the children are not financially able to participate, students might feel embarrassed or inadequate. Some teachers choose to celebrate, while others do not (Chen, 2018; Gooch & Brunetti, 2013) because of the reasons mentioned above.

So What Can Teachers Do?

Regardless of the economic status, religious beliefs, or family traditions, all students have assets[5] ("Assets," 2019) that enhance their contributions to class to create inclusion and not isolation. They can bring their humor, creativity, musical talents, and so much more. These can be valued and implemented within classroom activities instead of the known saying of "Santa or the Elf on the Shelf is watching you." There are several ways to think about how to approach holiday celebrations in the classroom. In this chapter, we discuss seven ideas to consider for inclusive classrooms:

1. Alternative schoolwide celebrations
2. Gain a deeper understanding of students and their families
3. Check with colleagues and administration regarding school expectations or guidelines

---

5   See Merriam-Webster—Asset in the Online Sources section at the end of the chapter.

4. Make celebrations about more than food, music, or popular icons
5. Plan ahead of time
6. Have an approach that is academic and not devotional
7. Educate with theological inclusivity

Alternative schoolwide celebrations may take the place of specific holiday celebrations. Many districts around the United States have moved forward with prohibiting schoolwide traditional holiday celebrations for several reasons including cultural appropriation, economic concerns, religious biases, and loss of academic hours.

One alternative schoolwide celebration is known as "Friendship Day." This celebration encourages students to be kind and accepting of others. Many times, this celebration takes the place of Valentine's Day ("Planning Ahead," 2016). Through this experience, students develop empathy, respect, and a positive rapport with peers. Students can write thoughtful notes to someone, or as a class, they can complete random acts of kindness in their communities. As part of this "Friendship" or "Kindness" Day, random acts of kindness can become a tradition that includes all students and develops a sense of caring for combating bullying.

Another holiday substitution can be "Historical Figures" Week instead of Halloween. The students can dress up like book characters, heroes, or historical figures. Alternatively, some schools now use Drug Abuse Resistance Education (D.A.R.E.) week for dress up days instead of celebrating Halloween, which provides all students the opportunity to participate. Hat Day, Crazy Hair Day, Funky Sock Day, and many more ideas can be found in the 2018 winter edition of *New Teacher Advocate* (Evans-Santiago, 2018).

When these alternative activities, traditions, and celebrations are included, student engagement increases and student isolation decreases. Alternative holidays could also ensure that students with low incomes are able to participate with minimal financial hardships when planned accordingly. For instance, students could wear certain colors for dress up days instead of purchasing costumes. By doing so, students' assets are supported through creativity, thus promoting self-efficacy and pride.

Learn about your students and their families so you are able to incorporate authentic and personal celebrations. Each year, teachers have new students, and with each new group of students, various cultural backgrounds enter the classroom environment. Therefore, teachers knowing *who* is in their classrooms each year to teach students' cultural backgrounds effectively is imperative.

Not only is knowing students important, but so, too, is communicating with students' families. The first communication with parents or family members should be positive to decrease negative feelings (Jones, 2014).

Also, receiving families into the classroom through pictures, visits, or volunteering is crucial. This creates a welcoming environment where families and students alike know their cultural experiences are valued in your classroom. When this occurs, students' cultural competencies and confidence increases, which, in turn, produces a productive and culturally sensitive classroom. Remember that we, as teachers, have the power to make or break a student's ability to succeed.

Finally, take time to allow students to share their cultures with the class and find ways to celebrate each student. This can be done with teacher-led or student-led activities such as student of the week sharing or "all about me" student projects. Scholastic[6] (DePasquale, 2017) provides insight and sample surveys for secondary students to use, and Education World[7] (Provini, 2017) provides a variety of surveys for different age groups. If the survey questions are not meeting expectations, edit the survey or create your own to guide your instructional techniques. Another way to get to know students is to oversee weekly or monthly student-led meetings. These meetings would provide a safe, comfortable setting. One suggestion is to hold weekly meetings on a Friday afternoon at the end of the day. Spend the last 20 minutes in a circle sharing a "good thing" and a "bad thing" for various grade levels. They do not have to speak if they choose not to, and a talking stick[8] (Jannita, 2015) should be used to enforce safety norms for language, respect, and secrecy. Older students could do weekly or monthly "speed dating"–inspired conferences where they connect with a student, answer a few questions based on the topic, and then switch to meet with a certain number of students at each session.

---

6   See Scholastic in the Online Sources at the end of the chapter.
7   See Education World in the Online Sources at the end of the chapter.
8   See Discovery Education in the Online Sources at the end of the chapter.

Although there are several <u>other ways</u>[9] (Teach Thought Staff, 2018) to get to know your students, those mentioned above are just a few that can be implemented within the classroom and help build those necessary relationships. Overall, when knowledge of individuals is obtained, the celebrations within the classroom become more personal (Teaching Tolerance, 2019b).

Check with colleagues and administration for school expectations or guidelines. Schools may have holiday traditions or class party celebrations. Some teachers decorate wildly for certain holidays and may not acknowledge any other holiday. There are districts with policies of autonomy for choosing what to celebrate at school, but most often, Christmas and Halloween are traditionally favored. Based on experience, I have seen costume parades and Christmas programs annually. However, addressing classrooms from a culturally relevant lens, celebrating seasons is a positive alternative.

But then there is also the question of how to maneuver the work environment. Take notice of the administration and staff celebratory practices and ask whether there are dress-up themes or contests together as a whole. Years ago, my school in San Bernardino, California, had a Christmas assembly with performances, and the faculty and staff dressed up in a theme. One year, we dressed in costumes based on *The Grinch* and performed a song together at the annual Christmas program for the kids. Participating was optional, and myself, along with five other teachers, chose to do so. But, at this assembly, my student who did not celebrate was present. This type of celebration, retrospectively, leaves some students out. Although it was a choice, as a new teacher I felt obligated to join the team with these activities to make it fun for the students. But would it have been more culturally accepting if we had performed in a winter program instead of a Christmas assembly? The school climate may come from traditional celebrations, so learning what is already being done and what they are willing to adjust or change are key.

As a new teacher, listen to colleagues' conversations about the holidays. Ask a professional learning community what they do in their classes for students who may not celebrate. Request holiday celebration policies from your principal or lead teachers for easy adherence to the policies. Many teachers are beginning to use large trees in their classrooms and decorate them based on

---

9   See Teach Thought in the Online Sources section at the end of the chapter.

the seasons. An example of decorating a tree during the winter season could include snowflakes, penguins, icicles, white lights, or snowballs. The holiday lessons could include show-and-tell or sharing with one another, and the winter party would not include a holiday theme, just treats and popular music. During other seasons, such as spring, the same tree could be decorated with flowers, umbrellas, and raindrops. Seasonal activities could be applied without using specific religious symbols throughout the year.

When peers and administration create a holiday celebration culture, finding balance and ensuring students are not singled out or isolated during these times is imperative. If your administration and peers support autonomy, then you have the freedom to celebrate what you choose in your classroom to welcome and support all students and their cultural traditions. Several schools and districts are beginning to adjust their holiday celebrations to a more equitable schoolwide celebration where any student can participate regardless of income or religion. If you work at a school where the festivities are more equitable, although you may celebrate a specific holiday or have a bias toward a certain celebration, adhering to the celebration culture at your school site is important.

As has been noted in other chapters, biases in educational settings could favor a particular person and may not provide adequate equity to all groups of people. If the school culture is more biased, be sure to discuss the varieties of festivities and teach students how to appreciate others for their beliefs that may differ from the school's overall celebratory practices.

Make cultural celebrations more than food, music, or popular icons. Teachers sometimes get caught up in singing and eating; therefore, the cultural beliefs, histories, or traditions are silenced. Understanding the traditional cultures of students and those within the United States provide an avenue for acceptance and appreciation of difference. One's knowledge about a person should not be limited to what he or she eats or the songs connected to his or her traditions. Therefore, when teaching, encouraging students to ask questions, inquire, and develop a wider view of cultures is important. This inquiry process has many positive impacts, but most important, it will develop students' social skills when meeting people that may be different from themselves.

Additionally, thematic units throughout the year could contribute to acceptance and diversity within your classroom. Examples of themes include friendship, caring or kindness, thankfulness, remembrance, and forgiveness.

The students could have the platform to share what their own families do with these different themes. By understanding that schools celebrate holidays and that it may be difficult to steer away completely from them, it may be easier to create themes. The theme of remembrance could occur during the first week of November for the Day of the Dead, or *Dia de los Muertos.* The students could then take the time to reflect and acknowledge their ancestors who have helped pave the way for them and who connect with them the most. If kindness week or month is implemented, the students could do random acts of kindness based on their own cultures by having secret pals. Or the students could vote on a class act of kindness to do for other students or staff on campus.

A fifth-grade teacher in Bakersfield City School District supported her students' idea of creating bookmarks for other students in the school. The bookmarks were filled with kind words and colorful pictures. They then placed them in random books in the library in hopes that if the student checked the book out, they would receive their kindness bookmark. Kindness Week could be an alternative to Valentine's Day.

Another teacher in Panama Buena Vista Union School District (Bakersfield, CA) used Globe Trot Scott (Kuster, 2018) to help teach her first-grade students about holidays around the world. The students watched Globe Trot Scott, a fictional world traveler, in videos, sang songs about the culture, read stories, colored flags, identified the countries on a map, wrote in their journals about what they learned, and experienced small sensory items included in the kit. All these activities support the idea of moving past more transparent aspects of culture.

As educators, appreciating the whole child is important. When developing social emotional skills, inquiry, empathy and appreciation of people with different qualities, we develop enlightened citizens.

Plan ahead. To accurately respond to diversity and avoid biased actions or remarks, planning is essential. There is a <u>directory of world religions</u>[10] (BBC, 2014) that gives facts about various holidays. This provides the opportunity to learn about the holidays and set your own opinions aside. We as teachers can be biased when teaching about holidays. An example of a holiday bias is picking your favorite holidays to celebrate in class. This could directly exclude students who observe different holidays or who do not commemorate the occasion at all.

---

10   See BBC in the Online Sources section at the end of the chapter.

Another example of a holiday bias that we tend to gravitate toward is reenactments (Teaching Tolerance, 2019d). The most common reenactment in schools is Thanksgiving. Students make their Native American and Pilgrim costumes and have a feast together in their classrooms or as a school. But do these activities provide accurate knowledge of cultures for our students?

Research the history behind holidays and find the most accurate information possible. Educational textbooks have historically promoted one side to every story, so as teachers, our responsibility is to learn historical facts from both sides. Several texts provide insights to historical holidays such as books by James Lowen, blogs from multicultural academics, and websites such as Teaching Tolerance (2019a) or Teaching for Change (2010). Another shelf-worthy book is *Beyond Heroes and Holidays* (Lee, Menkart, & Okazawa-Rey, 2008), which provides educational tools and activities for all grade levels to incorporate within the classroom to address social justice topics.

Educational insights of various cultures and religious celebrations should be accompanied with, or instead of, reenactments. Biases should be minimal to nonexistent when planned ahead. We want to be careful to not teach acceptance of <u>cultural appropriation</u>[11] ("Cultural Appropriation," 2019), but instead cultural appreciation.

Have an approach that is academic and not devotional. Teaching about religion does not mean that one is advocating for a specific religion. Teach the basics of various cultural celebrations to promote difference and acceptance. Historical perspectives provide reasons for traditional celebratory practices and increase individual's knowledge of cultural diversity. Helping students connect health and dietary restrictions could be coupled with understanding various religious diets. Literacy opportunities such as books, discussions, and nonfictional articles could contribute to the learning environment without <u>devotional</u>[12] ("Devotion," 2019) obligations.

A fourth-grade teacher in Greenfield School District (Bakersfield, CA) taught her students about Day of the Dead, Kwanzaa, Hanukkah, and several other December holidays that she could. She wanted students to be exposed to the various cultures that surround them and experience the fulfillment of

---

11   See Cambridge Dictionary in the Online Sources section at the end of the chapter.
12   See Merriam-Webster—Devotion in the Online Sources at the end of the chapter.

understanding differences. They were all able to participate in creating artwork and learning of various candles' cultural meanings. Although some of them were religious-based, she shared information that was explanatory without devotion. Students were also able to share what they learned in class with their own families at home. They not only learned about holidays, but the lessons also provided a positive social environment for relatability and self-confidence.

Although devotion is important to many religious practices, it is not the only piece of the cultural puzzle. To maintain equity when educating students about various traditions, the customs should be taught with structure or an outline to maintain a balance between academics and devotion.

Educate with theological inclusivity. Do not promote or denigrate any religion. Positive exposure with religions can lead to an appreciation for various holidays, and students may feel excited or curious to learn more about different cultures. We unintentionally spend more time on lessons that we enjoy or relate to and less time on unfamiliar or difficult topics. When teaching about various religions, try to spend the same amount of time implementing each lesson to avoid unintentional biases. A two-day lecture on Christianity compared to a one-day lecture on Islam demonstrates partiality.

Teaching Tolerance (2019c) provides various lessons for all areas of social justice, including a lesson titled "My Way Is Not the Only Way."[13] This lesson provides opportunities for students to analyze their own religious or non-religious beliefs and share/compare with other students in their class. Another lesson that may support religious teachings in class is "One Nation, Many Beliefs," which defines religion and provides text that helps students read statistics of populations and the variety of religions within the United States. These lessons could provide a basis for the variety of cultural teachings that may take place throughout the year.

These articles provide support to say that there are so many religions and we may not be able to learn about all of them. Thematic celebrations, birthday months (not days), and seasonal art throughout the year are examples of nonreligious, inclusive, celebratory practices. Research and learning from others give a platform to support academic and celebratory decisions within your classroom. Table 7.1 provides a generated list of alternatives to holidays.

---

13   See Teaching Tolerance in the Online Sources at the end of the chapter.

TABLE 7.1

ALTERNATIVE OR INCLUSIVE ACTIVITIES

Traditional Holidays (Aug.–May)	Alternative or Inclusive Activities
Halloween	Seasonal/nature activities (pumpkins, scarecrows, bats) D.A.R.E Week (days: mismatched socks, crazy hair, sports, school colors, backward) Hero/History dress-up day Book character dress-up day
Thanksgiving	Seasonal/nature activities (fall leaves, corn/popcorn activities, squirrels) Appreciation Week/Day (Who or what are we grateful for?)
Christmas	Seasonal/nature activities (snowflakes, icicles, snowmen, snowy owls) Learn of all the December holidays celebrated and do activities for them Gingerbread houses Giving to others/help those in need
Valentine's Day	Seasonal/nature activities (snow globes, penguins, bears) Friendship Day/Week Kindness Cards Appreciation Month Secret Pals Learn about the history of the holiday Treats Day (bring a sweet or sweet alternative to share with everyone)
St. Patrick's Day	Seasonal/nature activities (rainbows, clovers, spring buds or flowers, deer, ducks) Learn about Irish traditions and culture Learn about the history of the holiday Discussions/activities around having or not having a pot of gold—empathy, caring, love
Easter	Seasonal/nature activities (grass, blossoms, sun, rain, bunnies, chicks) Baby-chick-hatching project from a family farm Grow plants with a seed Track/follow a bird or other animal cam as it is born or grows Giving to others/help those in need Treats Day (bring a sweet or sweet alternative to share)

Conclusion

There are several ideas and approaches to celebrating holidays within class-rooms, but making sure that you research and prepare for whatever is celebrated with your students is important. Teachers have a "critical role and ability to broaden awareness" (Abo-Zena, 2012, p. 19) and promote acceptance in their classrooms through various avenues. Children have a right to participate in school activities, and marginalization minimizes their voices (Burger, 2019). Remember that not all students can afford to participate in these holiday cele-brations. When there are alternative craft and costume activities that include common items from home or can be created with school materials, it equals the playing field for all students. Classrooms need to be a safe space regardless of their income, religion, or cultural beliefs.

Through the life lesson that I encountered while teaching my fourth grad-ers, I made a mistake by not understanding the cultures within my classroom. I made religious assumptions based on their Latino heritage instead of inter-viewing my students or listening closely to their personal life stories. I created a classroom based on my experiences instead of theirs, and although I had great intentions, I excluded a student with my holiday celebratory actions. As educa-tors, we must reflect on religion and how microaggressive biases can isolate or exclude individuals in our classes. Your position as an educator is immeasurable in that you have the power to make or break a student's ability to succeed.

Reflection Questions and Activities

1. *Interview or survey a student and a parent. What did you learn about that family? What are the assets that this family brings to your classroom environment? Based on what you learned, how will this influence your future communication avenues and activities in your classroom?*

2. *Take a walk around the community various times of the year. Notice the activities, community interactions, holiday decora-tions, and music played in cars or homes. What do people in your*

classroom community enjoy? How do they interact and communi-cate with one another? How might you bring that into your lesson implementations?

3. *What holiday biases do you possess? How might you address your cultural biases to ensure your classroom is equitable for all stu-dents in your class?*

Online Sources

BBC: http://www.bbc.co.uk/religion/religions/

Chabad.org: https://www.chabad.org/holidays/default_cdo/jewish/holidays.htm

Discovery Education: http://blog.discoveryeducation.com/blog/2015/04/27/sos-talking-sticks/

Education World: https://www.educationworld.com/a_curr/back-to-school-student-survey-questionnaire.shtml

Gallup: https://news.gallup.com/poll/224642/2017-update-americans-religion.aspx

Kirwin Institute: https://www.youtube.com/watch?v=lWb4i-ZPE0Q

Merriam-Webster—Asset: https://www.merriam-webster.com/dictionary/asset

Merriam-Webster—Devotion: https://www.merriam-webster.com/dictionary/devotion

Merriam-Webster—Microaggression: https://www.merriam-webster.com/dictionary/microaggression

Scholastic: https://www.scholastic.com/teachers/blog-posts/john-depasquale/2017/Student-Interest-Surveys-Getting-to-Know-You/

Teach Thought: https://www.teachthought.com/pedagogy/the-first-6-weeks-strategies-for-getting-to-know-your-students/

Teaching Tolerance: https://www.tolerance.org/classroom-resources/tolerance-lessons/my-way-is-not-the-only-way

References

Abo-Zena, M. M. (2012). Faith from the fringes. *Phi Delta Kappan, 93*(4), 15–19.

Asset. (2019). In *Merriam-Webster*. Retrieved from https://www.merriam-webster.com/dictionary/asset

BBC. (2014). *Religions*. Retrieved from http://www.bbc.co.uk/religion/religions/

Berry, D. R. (2011). A not so merry Christmas: Dilemma for elementary school leaders. *Kappa Delta Pi Record, 47*(1), 10–13. doi:10.1080/00228958.2010.1051655

Burger, K. (2019). The subjective importance of children's participation rights: A discrimination perspective. *American Journal of Orthopsychiatry, 89*(1), 65–76.

Chabad.org. (2019). *Jewish holidays.* Retrieved from https://www.chabad.org/holidays/default_cdo/jewish/holidays.htm

Chen, G. (2018, December 14). The guide to a politically correct holiday classroom party [Blog post]. *Public School Review.* Retrieved from https://www.publicschoolreview.com/blog/the-guide-to-a-politically-correct-holiday-classroom-party

Cultural appropriation. (2019). In *Cambridge Dictionary.* Retrieved from https://dictionary.cambridge.org/us/dictionary/english/cultural-appropriation

DePasquale, J. (2017). Student interest surveys: Getting to know you. *Scholastic.* Retrieved From https://www.scholastic.com/teachers/blog-posts/john-depasquale/2017/Student-Interest-Surveys-Getting-to-Know-You/

Devotion. (2019). In *Merriam-Webster.* Retrieved from https://www.merriam-webster.com/dictionary/devotion

Evans-Santiago, B. (2018). Culturally inclusive celebrations: Three fun alternatives to parties. *New Teacher Advocate, 26*(2), 4–5.

Gooch, H., & Brunetti, J. (2013). Should holidays be celebrated in class? *California Educator 17*(4). Retrieved from https://www.cta.org/en/Professional-Development/Publications/2013/01/Dec-2012-Jan-2013/Should-holidays-be-celebrated-in-class.aspx

Hossain, S. (2017). Understanding the legal landscape of discrimination against Muslim students in public elementary and secondary schools: A guide for lawyers. *Duke Forum for Law & Social Change, 9,* 81–105.

Institute for Social Policy and Understanding. (2017). *American Muslim poll 2017: Muslims at the crossroads.* Washington, D.C: Institute for Social Policy and Understanding.

Jannita. (2015, April 27). SOS: Talking sticks [Blog post]. Retrieved from http://blog.discoveryeducation.com/blog/2015/04/27/sos-talking-sticks/

Jones, F. (2009). Tools for teaching (3rd ed.). Santa Cruz, CA: Fredrick H. Jones & Associates, Inc.

Kirwan Institute for the Study of Race and Ethnicity. (2016, October 7). *Implicit bias 101* [Video file]. YouTube. Retrieved from https://www.youtube.com/watch?v=lWb4i-ZPEoQ

Kronenfeld, J. (2017, September 13). *ADL reminds schools not to penalize children for high holiday absences.* Jewish News. Retrieved from http://www.jewishaz.com/arts_features/adl-reminds-schools-not-to-penalize-children-for-high-holiday/article_874796f6-989f-11e7-9a81-ab2a0917b3ae.html

Kuster, L. (2018, November 24). Holidays around the world [Blog post]. *Lyndsey Kuster*. Retrieved from https://lyndseykuster.com/2017/11/24/holidays-around-world-free-download/

Lee, E., Menkart, D., & Okazawa-Rey, M. (2008). *Beyond heroes and holidays: A practical guide to K-12 anti-racist, multicultural education and staff development* (4th ed.). Washington, DC: Teaching for Change.

Microaggression. (2019). In *Merriam-Webster*. Retrieved from https://www.merriam-webster.com/dictionary/microaggression

National Association for the Education of Young Children. (2017). *Anti-bias education: Holidays*. Retrieved from https://www.naeyc.org/content/anti- bias-guide-holidays/december-holidays

Newport, F. (2017, December 22). *2017 update on Americans and religion*. Retrieved from https://news.gallup.com/poll/224642/2017-update-americans-religion.aspx

Ochieng, A. (2017, March 29). *Muslim schoolchildren bullied by fellow students and teachers*. Retrieved from https://www.npr.org/sections/codeswitch/2017/03/29/515451746/muslim-schoolchildren-bullied-by-fellow-students-and-teachers

Planning ahead: December holidays in an inclusive classroom. (2016). *Curriculum Review, 56*(3), 11–12.

Provini, C. (2017). *Back-to-school surveys: Get to know students*. Retrieved from https://www.educationworld.com/a_curr/back-to-school-student-Survey-questionnaire.shtml

Rimm-Kaufman, S. E., Curby, T. W., Grimm, K. J., Nathanson, L., & Brock, L. L. (2009). The contribution of children's self-regulation and classroom quality to children's adaptive behaviors in the kindergarten classroom. *Developmental Psychology, 45*, 958–972. https://doi.org/10.1037/a0015861

Teacher Thought Staff. (2018, October 9). *The first 6 weeks: Strategies for getting to know your students*. Retrieved from https://www.teachthought.com/pedagogy/the-first-6-weeks-strategies-for-getting-to-know-your-students/

Teaching for Change. (2019). *Building social justices starting in the classroom*. Retrieved from https://www.teachingforchange.org/

Teaching Tolerance. (2013, April 16). *Problems with Christmas curriculum*. Retrieved from https://www.tolerance.org/magazine/problems-with-christmas-curriculum

Teaching Tolerance. (2019a). Retrieved from https://www.tolerance.org/

Teaching Tolerance. (2019b). *Culture in the classroom*. Retrieved from https://www.tolerance.org/culture-classroom

Teaching Tolerance. (2019c). *My way is not the only way*. Retrieved from https://www.tolerance.org/classroom-resources/tolerance-lessons/my-way-is-not-the-only-way

Teaching Tolerance. (2019d). *Religious holidays*. Retrieved from https://www.tolerance.org/professional-development/religious-holidays

CHAPTER EIGHT

NURTURING THE REVOLUTION: ANARCHY AND DEMOCRACY IN THE ELEMENTARY CLASSROOM

Brittney Beck

During my first year of teaching in a rural community in North Carolina, I taught first grade at a PreK–5 school that was considered failing according to the state's grading system. Pressured by the district administration to improve the school's grade, the principal used extreme tactics. Understanding the school grade was largely based on student performance on the English language arts (ELA) and mathematics standardized tests they took in third and fifth grades, the principal decided to shift human and material resources to these grades and subjects. In particular, she removed all the K–2 teacher aides from our classrooms and redesignated them as tutors for third and fifth graders. This principal also demanded that K–2 teachers focus solely on ELA and mathematics content and engage a narrow pedagogy that would prepare students for the multiple-choice tests they would begin taking in third grade. With these approaches, I knew that any short-term gains in student achievement would come at the cost of students' humanity and sense of possibility in education. However, as a new teacher, I was also vulnerable in the system. Because I did not have tenure, my contract could be nonrenewed without cause in my first 3 years. Therefore, fearful of the loss of my career path in a similar way I imagine my principal was fearful for the loss of hers, I, unwillingly, complied.

On the first day of school, as I stood in a 50-year-old high school–sized classroom that had been retrofitted to become an elementary school after integration, I assessed the state of the 28 first graders before me and no- ticed how they already seemed downtrodden. Many of them looked like they had not slept soundly, and most were still sneaking the breakfast they had tucked into their pockets in the cafeteria when the 25 minutes to go through the lunch line and eat the meager, technically nutritious meals we offered were not enough. I remember watching one frail girl walk into the classroom, wobbling fiercely, but with joyful persistence. This girl would slowly lose the ability to walk over the course of the year, and I would eventually carry her. I would also run with her in my arms to the nurse's office—a nurse who was split between three elementary schools in the district—as the girl breathed faintly and her body burned from a pneumonia-induced fever. I would praise every breath until the ambulance came, and I would not learn until much later that she had a form of muscular dystrophy that was largely unmoni- tored and increased her risk for respiratory complications. I share all this to emphasize the palpable and visceral needs my students demonstrated from the moment I met them. Yet I still moved forward with the ELA- and mathematics-testing preparation packets given to me by my principal as my main form of instruction.

My attempts to build a classroom community and foster a joy for learning were negated by my efforts to force them through lessons that were not reflec- tive of their minds, bodies, or spirits. When students refused to comply, the tension and frustration increased, and I would often punish and take away instead of nurture. After a month of using the students to help me remain in good standing with my principal so she could remain in good standing with the district, I broke down in the classroom after a particularly traumatic morning. The busses were early, and I had not had a chance to go to my classroom prior to meeting my students at the bus stop. As we walked into the classroom together, my students started to collectively gasp and awe. I maneuvered past them to see a pile of newborn baby mice in the middle of our reading carpet. Mice were a common occurrence in the school—as were bats, which, along with asbestos in our school's crumbling walls, often prevented us from using the gym. The students had even named one of the elusive mice that frequented our classroom space—"Junie," after a character in one of their favorite books. These mice, however, were different and needed immediate attention. As adorable baby animals, they had also captured the hearts of my students, and I had to gently tell them we could not raise them as I called the front office to ask for help in handling their removal. The janitor came into my classroom with a shovel, which I thought he was going to use to pick up the mice and take them outside. However, as 28 first graders watched with anticipation and concern for these baby creatures, the janitor used the shovel to crush the pile of mice and then pick up their remains. I felt like the wind had been knocked out of me and I froze. I'm not sure how long it took for me to tune back in to my students, yet as I did, I saw their expressions of fear, pain, and anxiety. I did not have words or a plan to accompany the tragic scene that had just unfolded before all of us; all I had was an ELA lesson that would prepare them for a test they would take in third grade.

Once I regained the ability to speak, I gently turned to them and said, slowly and nervously, "What do you feel like doing right now?"

Closed-Door Anarchy

For the remainder of the day after what would become known as the "baby mice incident," my students made all the decisions. We read stories that featured mice as the main characters, drew pictures of mice, and, with my assistance, wrote a letter to the janitor expressing how his actions made them feel and what he should do differently next time to protect and care for the animals in our school. At times, they felt like being outside, watching clips of cartoons, or having a quiet moment to themselves to cry. I created opportunities for all their requests, and by the end of the day, I felt a shift in my energy, in their energy, and in our energy as a collective. My students had read, written, and engaged in mathematical thinking, yet did so in a way that was responsive to

a lived community need. I did not have to force or punish or threaten consequence—the motivation to improve in the academic disciplines was seen as a
way to express themselves and change an injustice they had witnessed. As the
remainder of the year unfolded, I would be in cahoots with my students and
only pick up those testing packets during formal classroom observations.

Instead of trying to hold in all the pressure I was feeling about the school's
grade and the testing that would start for them in a couple of years, I engaged
them in conversation about it and elicited their opinions. Together, we developed a way of operating in the classroom that I would think of as "closed-door
anarchy." I explained to them how schools are graded, how the scores they will
earn on tests in third and fifth grade help determine the school's grade, and how
some adults thought our testing-based instruction was the best way to prepare. I
then asked them how they felt about the way in which we had been learning over
the past month. They used words like *boring, worried,* and *tired* to describe their
experience, and I felt the same. Therefore, I made a deal with them. I promised
to make our learning more fun, more engaging, and more relevant to their needs
and interests. However, when the principal would come for an observation, we
would have to go back to the old way of doing things for that lesson. Recognizing that the students tended to be intimidated by the principal—a fact the
principal knew and used to her advantage in her interactions with them—I also
opened the principal as a point of dialogue. The students mostly communicated
feelings of fear—they were "scared to talk to her," "worried she would hit them"
(corporal punishment was still happening in very unofficial ways), and "didn't
want to mess up" around her. I explained how it is good to want to do the right
thing but that it is not okay to feel threatened by someone there to care for you
and your work in school.

Through these conversations, I ultimately wanted to first validate that what
my students had experienced in this first month of first grade was not okay, that
adults have the capacity to be wrong, and that there are ways we can handle our
emotions and actions to improve our individual and collective experience in
school in ways that do not make us feel less safe. Thus, in my mind, I used the
term *anarchy* to acknowledge that I was no longer recognizing the authority
of my principal or district as having complete governing capacity over what
happens in my classroom. However, knowing my and my students' vulnerable
places in the system of education, I chose to soften the outward-facing impact

of anarchy by finding the wiggle room to disobey only when it would most likely go unnoticed. My lesson plans and formal observations were reflective of my principal's approach to testing-based instruction, yet everything else was not. For me, this tempered anarchy was essential in helping me explore nobler purposes of education and my role as an educator. Without this early anarchy, I fear I may have become entrenched in a system of education that positions children and teachers as conduits for the purposes and gains of others. I would later learn in my graduate studies that I was developing an awareness of navigational and resistance capital as a White educator in a community that predominantly served students of color (Yosso, 2005).

Navigational and Resistance Capital

Yosso (2005), operating through the lens of critical race theory, identifies the existence of at least six forms of cultural capital that are nurtured by communities of color and that often go unrecognized by White educators in the context of schooling: aspirational, navigational, social, linguistic, familial, and resistance (see Delgado Bernal, 2001; Solórzano & Delgado Bernal, 2001; Stanton-Salazar, 2001). These forms of capital, however, do not operate in isolation from each other and are ever-evolving in community life. For the purposes of this chapter, I zoom in on navigational and resistance capital, which became most relevant to the curricular and pedagogical shifts I made in my first years of teaching.

Navigational capital refers to the knowledge and competencies required to "maneuver through social institutions" and acknowledges both "individual agency within institutional constraints," as well as the "social networks that facilitate community navigation" (Yosso, 2005, p. 81). Historically, examples of navigational capital include students who were able to perform well in school despite the traumas and inequities of school segregation or marginalization. Closely tied to this form of capital is resistance capital, which refers to "knowledges and skills fostered through oppositional behavior that challenges inequality" (Yosso, 2005, p. 82). Inherent in resistance capital is the idea that knowing how to navigate—and perform well—in a system not designed for your success is not enough. Instead, navigation may be coupled with challenging the system itself. For those who adhere to Freire's (1970) critical consciousness, this resistance can be transformational for both the person resisting and the system being resisted. This transformative form of resistance capital includes possessing deep knowledge of structural racism, sexism, or homophobia and designing intentional acts to change those structures.

Although I did not recognize it at the time, my first-grade students had been engaging their navigational and resistance capital every day in my classroom during that first month of school. Despite the narrowed form of the curriculum they were experiencing, their feelings of boredom and worry, and the persistent hunger, sleeplessness, and neglect many endured outside of school, they were still figuring out on their own and with each other how to do well in the classroom. They were still resisting structures and processes that did not feel relevant or fair to them. This resistance often came in the form of not following directions, expressions of anger at me or other students, or refusing to complete an assignment. All these forms of resistance dissipated on the day of the "baby mice incident," and I was able to step back and observe their navigation of a day without my interference. In these moments, I, too, as their teacher, had been discovering my own power to navigate and resist an unjust system of education that I was being socialized to accept and perpetuate. Tapping into the reservoir of knowledge and competencies I gained while studying political science and engaging in civic action in college, I used the anarchist split from the principal's and district's governance to begin nurturing a more democratic form of education in my classroom rooted in students' realities and positioning students as capable, compassionate change makers.

Democratic Education

Based on my engagement with and research of democratic education over the past 14 years, I have come to define democratic education in terms of what I teach, how I teach, and why I teach. I concur with Dewey (1916) that "democracy is more than a form of government; it is primarily a form of associated living, of conjoint communicated experience" (p. 87). As such, individuals in a democratic community must consider how their actions impact others and how others' actions give meaning to their own. Dewey (1916) posits that this way of understanding democratic living has the potential to break down "those barriers of class, race, and national territory," which have kept populations from recognizing the complete consequence of their interactions. Toward this understanding, a democratic educator teaches about real classroom, school, and community issues through deliberative dialogue and civic action to foster students' development as just, compassionate, and informed citizens in a pluralistic, democratic society. Within this definition, I also acknowledge Ayers (2009) understanding of democratic education as a practice that cannot be disconnected from the democratic community in which education is happening and that, ultimately, democratic education has the potential to improve the democratic life of our community at local, state, and national levels. In this section, I more deeply explore each dimension of democratic education and offer examples of ways to animate this idea in classrooms.

What I Teach: Real Issues

Historically, most teaching and learning in K–12 education occurs in abstraction. That is, students are working to master remote skills in neatly divided disciplines, and their success is determined by the extent to which they can demonstrate these skills on paper-based assessments that are rarely kept, referenced, or particularly impactful after a grade has been given. This approach characterized my first month of teaching first grade. My students were not learning to engage the material and ideological realities of their lives to learn about themselves or their world. Instead, they were learning to perform to a narrow, static standard to appease a system of education that was designed without them in mind (Au, 2007, 2016). To address this relevancy gap, I argue students must be given opportunities to engage their budding competences in reading, math, science, and social studies in ways that enable them to address the issues that are impacting their lives in and outside of the classroom.

There are, however, two frequent barriers to this work: the perception that elementary students are "too young" or "not ready" to address real issues and teachers are not ready to address real issues with their students. Yet beginning to experiment with real issues does not mean you have to immediately begin talking about how race, class, gender, sexuality, ability, and immigration status shape students' experience. In fact, I implore you to not address those topics before you first become educated on how these societal stratifications influence and are influenced by schooling. Instead, begin with smaller shifts. Consider, for example, that your students are consistently getting into fights on the playground. Your morning community meeting can address the following prompt that includes a real problem and real data from your classroom:

> Last week, 8 students in our classroom got into a fight at recess. This week, 12 students in our classroom got into a fight at recess. From last week to this week, did the number of fights at recess increase or decrease? In your opinion, what caused these fights? How can you help reduce the number of fights that happen at recess?

From this one problem, a teacher can likely meet all their behavioral and academic goals for the entire week. In reading, students can write opinion pieces regarding their perspective on the fights that are occurring and their complicity in contributing to them by their action or inaction. In math, they can collect classroom or schoolwide data regarding the number of fights happening each day to track progress toward reducing fighting at recess. They can also interview students to dig deeper into the numbers. In social studies, students can learn about how a bill becomes a law and then use the qualitative and quantitative data they collect to inform and propose a new classroom or schoolwide policy to help address the root cause of the fighting. In science, they can perform an experiment to see if their proposed anti-fighting solution is working and iterate their policy recommendations accordingly.

Although small, the issue of fighting at recess is often a persistent one for both teachers and students, and the ability to address the root cause of interpersonal issues is important whether you are adjudicating fights between two first graders or two nations. Duncan-Andrade (2009) challenges the narrative that education should be used to escape circumstances such as poverty as narratives of escape harbor deficit-based views of students' families and community. Instead, he argues, education must be used to end poverty. Imagining an education that prepares our children to end community atrocities requires a concerted effort to engage these issues in the classroom and the acknowledgement that our students are already shouldering the weight of the injustices we, as a collective, have perpetuated. Treating students as anything less than sense-makers in this context is treating them as less than human and reduces their capacity to understand the full import of their humanity.

How I Teach: Deliberative Dialogue and Civic Action

Gaining the right to vote at 18 does not automatically come with the proper knowledge and competencies to shape our community to reflect our needs. As former Supreme Court justice Sandra Day O'Connor argues, "Knowledge of democracy is not passed down through our gene pool. It must be taught and learned anew by each generation of citizens" (Schiesel, 2008). Therefore, the skills of democracy must also be an explicit part of curricular and pedagogical development. In the scholarship on democratic education and in my experience, three core, interrelated competencies are essential in the democratic education classroom: the ability to engage in deliberative dialogue, the ability to deliberatively dialogue about controversial matters, and the ability to take civic action. Notably, without the engagement of real issues, the capacity of students to hone these skills is limited.

Deliberative dialogue differs from traditional elementary classroom discussion in three key ways. First, elementary teachers are most often accustomed to using dialogue as a way to help students understand a particular instructional point. That is, there is a conclusion teachers hope students will draw from a text or task. With a deliberative dialogue, however, the core question posed by the teacher is truly open-ended, meaning that the teacher does not have a prescribed conclusion for either him- or herself or the students. Second, the goal for participating in the dialogue is thus not to reach one neat conclusion or set of conclusions, but for all participants in the dialogue to better understand the nuances of the issues being explored, to better understand the perspectives of multiple stakeholders, and to ultimately have the opportunity to refine their thinking. Last, a deliberative dialogue should end with participants searching for common ground among their differing perspectives and determining a path of action they will take as individuals and as a collective.

By its nature, a question that invites multiple perspectives is often one that invites controversy. Yet, drawing from Hess (2009), the idea of what is controversial may change over time and vary by context in a process she defined as "tipping" (p. 28). For example, the topic of women having the right to vote was once viewed by the public as a highly controversial issue. Today, 100 years later in the United States, the ability of women to vote is no longer a widely accepted point of controversy. This shift means that the contemporary issues we hold as controversial are, too, likely to change over time. Significantly, inherent to the tipping of these issues from controversial to not controversial is citizens' choosing to engage in deliberative dialogue and taking civic action to raise awareness and call for change.

For me and the teachers with whom I work, the idea that controversy is variable and that teachers have the opportunity to impact what is defined as controversial is helpful in making a deliberative dialogue about a controversial issue feel less intimidating. I also pose the question to both teachers and students, "Controversial to whom?" The issue of marriage between two women is not controversial to the 6-year-old in the classroom who has two moms and sees them only as their loving family. There is a pedagogy of nice in which teachers feel like they should remain neutral, yet nothing is neutral—the choice to not talk about something in the classroom, to not engage a family with two moms in the classroom, is still a political decision. Furthermore, studies suggest that classrooms in which teachers activate ideological differences help students normalize controversy (Hess & Ganzler, 2007) and ultimately foster the development of students who have a "greater interest in politics, improved critical thinking and communication skills, more civic knowledge" and who are more likely to vote and volunteer (Gould, Levine, McConnell & Smith, 2011, p. 16).

The point of this deliberative dialogue around controversial issues is not simply to gain knowledge about and awareness of the issues but to ultimately take informed civic action. Civic action is multifaceted and can be defined by any public or private action we take to help solve an issue of community concern. Voting is generally the first, most dominant, and arguably the most important expression of civic action. Yet elementary students cannot vote in public elections (yet). Therefore, we, as educators, must draw from other forms of civic action that still engage students' political voice: volunteering, writing letters to the editor or government officials, protesting, and creating educational campaigns, amongst many others. The College, Career, and Civic (C3) Life Framework[1] (National Council for Social Studies, 2013) is used in the

---

1   See National Council for Social Studies in the Online Sources section at the end of the chapter.

context of social studies but offers a scaffold for helping students move from learning about an issue to taking action the issue. At the beginning, you can offer a series of civic options at the end of a lesson or unit for students to use as a way to apply what they learned in real-world contexts. However, as students become more adept at civic action, you can eventually release the responsibility and allow them to choose the type of civic action they would like to take. During the times in which I have engaged civic action in the classroom, I have often had kids ask to stay in from recess or to eat lunch in the classroom so they could continue to work on their projects because they felt the relevancy, the urgency, and the potential for impact.

Why I Teach: Fostering a Just, Compassionate, and Informed Community

At the start of each education course I teach, I pose the question, "Why did you choose to become a teacher?" The response I hear most often includes the phrase "Because I love kids." Once everyone in the room has shared, I often respond, to their surprise, "Loving kids is not enough." I explain they need to love justice and their role in the realization of it for the students and families they serve, for their colleagues, and for themselves. I also emphasize the need for them to define love as critical, as disruptive, and as a love that does not always feel easy or safe. Rury (2012) argues that "education clearly affects the course of social development, and schools also invariably reflect the impact of the larger social context" (p. 1). Whether they know it or not—whether they accept it or not—teachers influence and are influenced by broader societal conditions. Indeed, the historical roots of schooling were designed to aid the social experiment of our revolutionary form of government—a government that is of, for, and by the people.

This history has been largely marked by tragedy, assimilation, and subtractive contexts for people of color. As a result, schooling contributes to what Levinson (2010) defines as the civic empowerment gap, which translates to the fact that students of color and students from high-poverty backgrounds are less likely to be civically empowered through their K–12 education and thus less likely to shape the community to reflect their needs. In other words, for people of color and high-poverty populations, our government is less of, for, and by them than White, more affluent populations. As I think about my purpose for democratic education—to foster the development of just, compassionate, and informed citizens—I am always attentive to how my curricula and pedagogy shape and are shaped by these broader racial and class contexts.

Conclusion and Next Steps

These types of curricular and pedagogical shifts often demand that a teacher must use the base or scripted curriculum they were given as a foundation for reimagining student materials, activities, and assessments. These shifts also require a commitment to intensive self-reflection regarding a teacher's comfort and level of knowledge regarding issues of community concern, as well as taking civic action within their realms of influence. The guides by Teaching Tolerance offer a way to help you and your students consider levels of comfort for talking about controversial issues and to establish norms for deliberative dialogue:

Let's Talk[2] (2019)
Civil Discourse in the Classroom[3] (2017)

Reflection Questions

1. As a student or a teacher, have you experienced a time in which you were asked to do something not relevant to you and/or aligned to your values? How did you handle this situation?

2. As you think about teaching real classroom, school, and community issues in your classroom, what topics are in and outside of your comfort zone? Why?

---

2   See Teaching Tolerance, Let's Talk, in the Online Sources at the end of the chapter.
3   See Teaching Tolerance, Civil Discourse in the Classroom, in the Online Sources at the end of the chapter.

3. To best foster civic engagement in your classroom, you, too, must be civically engaged. Do you contribute to addressing issues of community concern? Why or why not?

4. One barrier to beginning to talk about real and/or controversial issues in the classroom is not knowing your rights and responsibilities as a teacher. Research your state and local codes of ethics for your profession, as well as policies designed to protect those historically marginalized based on race, class, gender, sexuality, ability, and immigration status. Create a concept map of your choosing that communicates the extent to which your curricula and pedagogy are achieving the intended outcomes of these codes and policies. In your map, also indicate the protections of marginalized populations that are not yet part of policy but that you feel should be.

5. Choose an existing lesson that is part of your curriculum. How can you adjust the content to address a real issue, the activities to include deliberative dialogue, and the assessment to include civic action?

Online Sources

National Council for Social Studies: https://www.socialstudies.org/sites/default/files/c3/C3-Framework-for-Social-Studies.pdf

Teaching Tolerance, *Let's Talk*: http://www.tolerance.org/sites/default/files/general/TT%20Difficult%20Conversations%20web.pdf

Teaching Tolerance, *Civil Discourse in the Classroom*: https://www.tolerance.org/sites/default/files/2017-07/Civil_Discourse_in_the_Classroom.pdf

References

Au, W. (2007). High-stakes testing and curricular control: A qualitative metasynthesis. *Educational Researcher, 36*, 258–267.

Au, W. (2016). Meritocracy 2.0: High-stakes, standardized testing as a racial project of neoliberal multiculturalism. *Educational Policy, 30*(1), 39–62.

Ayers, W. (2009). Teaching in and for democracy. *Kappa Delta Pi Record, 46*(1), 30–33.

Delgado Bernal, D. (2001) Living and learning pedagogies of the home: the mestiza consciousness of Chicana students. *International Journal of Qualitative Studies in Education, 14*, 623–639.

Dewey, J. (1916). *Democracy in education: An introduction to the philosophy of education.* New York, NY: The Free Press.

Duncan-Andrade, J. (2009). Note to educators: Hope required when growing roses in concrete. *Harvard Educational Review, 79*, 181–194.

Freire, P. (1970) *Education for critical consciousness.* New York, NY: Continuum Publishing.

Gould, J., Jamieson, K.H., Levine, P., McConnell, T. & Smith, D. (2011). *Guardian of democracy: The civic mission of schools.* Philadelphia, PA: Lenore Annerberg Institute of Civics of the Annenberg Public Policy Center, Campaign for the Civic Mission of Schools.

Hess, D., & Ganzler, L. (2007). Patriotism and ideological diversity in the classroom. In J. Westheimer (Ed.), *Pledging allegiance: The politics of patriotism in America's schools* (131–138). New York, NY: Teachers College.

Hess, D. E. (2009). *Controversy in the classroom: The democratic power of discussion.* New York, NY: Routledge.

Levinson, M. (2010). The civic empowerment gap: Defining the problem and locating solutions. In Sherrod, L., Torney-Purta, J., & Flanagan, C. A. (Eds.), *Handbook of research on civic engagement*, 331–361. Hoboken, NJ: John Wiley & Sons.

National Council for Social Studies. (2013). *College, career, and civic life C3 framework for social studies state standards.* Retrieved from https://www.socialstudies.org/sites/default/files/c3/C3-Framework-for-Social-Studies.pdf

Rury, J. L. (2012). *Education and social change: Contours in the history of American schooling.* New York, NY: Routledge.

Schiesel, S. (2008, June 9). *Former justice promotes web-based civics lessons. The New York Times.* Retrieved from https://www.nytimes.com/2008/06/09/arts/09sand.html?mtrref=undefined&gwh=AF3D144ABDE072726DB72414B9CB9FE6&gwt=pay&assetType=REGIWALL

Solórzano, D., & Delgado Bernal, D. (2001) Critical race theory, transformational resistance and social justice: Chicana and Chicano students in an urban context. *Urban Education, 36*, 308–342.

Stanton-Salazar, R., & Spina, S. U. (2000) The network orientations of highly resilient urban minority youth: A network-analytic account of minority socialization and its educational implications. *The Urban Review, 32*, 227–261.

Teaching Tolerance. (2017). *Civil discourse in the classroom.* Retrieved from https://www.tolerance.org/sites/default/files/201707/Civil_Discourse_in_the_Classroom.pdf

Teaching Tolerance. (2019). *Let's talk.* Retrieved from http://www.tolerance.org/sites/default/files/general/TT%20Difficult%20Conversations%20web.pdf

Yosso, T. J. (2005). Whose culture has capital? A critical race theory discussion of community cultural wealth. *Race Ethnicity and Education, 8*(1), 69–91.

CHAPTER NINE

Cultivating Diversity Through Multicultural Literature

Mahmoud Suleiman

Standing in front of my fifth-grade class many years ago was an experience of intrigue and curiosity not so much for me but for my students. After learning names, hobbies, and ambitions of what they wanted to be when they grow up, I asked each one to share a story about their life experience, that is, tell their story. Everyone loved telling their story and listening to each others' stories! They learned a lot about themselves and each other. Hearing their stories was also fascinating as they taught me a great deal about their identity and pride, backgrounds, life experiences, cultural schemata, expectations, and aspirations. Their self-disclosure reflected rich experiences that could never be ignored in my classroom. The stories would shape my learning and teaching for several months afterward.

I deciphered their curiosity as they were wondering about the sound of a foreign language in my spoken English and my looks as the "other" non-White Caucasian. One of the students asked me if I could share one of my stories. Another asked, "Do you have a language like English?" Another wondered where I originally came from. I felt stuck between the two worlds—mine and theirs—wondering how to begin and where to start.

Yet, I could not evade their curious questions as I told them that my story, despite similarities, was quite different from theirs.

As I learned about their dreams of what they wanted to be when they shared their stories, I thought I should also share with them my dreams when I was at their age! So I began telling them about a social science lesson that resonated in my memory when I was in fifth grade attending school in a small village on the hills of the West Bank not far away from Jerusalem. I shared with them that I learned about peoples and countries around the world as well as various cultures and social patterns. In particular, I shared with them a social studies lesson that taught me about various continents across the globe, major oceans, rivers, deserts, mountains, climates, and other information that quite honestly seemed abstract to me at the time as I naively wondered why I needed to know such things in the first place! Still, I gave them examples of how I learned about North and South American continents, their demographics, histories, geographical features including the mountain ranges, rivers, lakes, and deserts, such as the Mojave Desert and deserts of Arizona.

Then I realized more questions were triggered in their minds when they started asking about what I would call parallel experiences. For example, one student asked if my people had heroes such as American heroes and historical figures. Another wondered where the Holy Land was because she thought it was somewhere in the state of Pennsylvania. To my surprise, many kids in the class thought that Jesus was born in Maricopa County (Arizona), especially when I explained that I grew up near some of the most ancient cities such as Bethlehem, where Jesus was born; Nazareth; Jerusalem; and others.

It did not take long to learn that my lesson plan, which I worked on several days earlier, was not the right one at least for that day. I found myself engaging students in literary discourse listening to their stories and hearing mine. At the same time, I realized that learning and unlearning were taking place.

Literature and Universal Human Experiences

Early in their lives, children love hearing stories and literature being read to them. Literature captures their attention and imagination and engages them cognitively, emotionally, socially, and intellectually. At the same time, engaging young learners in literary discourse has promising consequences given the multifunctional roles of literary engagement.

Because literacy constitutes a wide range of dimensions, from linguistic to cultural and social domains, students need to have multiple ways in which they engage in learning/teaching situations. Such opportunities need to be authentic and connected to the cultural and social experiences of learners. Such opportunities can also serve as a pathway for academic, cognitive, social, and civic development. Literary engagement is one of the most effective and authentic ways to promote literacy and academic skills of all students, especially in diverse settings.

For thousands of years, literature has played a large role in recording our experiences, feelings, interactions, and aspirations (Knickerbocker & Reninger, 1979; Reimer, 1992). At the same time, it has portrayed the world of reality around us, thus promoting a deeper understanding of the universal human experience.

In this chapter, I explore several aspects of the place of literature in curriculum and instruction. In particular, I focus on the following:

1. Having a rationale for integrating multicultural literature in pluralistic schools
2. Examining the role of multicultural literature in learning–teaching situations
3. Enhancing educational outcomes through literary engagement in diverse settings
4. Seeking to engage students in multiple ways through multicultural literature
5. Cultivating students' assets and cultural capital through multicultural literature
6. Selecting rich authentic literature that is culturally responsive to students' needs

7. Drawing implications for teachers to capitalize on the power literature to engage students

Rationale for Integrating Multicultural Literature

Integrating literature in curriculum and instruction is a universally common practice in schools everywhere. It is a vehicle to engage students beyond building language and academic skills (Norton, 2009; Vasquez, 2003). The goals of literature-based programs are far-reaching to embrace skillful interaction and competent performance in schools and beyond; that is, they aim to engage students to survive and thrive as they develop lifelong practical skills and critical thinking abilities. Literary works often chronicle and portray human experiences and anecdotes that can impact readers to change their behaviors and broaden their knowledge about the world around them. Several philosophical foundations provide a rationale for including literature in the educational process, especially in linguistically and culturally diverse settings. Such foundations can provide a sound rationale for enriching curricular choices and pedagogical options for students and teachers alike. Thus, some of the philosophical underpinnings of integrating literature, in general, and multicultural literature, in particular, include the following:

- All literature is multicultural and has universal appeal.
- Literature imitates life, and life imitates literature.
- Literature is didactic: It informs and entertains.
- Literature closely relates to language and vice versa.
- Literature has many genres, including electronic forms.
- Literature engages readers in many ways (cognitive and affective).
- Literary engagement promotes social and emotional learning.

As far as literary and literacy engagements are concerned, students should meaningfully participate in the process that builds on their needs, abilities, and expectations. Literacy needs are universally grounded in both the affective and cognitive domains of education. Achieving the balance between those domains should be the basis for any successful literacy programs. The literature-based programs that integrate relevant and rich genres can have a key role in achieving such balance.

I would like to emphasize the construct that *all literature is multicultural.* Most agree about the premise of this statement given the nature, purpose, value, and appeal of literary works. After all, literature provides a sociocultural account of human experience and interaction among individuals and groups in a given place at a given time. It provides a frame of reference for global, universal patterns of human interaction. In fact, literature writes us as much as we write it; it re-creates us as much as we create it. Also, it is a window on the human mind and soul; it is a revelation of how we interact and live. More important, literature serves to reflect our experience and perspective regarding the world around us. In short, literature helps the understanding of oneself and others.

The Role of Multicultural Literature

For many years, critics pointed out that the school curriculum reflects monolithic social values that are not congruent with the values of all students in the classroom (Chisholm, 1994; Nieto, 2004). This sameness in education through a monocultural curriculum, including literature-based approaches, guarantees inequity to a large number of students in today's classrooms (Cortes, 1995). Nonetheless, one of the basic premises of the American educational public system is to integrate multiculturalism into all facets of learning. This is articulated in the frequently quoted suggestion by Lewis and Doorlag (1987), who maintain the following:

1. Commonalties among peoples cannot be recognized unless differences are acknowledged.
2. A society that interweaves the best of all its cultures reflects a truly mosaic image.
3. Multicultural education can restore cultural rights by emphasizing cultural respect and equality.

4. Multicultural education enhances the self-concepts of all students because it provides a more balanced and realistic view of American society.

Several general goals of multicultural education are implied in its definitions, dimensions, and approaches (see, e.g., Banks, 1995). Some of these goals involve teachers while others involve students. Thus teachers and educators in today's schools have the greater responsibility to ensure the achievement of these goals by (a) developing positive attitudes and human relations among all students who represent various groups and races both in the mainstream and minority populations; (b) acquiring knowledge and skills in order to appreciate and value racial, ethnic, and cultural diversity around us; (c) eradicating negative symptoms of stereotypical images fostered by ethnocentrism; (d) bridging the gap of racial and cultural differences through the process of understanding and empathy; (e) developing historical understanding of their multiethnic society; and (f) developing skills to cope with our changing society and to prepare students to function properly in its democracy. In any educational reform, these goals underscore the need to address linguistic diversity and meet the literacy and academic needs of all students, especially English-language learners.

Having this in mind, Gates and Mark (2006) argue that there is a need for an effective restructuring in schools. Some of the ingredients for such successful reform include the following:

- Implementing a culturally diverse curriculum
- Balancing the combined focus between language and literature
- Prompting students' ability to deconstruct their own "knowledge"
- Integrating cognitive and affective learning
- Creating of space and place for girls' voices
- Developing a pedagogy that promotes self-esteem, open-mindedness, and collaboration
- Creating a supportive and challenging learning environment

- Recognizing and becoming aware of racism and prejudice in society and school
- Creating a context for reflection, challenge, collaboration, and support in the classroom

Because the school curriculum has largely revolved around ethnocentric mainstream representation, these conditions for success must be created. The literature used in schools has generally reflected a monocultural focus that has enhanced provincialism and stereotypes and has deprived most students of optimal learning opportunities to gain more insight about the collective human experience. On the other hand, culturally relevant practices and activities, such as integrating multicultural literature, serve as an important avenue to bring about desired change in schools and society at large (Gates & Mark, 2006). To bridge the gap between provincialism and multiculturalism in schools, literature reflecting diverse human experiences should be an integral part of the school curriculum and daily activities (Norton, 2009). This will, in turn, achieve a dynamic balance between the mainstream culture and other cultures (and languages) represented in the classroom (Freeman & Freeman, 1993, 2004). In addition, it will bring about the desired change, promote cultural awareness, augment knowledge, foster empathy, and empower all students.

Although the role of multicultural literature is to represent certain distinctive groups accurately and immensely, numerous promising educational consequences and outcomes are seen as a result of engagement in multicultural literature. These outcomes are consistent with the aspirations and dreams of diverse student populations and the groups they represent.

Outcomes of Multicultural Literary Engagement

There are many outcomes of literacy and literary engagement using multicultural literature. These outcomes can be immediate and enduring, individual and collective, cognitive and affective, ethical and moral, and linguistic and academic, as well as educational and entertaining. The study of multicultural literature should rest on a set of desired promising consequences that are empowering to readers and learners (Levin, 2007; Tompkins, 2012). For the most part, multicultural literary and literacy engagements result in the following:

- Affirming the intellectual and physical being of learners
- Affirming pluralism of human experience
- Promoting empathy among various groups
- Fostering respect among diverse learners
- Crossing culture gaps and enhancing human values
- Bringing about desired change in all learners
- Allowing readers to see themselves through others
- Empowering readers and promoting social action
- Combating prejudice and stereotypes
- Maximizing the potential of learners
- Enhancing self-esteem and a positive self-image

These outcomes underscore the need for integrating multicultural literature and its impact on learners in diverse settings. Gates and Mark (2006) maintain using multicultural literature enables teachers to apply ethical traditions as a vehicle for developing awareness and understanding of cultural diversity and the issues of racism and prejudice. Thus, two reasons for the importance of the study of multicultural literature can be identified: One, "it offers a mirror through which children can see representations of themselves, and it provides a window by which children not of the represented culture can see into worlds and experiences not personally accessible to them" (Gates & Mark, 2006, p. 9). Similarly, discovering the world of reality is an ongoing journey that can be facilitated and mediated by a multiphase process of multicultural literary engagement (Norton, 2009). Several dimensions of literacy can be attained through the volume of multicultural literary experiences we encounter.

Unquestionably, literacy development through literature transcends the development of language skills and abilities to communicate (Brett & Gerdean, 2005). This is especially true when we read and study multicultural literature replete with extra-linguistic cues and cultural icons. These mostly echo the realities of linguistically and culturally diverse students, their cultural schemata, as well as their intellectual and societal expectations, as they engage in the educational process to become productive citizens.

Literacy Engagement: Beyond Linguistic Cues

Literacy and literary engagements involve many psycholinguistic processes that involve substantiating meanings based on extra-linguistic cues within the text. This meaning-making process requires critical literacy, higher order thinking skills, metacognitive processing, and a wide range of engagement strategies to comprehend the underlying loaded messages and themes. This becomes more demanding when interpreting and comprehending culturally based literary genres and experiences. Thus, multicultural literature transcends linguistic cues to embrace many other overt and covert messages (Brett & Gerdean, 2005; Steiner, Nash, & Chase, 2008). Some of these are discussed in the following.

Morally relevant themes. Like almost every piece of authentic literary genre and work, multicultural books integrate morally relevant content. This can be an explicit or implicit process. Thus, it is not surprising that throughout literary engagements, students are constantly asked to examine and identify the "moral" of the story that revolves around the notion of poetic justice involving conflict between good and evil, right and wrong, virtue and vice, and the like.

Ethnically relevant experiences. In an authentic literary piece, people in action act on their moral obligations as human beings—a pattern that may be culturally bound and yet universal. As the events of the story unfold, readers become enticed to explore the themes and morals of the piece in relation to who the actors are. As such, they become cognizant of the unique distinguishing ethnic realities and traits that describe the characters of the story. Consequently, readers learn about the unique ethnicity of the actors that may be different from theirs but universally significant. Readers' experiences are enriched by learning from those of others, who try to solve similar problems all of us can relate to.

Culturally relevant values. Literature is a viable way to depict cultural and social values, especially when such values are relatively different among individuals and groups. Common and shared values can be highlighted in intriguing ways using multicultural literature. At the same time, enhancing common values can easily be transmitted and enforced through the literary work at hand. Although value systems vary from one culture to another, they intersect in many ways at the universal levels. After all, human experience is timeless and is not bound by any geographical or physical barriers. Human experiences and values travel from one place to another using the literary genres as vehicles of such cultural journeys.

Geographically relevant settings. Events in stories and literary works do not occur in a vacuum but have a place and setting within the boundaries known to us as humans. The geographical barriers can be crossed through literary engagements as we learn about human behaviors, cultures, and interactions in places remote or close to ours. Nonetheless, the global distances are bridged through the literary media. Readers of literature are taken to places they have never visited and experience the settings of different physical worlds different from theirs. In short, literature promotes our understanding of the geography of the places where our fellow humans interact within their social units—all of which compose the collective human experience of the past, present, and future.

Historically relevant cues. Time is a critical element in any fabric of a literary work. Literature serves accordingly as a chronicle of human experiences across places, cultures, and times. It serves as a window on the past, a mirror of the present, and a telescope for the future. We frequently appreciate and understand the present through reading about the past human experience and attempt to map our future as we move beyond the present times. History may explain our present and predict our future. As human experiences are echoed over time, literature seems timeless and immortal in its appeal to our reason for learning lessons from the past and present.

Logically relevant solutions. Literacy development through literary engagement helps in examining real-life problems and challenges facing all of us as humans. It also inspires us to create solutions for shared problems as we seek to overcome challenges in many walks of life. The sound life choices we make might be an outcome of the meaningful literary engagement with embedded morals, messages, and the proven and tested human experiences depicted in a given place, culture, and time.

These levels of engagement form the basis of setting learning goals and outcomes. Teachers should integrate these in lesson planning, delivery, and assessment. The mere emphasis on limited aspects of language (e.g., vocabulary, grammar, etc.) when working with English-language learners is not sufficient and can, by all means, be limiting. Instead, the focus should include the development of academic and linguistic skills within a higher level of conceptualizing literacy and literary processes. This requires students to think beyond the overt linguistic nuances to include more complex cueing strategies that appeal to the multiple avenues of intelligence and students' cognitive and social abilities (Suleiman, 1996). Multicultural literature is a nice way of harnessing such processes given its multiple levels of appeal.

Multicultural Literature Appeal

The art of creating literature involves exceptional skills on the part of the writer. The author's ability to weave in multiple themes, episodes, symbols, events, characters, plots, and other elements within the hierarchical structure of an authentic literary work can be reflected in the many ways such work appeals to readers. Of course, in crafting culturally relevant literature, the writer has an obligation to make that appeal more meaningful and universal. Eliciting the different expectations for an appealing authentic piece is worthwhile. Multicultural literature appeals to readers in many ways that include the following:

- Aesthetic appeal
- Ethical appeal
- Logical appeal
- Emotional appeal
- Linguistic appeal
- Moral appeal
- Cognitive appeal
- Social/civic appeal
- Scientific appeal
- Universal appeal

For diverse student populations, these appeals constitute a foundation for interpreting the literature-based curriculum given their unique multifaceted cultural and linguistic schemata and experiences. Literacy and literary activities based on these levels can have promising consequences in not only promoting linguistic but also academic, social, intellectual, and other skills needed for effective learning and interaction. To maximize learning outcomes, a literature-based curriculum should integrate meaningful content, have multiple forms of appeal, and, most important, must be carefully selected in terms of humanistic parameters and guidelines.

Selection of Multicultural Literature

Teachers and educators working with diverse student populations should select multicultural literature that is authentic, relevant, and sensitive to the reality around us. They also should make informed choices about the kinds of literary works that are responsive to students' needs and expectations (Bishop, 1992). There are widely circulated accounts of what authentic multicultural literature should look like. For example, Brandt (1997, p. 53) outlines the following criteria:

Marks of Quality in Multicultural Literature

1. **Overall quality.** Multicultural literature must meet the same standards as any other book you would choose. Would the story hold a young reader's interest? Was it well written? Did the illustrations complement and enhance the text?
2. **Accuracy.** Make sure that multicultural books are factually accurate. Or, in the case of folktales or legends, make sure your students understand that they are not intended to be interpreted literally.
3. **Illustrations.** Young readers rely heavily on a book's pictures to convey the story. Look carefully at the characters shown. Do they have a standardized look, with variation only in the shades of their skin color? Do they have exaggerated features? Are there stereotypes? The most powerful illustrations in multicultural literature portray members of a particular

culture as unique individuals engaging in traditional and non-traditional activities. They are rich with culturally authentic styles and colors, indicating that the artist is a member of the community portrayed or has done careful research on the community. Also, illustrations should add valuable details that might not be described in the text, such as a character's clothing or furniture.

4. **Theme.** Think about the main character's struggle in the story. Is the main issue one that affects only members of a single cultural or racial group? If so, the book might be the one that your students will not relate to. Typically, the most engaging themes are central to the experience of being human, not just central to a single culture.

5. **Perspective.** Books that depict the author's or illustrator's own experience in a particular culture are less likely to stereotype than books that attempt to portray a culture as a whole. Did the author draw upon their own memory in order to create the book? (Check the backgrounds of the author and illustrator.) Did they successfully portray the characters' language, thoughts, and emotions?

6. **Balance.** Many multicultural books portray members of a cultural group in exotic costumes, explain traditional ceremonies, or tell classic folktales. While this information is helpful, you'll also want to include books that depict the culture in daily life, both in modern times and throughout history, to get a balanced look at the culture.

7. **Reviews and awards.** Has the book received any literary awards? Scanning children's book reviews is a good way to discover the best new multicultural literature.

These criteria can be helpful guidelines regarding the authenticity, accuracy, and balance in the selection of multicultural literature. Well-selected multicultural literature has many advantages to all students including mainstream learners. One advantage is promoting an understanding of the essence of humanity in all readers as they discover that people from various cultural groups are real people having similar emotions, needs, wants, aspirations, and dreams (Reimer, 1992; Tompkins, 2012). In fact, children identify meaningfully with the experiences of characters and sequences of events in the literature they read. When used effectively, according to Norton (2009), positive multicultural literature can "help readers identify cultural heritages, understand sociological change, respect the values of minority groups, raise aspirations, and expand imagination and creativity" (p. 2). Moreover, effective use of multicultural related activities "improves reading scores and improves attitudes among students from varying cultures" (Norton, 2009, p. 2).

Although the purpose of literature is multifaceted, it tends to be didactic. First, literature informs through intellectual engagement. When one reads a story, for example, he or she reads to learn and discover the meaning implicated in the sequence of events, the actions of characters, the lessons behind the story line, and the like. Second, literature evokes our feelings, emotions, and desires. For instance, when reading a story with a tragic ending, one is engaged emotionally: One might weep and develop empathy. Likewise, one may be moved to like or dislike, rejoice or reject, and cry or laugh. Moreover, literature influences us to act on what is humanistic, ethical, moral, and right.

The elements of literature and its structure vary based on genre, theme, purpose, and form. Generally, several literary elements are found in almost every form of literature, such as theme, plot, purpose, point of view, setting, and the like. The structure of these elements is usually crafted by the author in a complementary fashion based on the moral of the piece and the foci of its themes. To yield adequate appeal and involvement in readers, several guidelines are expected by readers.

For multicultural literature to be meaningfully functional in the lives of learners, each of the literary elements should be sensitive to the underlying premise of their existence and life experiences. Therefore, each element should accurately depict a given group or character, reflect universal human appeal, portray realistic events and actions, contribute to the understanding of truth, result in a pragmatic call for action, echo flashbacks of relevant experiences, and value the diversity of human global perspectives.

For multicultural literature to be meaningfully functional in the lives of learners, each of the literary elements should be sensitive to the underlying premise of their existence and life experiences. Therefore, each element should accurately depict a given group or character, reflect universal human appeal, portray realistic events and actions, contribute to the understanding of truth, result in a pragmatic call for action, echo flashbacks of relevant experiences, and value the diversity of human global perspectives.

Implications for Teachers

Apart from the content, multicultural literature has the power to transmit a large bulk of racial, social, cultural, geographical, and other facts and information (including scientific and academic content). The extent to which multicultural literature can enhance a deeper understanding of humans cannot be understated. Undoubtedly, it can provide multiple learning opportunities for all students in a culture-friendly environment when adequately used.

Multicultural education using culturally relevant and diverse literature should be part of everyday activities in today's classroom. To multiply learning opportunities through multicultural literature and cultivate more positive attitudes in the American school system, the following guidelines must be kept in mind:

1. Selection of authentic literature must be free of any negative stereotypes and misinformation. The criteria for selecting such literature must be met.

2. The objectives of multicultural literature should go beyond educational goals and the entertainment of children to embrace far-reaching social goals that include awareness combined with mutual understanding and appreciation of cultural differences.

3. Frequent and recurrent multicultural themes should foster an awareness of common human experiences while celebrating the uniqueness of cultural and thought patterns of target groups.

4. Literature response activities must transcend linguistic literacy to embrace other forms of literacy to develop multicultural competence and understanding.

5. A literature-based curriculum must involve affective and cognitive domains of learning in terms of the outcomes of multicultural literary engagement.
6. Response activities to multicultural meanings should focus on making oneself understood and comfortable in the learning/teaching environment.
7. Multicultural literature should include all genres, such as poems, fiction, and nonfiction, in addition to the industrially produced (e.g., electronic forms, film strips, movies) forms.
8. Multicultural literature should expose students to various cultural rhetorical devices and language modes to promote metalinguistic awareness and metacognitive skills.
9. Assessment in language arts programs must include an appraisal of ethnic and cultural knowledge.
10. Rich authentic literary, linguistic, and cultural cues must be part of the school environment and culture.

Finally, because the lack of knowledge about a given cultural and ethnic group may pose a challenge when teaching in diverse settings, students and teachers alike must be alerted and prepared for the unexpected when studying multicultural literature (Stafford, Sagehorn, & Suleiman, 1997). Unless the very best examples and decisions are made regarding the use of multicultural literature in diverse classrooms (Gates & Mark, 2006), education reform efforts will continue to flounder on how to cultivate pluralism and democracy in schools today.

A Case in Point

Teacher candidates and teachers should become avid multicultural readers and writers as they are trained to work with a diverse student population. They should be able to evaluate and examine each book and its utility and value based on the role of literature and its functions in our lives. One of the ways to do that is to chronicle and compile a multicultural annotated list that highlights the value of each book and its academic and literacy impact on learning. Such a list can serve as a quick reference that helps teachers make here-and-now instructional decisions and choices based on the unique diversity of their students. As such, teachers take multicultural literature beyond the traditional role of promoting linguistic skills to embrace a far-reaching set of goals that include content areas and academic skills. In other words, engagement in multicultural literature serves to promote multiple levels of literacy and academic skills. Table 9.1 outlines some examples that can be integrated into a culturally rich curriculum and instruction in diverse classrooms.

Generating such reference sources should include careful selections prior to integrating them into classroom activities. Published multicultural literature is frequently evaluated by professional organizations and are examined for any signs of bias, misinformation, and/or negative hidden messages about the cultural group depicted in the piece. Award-winning books and collections are examples of how some books are filtered or evaluated before consumption and use in schools. Additionally, these selections should be purposefully and strategically integrated into the scope and sequence of the curriculum and instruction, aligned with state standards and frameworks, and built on to move students' literacy and academic skills from one level to the next.

TABLE 9.1
MULTICULTURAL BOOKS AND OUTCOMES

Book	Annotation	Outcomes
Bodeen-Stuve, S. (author) & Hale, C. (illustrator). (1998). *Elizabeti's doll*. New York, NY: Scholastic Inc. Family—fiction. N. page. Print (Interest Level: K–3)	Watching her mother caring for younger brother Obedi, Elizabeti is enticed to have her own baby so she can nurture. Using a stone and naming her Eve as a symbolic "baby," Elizabeti imitates her mom with tasks of caring for a baby. Acquired maternal instincts are reflected in Elizabeti's behavior that echo sweet childhood moments across many cultures. The story captures a unique portrait of the Tanzanians traditions, lifestyles, values, dress, and other cultural patterns.	• Cultural literacy • Social values • Empathy
Hillerman, T. (1986). *The boy who made dragonfly*. Albuquerque: University of New Mexico Press. Historical myth retold. 75 pages (Interest Level: ages 7–10)	Haíwikíuh, a young boy, and his sister develop wit, wisdom, and leadership skills by mediation of a dragonfly and help from the corn maidens. They are provided with knowledge about how to care for the villagers and the bounties of the land. The book abounds in multiple cues and themes. It also provides rich learning experiences that are didactic and instigate intrigue and interest in young learners.	• Cultural literacy • Social values • Responsibility

Book	Annotation	Outcomes
Lee, V. H. (2005). *In the leaves*. New York, NY: Henry Holt. Farm life—fiction. N. page. Print (Interest Level: K–3)	The author creates a tale intended to meaningfully teach the Chinese characters. Taking his friends to a farm, Xiao Ming explains to them the iconic nature of the Chinese symbols and the meanings they represent using concrete elements around, such as field, fire, grain, and the like. Building on the innate assets of young learners, the author crafted this story to motivate children to learn about the unique Chinese written language in fun and engaging way.	• Cultural literacy • Aesthetics • Art and science • Critical thinking
Qamar, A. (2008). *Beneath My Mother's Feet*. New York, NY: Atheneum Books for Young Readers. Nonfiction. 208 pages (Interest Level: 9–11)	Based on gender roles and disparities, the author portrays the struggle of females through the plight of Nazia and her mom. After her father became disabled due to a work injury, Nazia was forced to quit school and join her mom to work to support the family. Shedding light on how young women marry and the place of women in the Pakistani communities, this story provides a unique perspective about certain beliefs and traditions in that region.	• Cultural literacy • History • Empathy • Social science
Tonatiuh, D. (2010). *Dear Primo: A letter to my cousin*. New York, NY: Abrams Books for Young Readers. Cultural Differences. 32 pages (Interest Level: 4–8)	Telling a story of two cousins living in two worlds, this story cast some light on shared values and cultural assets despite the different contexts of where they live. Charlie, who lives in the United States, and Carlitos, who lives in Mexico, exchange letters describing their daily routines and experiences. Readers become more sensitive to each reality and appreciative of both cultures.	• Cultural literacy • Universal experiences • Geography • History
Wheeler, L. (author) & Suarez, M. (illustrator). (2004). *Te amo, Bebe, little one*. New York, NY: Little, Brown. Mother and child rhythmic. N. page. Print (Interest Level: K–3).	This book provides a colorful picture of a motherly love for her child through the prism of a Hispanic mom interacting with her baby. The mother immerses her baby in rich Latino cultural icons such as language, rhymes and music, traditions, food, and dress. The timing is artfully set as the baby turns one and becomes immersed in his surroundings throughout the cycle of four seasons.	• Cultural literacy • Universal values • Global literacy • Respect

Conclusion

Ancient civilizations and their leading scholars and educators recognized the power of literature and its didactic function as a tool of learning about other peoples and cultures. In fact, the civic upbringing rested on the ability of its citizens to engage ethically, morally, and intellectually through literary and literacy engagement.

Whether implicit or explicit, goals of literary men and women have always revolved around constructing knowledge in terms of the symbolic truth embedded in fiction and nonfiction. As Knickerbocker and Reninger (1979) put it, literature offers a rich empirical account about the human experience through the objective observations of the writer which are essential for the individual's growth and development. Thus, the study of culture through literary genres is like the study of idealism. In their quest for self-actualization, humans try to approach a certain level of perfection in their life. Such a quest has always been made easy through the study of literature. That is, the more literature one reads, the more he or she learns about the human experience. Because literature is written in a given language and tends to reflect the values, belief systems, and traditions of that linguistic community, readers of that literature will be exposed to a "snapshot" of the global culture embedded in the text.

Because literature offers many shades of meanings about the universal experience of humans, it is well suited "to developing a deeper understanding of the multicultural nature of society" (Stice, Bertrand, & Bertrand, 1995, p. 409). In addition, it is a powerful vehicle for striking a delicate balance between cognitive and affective domains of human interaction. These elements are critical in meeting the needs of all students in our multicultural schools.

Because literature is a core component of the school curriculum, it should be carefully selected and implemented to engage all learners. Multicultural literature has the power to affirm diverse learners' identities, cultures, languages, and other aspects in learning teaching situations. It is a viable way to respond to students' academic and literacy needs and capitalize on their assets so long as it is relevant and appealing within the overarching universal frames of reference.

Reflection Questions

1. *Examine the literature-based curriculum at a given grade level and evaluate its relevance and goals in responding to all students' needs.*

2. *Select a multicultural book used in schools and apply the quality criteria outlined in the chapter and report on how such a selection can impact student learning.*

3. *Design an instructional unit based on a series of multicultural literature books to educate all students to become productive global citizens.*

Exploring the Internet

1. Explore the Internet and compile a list of must-click-on websites that include rich multicultural literary resources to be used in diverse schools.
2. Conduct an online search about viable electronic multicultural resources that you could use in your culturally responsive instructional planning and delivery.

References

Banks, J. (1995). Multicultural education: Historical development, dimensions, and practice. In J. Banks & C. Banks (Eds.), *Handbook of research on multicultural education* (pp. 3–29). New York: Macmillan.

Bishop, J. A. (1992). Multicultural literature for children: Making informed choices. In V. J. Harris (Ed.), *Teaching multicultural literature in Grades K–8* (pp. 37–54). Norwood, MA: Christopher-Gordon.

Brandt, J. (1997, March/April). Marks of quality in multicultural literature. *Learning, 25*(5), pp. 52–54.

Brett, L., & Gerdean, T. (2005). Looking beyond the pages: Representations of culture in story book choice in second grade. *WSU McNair Journal, 3,* 15–23.

Chisholm, I. M. (1994). Preparing teachers for multicultural classrooms. *The Journal of Educational Issues of Language Minority Students, 14,* 43–67.

Cortes, C. (1995). Knowledge construction and popular culture: The media as multicultural educator. In J. Banks & C. Banks (Eds.), *Handbook of research on multicultural education* (pp. 211–227). New York, NY: Macmillan.

Freeman, D., & Freeman, Y. (2004). *Essential linguistics: Everything you need to know to teach reading, ESL, spelling, phonics, and grammar.* Portsmouth, NH: Heinemann.

Freeman, D. E., & Freeman, Y. S. (1993). Strategies for promoting the primary languages of all students. *The Reading Teacher, 46,* 552–558.

Gates, P. S., & Mark, H. (2006). *Cultural journeys: Multicultural children's literature for children and young adults.* Lanham, MD: The Scarecrow Press.

Knickerbocker, K. L., & Reninger, H. W. (1979). *Interpreting literature.* New York, NY: Holt, Rinehart & Winston.

Levin, F. (2007). Encouraging ethical respect through multicultural literature. *The Reader Teacher, 61*(1), 101–104.

Lewis, R. B., & Doorlag, D. H. (1987). *Teaching special students in the mainstream.* Columbus, OH: Merrill Publishing.

Nieto, S. (2004). *Affirming diversity: The sociopolitical context of multicultural education* (4th ed.). New York, NY: Longman.

Norton, D. E. (2009). *Multicultural children's literature through the eyes of many children* (3rd ed). Boston, MA: Allyn & Bacon/Pearson.

Reimer, K. M. (1992). Multiethnic literature: Holding fast to dreams. *Language Arts, 69,* 14–21.

Stafford, K., Sagehorn, A., & Suleiman, M. (1997). Learning to teach, teaching to learn: Evaluative and pedagogical tools for teaching Native American literatures. In C. Grant (Ed.), *National Association for Multicultural Education proceedings* (pp. 161–170). San Francisco, CA: Caddo Gap Press.

Steiner, S. F., Nash, C. P., & Chase, M. (2008). Multicultural literature that brings people together. *The Reader Teacher, 62*(1), 88–92.

Stice, C., Bertrand, J., & Bertrand, N. (1995). *Integrating reading and the other language arts.* Belmont, CA: Wadsworth.

Suleiman, M. (1996). Multiplying learning opportunities through multicultural literature: Implications for teachers. *Kansas Journal of Reading, 6,* 35–42.

Tompkins, G. E. (2012). *Literacy for the 21st century: A balanced approach.* Englewood Cliffs, NJ: Merrill/Prentice Hall.

Vasquez, V. (2003). *Getting beyond "I like the book": Creating space for critical literacy in K–6 classrooms* (Kids Insight Series). Newark, DE: International Reading Association.

CHAPTER TEN

REVAMPING CURRICULUM THROUGH A "SOCIAL JUSTICE" LENS

Anni K. Reinking

Mainstream Curriculum: Community Helpers

A young first-year teacher was preparing to teach about community helpers in her third-grade classroom. She was collecting all the materials she had bought from the teacher store or printed from online. She hung a picture of a White female nurse, she cut out a picture of a White male firefighter, and she made sure to hang pictures of male astronauts and scientists. After a weekend of hanging all her materials for the upcoming unit, her students walked in Monday morning, and her lessons began.

She taught her lessons from a very Eurocentric way, as is evident from the pictures and materials displayed in the classroom. She had firemen, postmen, female nurses, male doctors, female teachers, and businessmen.

To begin her unit, she asked students to draw a picture of what they want to be when they grow up, understanding that they would be talking about community helpers. All the students drew pictures; some were more elaborate than others. Then they began to share their pictures. Tommy went, followed by Elizabeth, and Maria. Then it was Mark's turn. Mark held up his picture and said, "I want to be a nurse when I grow up because they make people feel better when they are sick. They go to school for a long time. I met a nurse the other day at the doctor's office and she was so nice."

The young first-year teacher listened politely and then said, "Well, Mark, wouldn't you rather be a doctor? Nurses are girls, and doctors are men."

Transformational Teaching: The Police Project

During a 12-week research project, Alicia often reflected to the researcher, who was a former teacher focusing on multicultural curriculum implementation in early childhood classroom. Alicia reflected, both verbally and in written form, that she desired to help students in her prekindergarten classroom understand the specific community they lived in. She would do a project on "anything they [students] are interested in. So I mean, regardless if people are mad or whatever, if they [students] want to know about it I will do a project on it." Alicia wanted to be honest with her students and help them learn about their community, their reality.

One day, after a long weekend, students in her class entered the classroom as they normally did. They hung up their coats and their bags and began playing. However, Alicia and her co-teacher began hearing a murmur of whispers focused on the same topic: "The police are bad." Instead of immediately correcting the students about police officers, Alicia interacted with them.

Quizzically, Alicia and her co-teacher began to engage in the murmured conversations to find out more. She asked questions, such as "Why do you think police are bad?" Or she might say, "Wow, that is an angry voice when you just said that [about the police]." Through these conversations, she began to understand the root of the students' comments.

What did they find out? Many of the students lived in the same Section 8 housing unit behind the school. Over the weekend, many police had come to their home because of an incident, and many people were handcuffed and taken away. The children had heard their parents talking about the police afterward and were bringing that into the classroom.

After learning this fact, Alicia reflected that she needed to start a positive conversation with the students in her classroom about the police. She even reflected that she felt a sense of urgency to engage her students in this topic of helpful police interactions because of the negative rhetoric regarding minority groups and police forces that seem to overtake news cycles and social media feeds.

So, Alicia started planning a unit on police, a unit focused on many perspectives, and a unit embracing the multicultural implementation of revamping mainstream curriculum.

The steps Alicia took during the project, which lasted approximately 4 weeks, included the following:

1. *Beginning conversations with students and recording the students' statements about police: what the students knew and what they heard. (This is a type of preproject assessment to gauge students' changed or unchanged mind-sets by the end of the project.)*
   - *During these first conversations Alicia heard many comments, and most of them focused on the idea that police are bad.*
2. *Reaching out to community members and police officers to come in to the classroom to speak to the children. The goal of these visits was to understand all the things police officers do, outside of arresting people.*
   - *Alicia began teaching her students that police do not just arrest people because they want to but that they arrest people who might make poor choices or do things that are against the law.*
3. *Teaching*
   - *Gathering and providing materials in the classroom that police officers use such as an orange vest and other child-friendly police gear.*

- *Writing observations of the interactions and conversations throughout the project. During these observations, Alicia documented student growth from negative to positive perspectives of police officers.*

4. *Finally, asking the students to make statements about police officers. The new statements students provided displayed a more positive perception of police officers. Additionally, students were no longer handcuffing each other and throwing peers in jail as a play scenario. Rather, they were acting as police officers who helped change tires or who came and checked on people who might need help.*

Interestingly, Alicia thought the project was over when she completed the student interviews and posted them on the wall of the hallway to show the school what her classroom has been learning. However, it continued, not with the students but with the staff members. In a reflection to the researcher, she wrote about some staff members who were adamantly against the displayed project because of the perceived negative portrayal of police officers. Conversely, some teachers found it enlightening and worthy of praise for helping students to understand a social misconception in the community regarding police officers. Overall, the conversation and learning did not end in the classroom but entered into the wider conversation in the school and among staff members.

Curriculum and Social Justice

Transformational teaching in urban settings has the power to change mind-sets, increase academic performance, and create a student who has the confidence to ask questions and explore his or her world. In Alicia's case, the transformational learning occurred when her students were able to widen their lived experiences and have a more positive outlook on police in their community. Through the outlined project, Alicia displayed her understanding of the importance of student-initiated projects. She also understood the needs of her students from a local and national level. A positive conversation about police was and is needed in the demographics of her students. Alicia took guidance from her students' experiences. She educated herself, and she gathered knowledgeable individuals who could help her change the mindsets of her 4- and 5-year-old students.

This transformational teaching can take place in all classrooms when teachers are knowledgeable about revamping curriculum, reflective on personal practices, and able to create a classroom culture of positive learning to change mindsets. Teachers, such as Alicia, who research, question, reflect, and implement projects based on students' lived experiences, which are sometimes considered taboo topics, are praised by some but seen as enemies by others. This guarded or uneasy feeling felt by some educators when discussions of differences or "touchy" topics are presented is not a new concept. It is a phenomenon that is present in all of society (Tatum, 1992). However, taboo topics should not be ignored in classroom but, rather, embraced and taught. One way to teach taboo topics is through the implementation of multicultural curriculum.

Multicultural Curriculum Implementation

Multicultural education is a multifaceted movement that encompasses a wide range of ideas, purposes, practices, and communities of interest (Banks & Banks, 1995; Gibson, 1976; Sleeter & Grant, 1987). For generations, it has been used as an "umbrella concept" for educational practices that include race, class, and gender, along with disability, sexual orientation, language, and religion (Pohen & Aguilar, 2001; Sleeter & Grant, 1994).

Since the civil rights movement, multicultural education has played an important role in society (Blum, 1999). The theory and practice behind multicultural education have advanced because it is a way to create equal education opportunities for students from diverse racial, ethnic, and cultural groups (Banks & Banks, 2001). Multicultural curriculum is also a way to create a welcoming environment for all families in the community.

The core multicultural curriculum implementation, as a way to positively recognize and implement culturally relevant pedagogy, is accomplished through five steps developed by Banks (1999) and added to by McIntosh (2000):

1. Curriculum of the Mainstream
2. Contributions Approach (Heroes and Holidays)
3. Additive Approach (Integration Stage)
4. Transformation Approach (Structural Reform Stage)
5. Social Action Approach (Multicultural, Social Action, and Awareness Stage)

FIGURE 10.1
MULTICULTURAL CURRICULUM IMPLEMENTATION

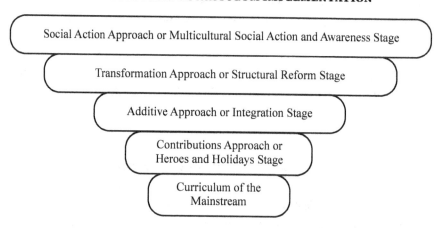

As evident in Figure 10.1, Curriculum of the Mainstream is the lowest and most surfaced avenue to implementing true multicultural curriculum into a classroom. The stages move all the way up to the social action piece, which is the most inclusive implementation practice.

Curriculum of the Mainstream is an approach in which the information is presented in a Eurocentric manner, or a manner that focuses on the White-majority view and mind-set of topics. Essentially, this is the traditional method of education due to the institutional and structural racism present in the education system. An example of this level would include a lesson only about the Pilgrims at Thanksgiving or predominately about White people's influences on, and perspectives of, society through the years.

The Contributions Approach is also known as the "Heroes and Holidays" approach because teachers only incorporate perspectives outside of the majority view when the individual is a hero, such as Martin Luther King, Jr., Cesar

Chavez, or Rosa Parks. Another example is around December when many places are not only incorporating Christmas traditions but also bringing in holidays such as Kwanzaa or Hanukkah through the "othering" process. The "othering" process is any action or thought leading to words that result in an individual or a group becoming mentally classified in someone's mind as "not one of us." Essentially, in this stage, teachers incorporate books and activities to celebrate the "Heroes and Holidays" during specific times of the year, which is in contrast to incorporating multicultural curriculum throughout the entire school year.

The Additive Approach is also known as the Integration Stage because teachers begin to integrate content, concepts, themes, and perspectives to the already established curriculum without changing the basic structure (Banks, 1999). Teachers who are at this stage of multicultural curriculum implementation would take the already-existing curriculum and add diversity concepts to the instruction. For example, a unit on transportation would incorporate pictures of women and men operating vehicles, along with people of various races. Another example would include a teacher encompassing male nurses and Black female doctors during a unit on professions or community helpers. Essentially, the unit title does not change content, but the depictions of various individuals is added to the already-existing unit to display diversity of a multicultural topic, such as race or gender.

The next approach is known as the Transformation Approach or the Structural Reform Stage. This is the stage that Alicia was in during the police project. During this stage, teachers change the curricular structure in the classroom to encourage students to view concepts, issues, themes, and problems from several cultural perspectives. From Alicia's example, she assisted the students in her classroom to see police officers from several perspectives, not just from the perspective they initially experienced in their neighborhood. Further examples of this approach would be to teach students about the Native American perspective while also teaching the Pilgrim perspective around the time of Thanksgiving. Or, teaching multiple perspectives of the story behind Christopher Columbus, rather than only the White, male, dominant perspective. The overall idea of the transformation approach is that all lessons are transformed to see multiple perspectives throughout the school year and not only for "heroes and holidays."

Finally, the most inclusive approach is the Social Action Approach or the Multicultural, Social Action, and Awareness Stage. In essence, this approach not only adds to the changes made in the transformational approach but also encourages students to question and act on social issues (Banks, 1999; McIntosh, 2000). Examples of this in an early childhood classroom might include writing to a large chain grocery store to persuade the executives to build a grocery store in a food desert in their community or to make blankets for veterans and/or homeless in their community. The goal of this stage is for students to see all the perspectives and to know that their voice and actions can make a change in their community and in a wider view of the world. Essentially, in this stage, students and teachers engage in social action with community members.

Fourth-Grade Social Action Approach

In 2017, an Islamic school in a Midwest town was vandalized. The fourth-grade students of a local public school found out about the vandalism, which consisted of Islamophobia graffiti on the school's sign. The teacher of the fourth-grade classroom, Mrs. Jones, encouraged the student-led conversation and facilitated a discussion about the vandalism at the school in their town. After a few weeks of conversations and following the news reports, the fourth-grade students asked their teacher a question: "Can we go visit Daarul Ulloom [the school]? We would like to make them cards, visit with them, and show them that we care about them."

Awestruck and excited, Mrs. Jones reached out to the principal of the Islamic school. After a few conversations, the field trip was planned. Mrs. Jones's students would visit the school to deliver their cards.

The day of the field trip, fourth-grade parents volunteered to help drive the students to the school, which was about 2 miles away. When they all arrived, they were welcomed with open arms. As the teacher put it, "It was a genuine act. It was awesome!"

When the students arrived, they helped clean up the graffiti, shared stories, and ended up making a video for a local news station about hate. From the fourth-grade perspective, it resulted in a touching segment discussing how hate is not okay and that everyone should be nice to each other.

This is social action teaching: student-led, student-voiced, student-engaged social action that made a difference in the rural town.

Social Justice, What Is It?

So teachers should engage their students in social action based in social justice, but what is social justice?

Social justice is advocating, striving, and working toward an equitable distribution of wealth, opportunities, and privileges within a society. The final approach in Banks's (1999) framework focuses on social justice action students can partake in whether it is writing letters to senators or working with community partners on service-learning projects. Although Banks's (1999) theory is not the only theory used to implement multicultural curriculum, it is one of the most respected and practiced. However, another researcher, Gorski (2010), gathered and organized six commonly shared ideas regarding multicultural education that are available in the scholarship. Overall, the six characteristics focus on educating students and advocating/teaching social justice. Gorski's (2010) six shared ideas are outlined and discussed next.

Gorski's (2010) Six Commonly Shared Ideas

1. Every student in an educational setting must **have an equal opportunity** to reach his or her maximum potential.
2. School buildings must prepare students to **participate** in their ever-changing multicultural society.
3. Students have the responsibility to learn how to interact and embrace changing demographics—**teachers effectively prepare and facilitate learning.**
4. Students must **be active in ending oppression.**
5. Education must **be student-centered and inclusive** for all.

6. Educators and advocates for educational *equity* need to **re-examine** how educational practices have an impact on student learning.

First, every student in an educational setting must have an equal opportunity to reach his or her maximum potential (Gorski, 2010). That means that teachers need to create environments where students can be and are successful, both academically and socially. Students must also be prepared in school buildings to participate in the ever-changing multicultural society they live in (Gorski, 2010). As school buildings become increasingly diverse, students have the responsibility to learn how to interact and embrace the changing societal demographics, just as teachers do through the process of learning and reflection. This preparation occurs as a result of teachers preparing to effectively facilitate learning for individual students, regardless of their perceived "differences." Teachers can do this by creating lessons through which all students can learn, as described by Banks's (1999) approaches to multicultural curriculum implementation.

Schools must also be active in ending oppression for all types of individuals (Gorski, 2010). Educators who create an environment where students are active and aware, both socially and culturally, are taking one step closer to ceasing oppressive environments in school buildings. The fifth common ideal among researchers and education professionals is that education must be student-centered and inclusive for all students. This stipulation falls in line with many of the previous ideas where students need to be the center of classroom instruction (i.e., student-centered). Finally, educators and advocates for educational equity need to reexamine how educational practices affect student learning (Gorski, 2010). Some of the specific educational practices that should be questioned or reexamined include assessments, classroom management strategies, pedagogies, materials, textbooks, children's books, and other artifacts in the classroom or school setting.

Revamping Curriculum

As a college professor, I teach a course focused on diverse learners. As part of the course, I engage my students in a process of revamping mainstream curriculum. The activity is outlined next. Examples are also provided for how students have completed this in the past to provide you an understanding of how to take your current curriculum and focus on social action. As a caveat, every example is not an exemplar, but being able to reflect on these examples is also part of the growth process.

Revamping Curriculum Activity

Choose a unit that is commonly taught in classrooms. Describe how the unit could start as Curriculum of the Mainstream and move through each level to reach the most inclusive level of Social Action Approach or Multicultural Social Action and Awareness. In Table 10.1 examples are provided.

Reflection Questions

1. *Reflecting on Gorski's six commonly shared ideas about multicultural education, which are you currently addressing? Which are you going to add to your action plan to focus on next?*

2. *After completing the revamping curriculum activity, what questions arose? What was difficult to include? Why?*

3. *How are you going to purposefully plan social engagement activities at the highest level of "social action" for the students in your classroom on a continuous, yearlong basis?*

TABLE 10.1

APPROACHES CREATING MULTICULTURAL CLASSROOM CURRICULUM

Approaches	Describe how you would change your curriculum to fit into the levels of multi-cultural curriculum implementation, with the understanding that the goal is the Social Action Approach.		
Multicultural Levels	**Farming**	**Community Helpers**	**Black History Month**
Contributions	Include students in an activity on farming (a farmer) explaining what a farmer (male) does. Include Johnny Appleseed.	Only celebrate heroes and holidays around nationally celebrated individuals such as Veteran's Day or Martin Luther King, Jr.	Only teach during Black History Month (February) the contributions of well-known Black people in history (e.g., Rosa Parks; Martin Luther King, Jr.; Barack Obama).
Additive	Add various animals and farm equipment. How do you use each of the pieces of farm equipment? How does farming influence our daily lives? Include George Washington Carver.	Recognizing under acknowledged contributors to society: male nurses, female emergency medical service providers, waste management, construction workers, housekeepers, etc.	Add in eras throughout history for a few months. Add a few more well-known Black people in history (e.g., Malcolm X, Sammy Davis Jr., Langston Hughes).
Transformational	Transform from farming to agriculture around the world. View farming from many points of view (e.g., farmer, manufacturer, store worker, customer).	Teach and discuss how all community helpers impact or make a community instead of acknowledging the work that is done. Who is in the community—community members, homeless people, visitors, storekeepers, volunteers, animals shelter workers, etc.?	Teach about Black history throughout the entire year, focusing on social changes, such as the civil rights movement.
Social Action	Plant a garden at the school or in a food desert. Research issues that face farmers and advocate for farmers to legislators.	Send care packages to firefighters, thank you cards to police officers, teachers, and veterans, and volunteer at a local animal shelter.	Participate in peaceful protests, such as one held by Black Lives Matter. Develop educational materials for peers and community members about Black history in America.

References

Banks, J. A. (1999). *An introduction to multicultural education* (2nd ed.). Boston, MA: Allyn and Bacon.

Banks, J. A. (2009). Multicultural education: Characteristics and goals. In J. A. Banks & C. A. M. Banks (Eds.), *Multicultural education: Issues and perspectives* (7th ed., pp. 3–26). Boston, MA: Allyn and Bacon.

Banks, J. A., & Banks, C. A. M. (2001). *Multicultural education: issues and perspectives. 4th ed.* Danvers, MA: John Wiley and Sons

Wiley. Blum, L. (1999). Race, community and moral education: Kohlberg and Spielberg as civic educators. *Journal of Moral Education, 28*(2), 125–143. Retrieved from https://doi.org/10.1080/030572499103179

Gibson, M. A. (1976). Approaches to multicultural education in the United States: Some concepts and assumptions. *Anthropology and Education Quarterly, 7,* 7–18.

Gorski, P. C. (2010). *Multicultural reform: Stages of multicultural curriculum transformation.* Retrieved from http://www.edchange.org/multicultural/curriculum/steps.html

McIntosh, P. (2000). Interactive phases of personal and curricular re-vision with regard to race. In G. Shin & P. Gorski (Eds.), *Multicultural resource series: Professional development for educators.* Washington, DC: National Education Association.

Pohan, C. A., & Aguilar, T. E. (2001). Measuring educators' beliefs about diversity in personal and professional contexts. *American Educational Research Journal, 38,* 159–182.

Sleeter, C. E., & Grant, C. A. (1994). *Making choices for multicultural education* (2nd ed.). Englewood Cliffs, NJ: Prentice Hall.

Tatum, B. (1992). Talking about race, learning about racism: The application of racial identity development theory in the classroom. *Harvard Educational Review, 62,* 1–25.

CHAPTER ELEVEN

Unpacking the Messiness in Critical Elementary Education

Laura Shelton and Jeannette Alacrón

I (Laura, Author 1) began my first year of teaching committed to tackling difficult content with my fifth-grade students. More than one person asked me why this was important to me, especially given that the first year of teaching is typically the most stressful. As the year progressed, I realized how complicated, messy, and exhausting this commitment could actually be. Throughout the year, I also participated in a new teacher support group that helped me learn to articulate and stick with my commitment to tackling complex social issues with students in a move toward justice education.

In the vignette, I share a learning experience that helped me grow in two areas. First, I learned the importance of anticipating the emotional support students may need to unpack complicated issues, such as race and racism, and recognized the work I had accomplished to build a warm and democratic learning environment. Second, I learned important strategies for communicating with parents when discomfort presents itself while teaching academic content knowledge such as the civil rights movement, activism, and the powers afforded the branches of government in the United States.

It is important to note that I am a White teacher because my intention is to provide a resource for other White teachers grappling with addressing race, racism, power, access, and equity in their classrooms. Although, ultimately, I have modified and used the unit more than once, my first attempt included significant discomfort and learning.

Building from an article I had read, I designed an integrated learning unit for teaching the three branches of government. I was particularly proud of the unit because instead of taking the traditional approach, we were going to understand the relationship between the powers of the branches in relation to the civil rights movement of the 1960s. Both topics are named in social studies teaching standards and are considered age-appropriate. Typically, teachers cover this content by showing a video and doing textbook readings about government and the balances of power, but I wanted students to recognize the ways in which everyday citizens can influence the government.

The unit opened with a gallery walk meant to engage students' thinking about the civil rights movement. Each learning station included primary source images, document-based questions, and collaborative grouping. The students were asked to make observations of the images and use the document-based questions to guide their interpretation of the content of the photos. Students worked together to unpack complicated and racialized topics while I moved from group to group to listen to discussions and ask clarifying questions as needed.

Students moved through different stations buzzing with excited commentary. "This kid is holding signs that say Whites only," exclaimed one student. "That's messed up," responded another. "This is so racist," added a third. Admittedly, I was a bit nervous as the reality of the students' discussions came to life. I began questioning whether my teacher preparation program had actually prepared me to teach complicated issues to fifth graders as students homed in on the shock of seeing historical images of people who were actively participating in White supremacy.

As I made the rounds, I noticed Jayden had left his group to sit alone with his head down at a table. I glanced at the image his group was analyzing, a police dog lunging at an African American man. Jayden was the only Black male student in our class, and his response worried me. I consider myself to be a White ally and honestly felt I was providing a pathway for understanding historical events and governmental powers from a different perspective. This response was unexpected. Where had I gone wrong? Was I harming Jayden?

"Are you okay, Jayden?" I asked bending down beside him to meet his eye level. Jayden sighed and turned his face away. "I just don't like learning about this stuff," he said quietly. Feeling surprised by Jayden's response, I asked, "Would you like to take a break and get some water?" Jayden left the room without saying a word. A few students noticed and began whispering about Jayden's sudden exit. The classroom became very tense, and I noticed my own discomfort in the moment. I began moving quickly through each station to minimize the discussion of Jayden's reaction. In the moment, I was flustered and had trouble deciding whether should have ever created this lesson in the first place.

When Jayden returned, he did not go back to his station; instead, he chose to sit alone. Students looked at him but continued filling out the graphic organizer. I noticed the shift in the room from excited buzz to awkward stiffness. As conversation and productivity waned, I drew the students together for a whole-group debrief of the observations they recorded in response to the images. Jayden remained disengaged, but I did not push him to participate. Overall, the whole-group debrief was productive, and the students generated important questions that would guide the next phases of the unit.

I was grateful for the few minutes that duty-free recess and lunch afforded for reflection when this challenging lesson was over. Although I was tempted to remain focused on the successes of the lesson, I could not shake the confusion I felt around Jayden's reaction to the content. Admittedly, I had grappled with including images depicting racialized violence, but ultimately, I naively believed that any representation of minority experiences would benefit the students of color in my class.

My Whiteness prevented me from anticipating the way a young African American male student would react to seeing violence perpetrated on another Black male. Having once felt confident about the unit and its content, I began to question my choices. I remained committed to teaching about complicated issues of social injustice, but I needed to reconsider how this might affect Jayden and other students of color. I decided to contact my mentor. During the conversation, we unpacked my motives for instructional choices, Jayden's reaction, and the next best steps. I had already begun to build a trusting learning community and relationships with parents. We decided that I should call Jayden's mom in a proactive move to get her thoughts on the experience and hopefully gain her support in helping Jayden move through the feelings he was processing.

The rest of the day was a bit nerve-wracking as I anticipated my conversation with Jayden's mom. After dismissal, I walked back to my empty room and closed the door to review my notes and prepare for the phone call. As I switched on the lamp, a stream of questions flooded my mind: Did I push the students too far? How can a teacher really know if a class is ready for challenging content? How can teachers help students with various racialized identities reflect on the complicated issue of race? Were other students having similar feelings, but just not saying anything? If I continue with the unit, will it be at Jayden's expense? I braced myself and picked up the phone. Although our conversation was difficult, Jayden's mom expressed her desire for him to understand complicated social and historical issues and offered her support in helping to move him through the content in ways that resulted in his making sense of the world and not in ways that made him feel inferior.

I share this vignette to highlight my journey with becoming a social justice-oriented educator. It is not an easy journey, and I hope that the framework and practical resources in this chapter will help others take the leap.

Engaging Theory and Action Research

During my (Laura Shelton) first year of teaching, I participated in a professional development support group composed of other first-year teachers who had graduated from the same university-based program facilitated by Jeannette Alarcón (Author 2). The group's main goal was to create a support network for new teachers who had voiced a commitment to equity, access, and justice in their teaching. We created space to hash out problems of practice, develop our teaching philosophies, and better understand the theoretical frameworks that informed our ideas about teaching and learning.

Although we employed several frameworks, this chapter draws on Picower's (2012) work for crafting definitions for the principles of social-justice education and Smalls-Glovers's (2019) work on understanding identity development for students of color and effective strategies for community building. Our group also engaged in teacher action research as we grappled with questions such as "How can teachers facilitate difficult, courageous conversations in academic content areas without further marginalizing students of color?"

We brought the vignette experience to the new-teacher group as a problem of practice that we could all wrap our heads around. We engaged in a group discussion aimed at how to both move forward with the unit planned and make changes to the opening lesson. We soon realized that although the content of the lesson was age-appropriate and classroom community was continually facilitated to build trust, work specific to helping youngsters understand intersections of identity and social issues had not been explicitly addressed. We returned to the Picower (2012) work we used to frame our definition of justice teaching/learning in elementary settings and decided that more concrete work with the first two principles could be a pathway to setting the stage for tackling complicated issues.

Picower (2012) developed the Six Elements of Social Justice Education to serve as guideposts for planning and implementing academic content highlighting justice issues. Picower's (2012) elements are self-love and knowledge, respect for others, issues of social injustice, social movements and social change, awareness raising, and social action. Furthermore, she posits providing "students with the historical background knowledge to recognize the strengths and resiliency of their communities" and allows them to see issues of social injustice as systemic in, rather than deficits of, their community (Picower, 2012, p. 2). She also cautions that jumping into complicated issues of injustice in the classroom without leading students to "value themselves" can "reinforce cross-group tension" because students have not developed ways to talk about and be sensitive to identities (Picower, 2012). As authors, we take this to mean that students experiencing self-love and knowledge and respect for others before they learn about issues of social injustice is imperative. Furthermore, we assert that to do this work successfully, partnerships with parents and families are key. In addition to focusing on building mutual respect, appreciation, and trust for others within the classroom, for teachers (particularly White teachers), becoming more familiar with the educational goals, parenting styles, and expectations that parents of color hold is necessary. We have found the work of psychologist, Dr. Ciara Smalls-Glover to be helpful.

Dr. Smalls-Glover (Lumanlan & Smalls-Glover, 2019) studies the ways in which parents of color teach their children about identity and social belonging. In a recent interview, she shared three key ideas for helping parents provide an environment for talking with children about issues of race, racism, and identity. We extend her ideas to include the classroom setting where children should be guided to unpack such persistent social problems. The three tenets are providing a balance of messages, creating a warm and democratic learning context, and ensuring content is age-appropriate.

The example provided shows the ways in which we attended to these tenets while the practical advice section provides some ideas for improving that practice. In particular, since the first year of teaching, we have become much more cognizant of providing hopeful messaging whenever we tackle oppressive messages. Furthermore, facilitating a warm and democratic learning environment via critical community building has become a cornerstone of our practice.

Bettez (2011) defined the idea of critical community building as an extension of traditional community building in that it specifically attends to creating spaces for difficult and honest dialogue. She describes three tenets: maintaining an open web of connections, engaging in active listening with critical question posing, and making a commitment coupled with accountability.

As mentioned previously, we realized that more explicit community and trust building needed to happen prior to introducing the concepts covered in the learning unit. Critical community building served as a tool for helping us do this. Maintaining a web of connections hones openness and inclusivity, builds bridges, and requires being conscientiously welcoming. Engaging in active listening requires sought-out dialogues across differences—aiming for space where both speaker and listener can learn. Finally, a commitment to mutual accountability fosters empathy for classmates' experiences and reactions. In the following section, we offer strategies and resources for building a learning community where difficult topics can be addressed. We also offer resources for finding links to academic content and standards that are helpful to new teachers for making the case for justice-oriented teaching.

Building a Learning Community

Teachers need to establish a solid foundation of classroom trust and help students develop a language for talking about and across identity and cultural differences. Jayden's emotional response and isolation described in the vignette were partly due to a lack of preparation for navigating complicated issues in classroom settings. In hindsight, the lesson should have followed students sharing about their families, celebrating their identities, deconstructing stereotypes, and creating norms for how they want to talk about difference. After students gained an appreciation for their identities, we would have been more prepared to move toward lessons that focus on developing respect for others. These two steps lead students to appreciate the diversity present within the class community and deconstruct stereotypes. Table 11.1 lists activities and strategies geared toward facilitating community building with an emphasis on self-love/ knowledge and respect for others.

TABLE 11.1
FACILITATING COMMUNITY BUILDING

Self-Love and Knowledge or Respect for Others	Activity	Description and Possible Work Products
Self-Love and Knowledge	Where I'm From Poems[1]	Have students write and share poems describing their family, objects, and communities that are important to them. These projects can culminate in a poetry salon where families are invited to listen to students perform their work. Students can even choose to participate in the I Am From Project[2] (n.d.) by submitting the final draft of their poems (Christansen, 1997).
Self-Love and Knowledge	Identity Tree[3]	Help students understand identities by creating an identity tree[3] and describing their own identities as well as the identities present in their classroom.

Self-Love and Knowledge or Respect for Others	Activity	Description and Possible Work Products
Respect for Others	Talking Circles and <u>Restor-ative Circles</u>[4] (International Institute for Restorative Practices, n.d.)	Teachers can facilitate talking circles and restorative circles for community building and problem solving. Utilizing circles in the classroom can help students share stories about their lives, and feel comfortable to be themselves, and problem solve as a community (Morrison & Vandeering, 2012). International Institute for Restorative Practices. (n.d.). 5.2. Defining restorative circles. Retrieved July 31, 2019, from https://www.iirp.edu/defining-restorative/5-2-circles
Respect for Others	Create a Talking Object	Students and teachers can co-create a talking object to be used in talking circles. The activity begins by the entire class sitting in a circle. The teacher says three things about themselves, wraps yarn around a stick or talking object, and then passes the yarn and object to the next student, who then repeats the process. This continues until the entire class has participated. At the end, the teacher describes how each person in the community has contributed to the talking object, and therefore, everyone's voice is present in each class meeting and talking circle. (It is important to use multicolored yarn so racial and cultural diversity can also be addressed when debriefing the activity.)
Respect for Others	*The First Six Weeks of School*[5] (Responsive Classroom, 2011)	This article and book by Responsive Classroom go through activities and planning ideas for each week of instruction in the first 6 weeks of school for each K–6 grade level. There are community-building ideas and ways to set up classroom routines and norms that involve high levels of student input that focus on respecting the classroom and community for everyone's benefit.

1 See Rethinking Schools in the Online Sources section at the end of the chapter.
2 See I Am From Project in the Online Sources section at the end of the chapter.
3 See Edutopia in the Online Sources section at the end of the chapter.
4 See International Institute for Restorative Practices in the Online Sources section at the end of the chapter.
5 See Responsive Classroom in the Online Sources section at the end of the chapter.

Although resources offered here primarily focus on two elements of social justice education, recognizing that the learning cannot stop there is important. For students to be empowered to create a more fair and just world, they must also learn about historical examples of the ways people have fought injustice. Furthermore, students and teachers must make connections to the present moment to participate in contemporary social change. Learning experiences that

promote civic engagement allow for what Banks (2017) describes as "transformative citizenship education," meaning that students "from diverse groups . . .
increase their academic knowledge, political efficacy, and political participatory
skills" (p. 373). Including all the elements for social justice education ensures
young students practice doing so. By incorporating real examples of civic engagement and creating opportunities for students to participate in social action,
they become empowered to make real changes, but none of this is possible without all students having self-love and respect for others.

Cultivating a classroom community does not end with students. It is
equally important for teachers to build a trusting community with families
as well. Teachers must acknowledge and value different forms of parenting to
build relationships with families that extend beyond sending report cards and
scheduling conferences. White teachers especially need to realize they are not
the experts on talking with students of color about race, and families can be a
resource for addressing such topics in the classroom. Facilitating discussions
across difference can feel intimidating, especially as a White teacher who is
still on her own anti-racist journey. Building trusting relationships with families takes time and ongoing effort throughout the year. Mary Cowhey (2006),
author of *Black Ants and Buddhists*, describes families as expert resources that
can be tapped into throughout the year. She suggests going on home visits at the
beginning of the year to get to know students and their families and continually
working to help families feel welcome at school by hosting family potlucks,
inviting families to participate in morning meetings, field trips, and other activities during the school year (Cowhey, 2006).

Linking to Academic Content

A common argument against covering complicated topics in the classroom
is that the topics deviate from the Common Core standards and/or state required content. This is especially true in the age of high-stakes testing. One of
the ways teachers can counter this argument is by referring to Teaching Tolerance's (2016) *Social Justice Standards*. As shown in Table 11.2, the standards
overlap nicely with Picower's (2012) Six Elements of Social Justice Education
and include four bands—identity, diversity, justice, and action—and are

written for K–2, 3–5, 6–8, and 9–12 grade bands. Teachers can use the standards to support the topics they choose to address. The standards are easily integrated with any content areas, particularly literacy and social studies (see Table 11.2).

TABLE 11.2
SOCIAL JUSTICE STANDARDS EXAMPLES

Teaching Tolerance Social Justice Standard Strand	Element of Social Justice Education
Identity	Self-Love and Knowledge
Diversity	Respect for Others
Justice	Issues of Social Injustice and Social Movements and Social Change
Action	Awareness Raising and Social Action

Additionally, covering complicated topics is naturally embedded within required grade-level content. For example, fifth-grade social studies standards include the founding of America, which is rampant with instances of power and oppression for students to critically examine. The unit described in the opening vignette of this chapter addresses the fifth-grade social studies standards requiring students to learn about the three branches of government. I chose to do this by learning about grassroots activism so that students could see examples of the ways people affect the government. Therefore, when planning integrated units of study, teachers should consider the following:

a. What are students talking about and wondering regarding these topics?
b. How is power represented, maintained, and/or described in the content material?
c. What power dynamics need to be considered within the classroom community?
d. How is the topic relevant to local and/or current events?

Considering these four questions can help teachers guide students through issues of controversy in developmental appropriateness because they are based on students' questions and require them to reckon with power structures and connect them to the present moment.

Conclusion

This chapter is intended to guide new teachers to prepare for and reflect on tackling complicated social issues with young learners in relevant and brave ways. Fortunately, a growing number of teachers voice an intention to attend to issues of equity, access, and justice in their classrooms. However, often they dive right into complex issues without taking the time to establish a warm and democratic learning environment. Teachers must create learning spaces where students can engage in authentic learning about themselves and others with the goal of creating understanding and respect for difference. To facilitate this work, we have provided resources to aid with planning and revealed a first-year teacher's reflections on the process of becoming a critical elementary educator. We believe creating a safe and welcoming classroom environment is the foundation necessary for authentic and timely social justice work with young learners.

Reflection Questions and Activities

1. *Make a plan for establishing trust at the beginning of the school year. What norms and procedures might you implement throughout the year that help students hone empathy and respect for others?*

2. *What are the ways in which you can showcase and celebrate students' identities in the classroom?*

3. *How can you help all students' voices be heard and valued in your classroom? What roles will families play in your students' development of self-love and knowledge?*

4. *Brainstorm reflective practices that you might engage as you learn to navigate controversial topics with students. What are the ways in which you can help students identify and dismantle biases in their perceptions of difference?*

Online Sources

Edutopia: https://www.edutopia.org/blog/fostering-identity-safety-in-classroom-shane-safir
I Am From Project: https://iamfromproject.com/
International Institute for Restorative Practices: https://www.iirp.edu/defining-restorative/5-2-circles
Responsive Classroom: https://www.responsiveclassroom.org/the-first-six-weeks-of-school/
Rethinking Schools: https://www.rethinkingschools.org/articles/where-i-m-from

References

Banks, J. A. (2017). Failed citizenship and transformative civic education. *Educational Researcher, 46,* 366–377.
Bettez, S. (2011, February 18). *Critical community building: Beyond belonging.* Keynote address at Southeastern Association of Educational Studies conference, Chapel Hill, NC.
Christensen, L. (1997). *Where I'm from.* Retrieved from https://www.rethinkingschools.org/articles/where-i-m-from
Cowhey, M. (2006). *Black ants and Buddhists: Thinking critically and teaching differently in the primary grades.* Portland, ME: Mary Cowhey
I Am From Project. (n.d.). Retrieved from https://iamfromproject.com/
International Institute for Restorative Practices. (n.d.). 5.2. *Defining restorative circles.* Retrieved July 31, 2019, from https://www.iirp.edu/defining-restorative/5-2-circles
Lumanlan, J., & Smalls-Glover, C. (2019, June 23). 093: *Parenting children of nondominate cultures.* Retrieved from https://www.listennotes.com/podcasts/your-parenting/093-parenting-children-of-eNlBftHu8zZ/
Picower, B. (2012) Using their words: Six elements of social justice curriculum design for the elementary classroom. *International Journal of Multicultural Education, 14*(1) 1–17.
Responsive Classroom. (2011, July 19). *The first six weeks of school.* Retrieved from https://www.responsiveclassroom.org/the-first-six-weeks-of-school/
Teaching Tolerance. (2016). *Social justice standards.* Retrieved July 31, 2019, from https://www.tolerance.org/sites/default/files/2017-06/TT_Social_Justice_Standards_0.pdf

Theme Three: Professionalism

CHAPTER TWELVE

ESTABLISHING PROFESSIONAL COMMUNICATION THROUGH CULTURALLY RESPONSIVE RAPPORT

Mahmoud Suleiman

I ran a small private elementary school where I served as principal and director of education for a few years in Arizona. The school demographics were very diverse and represented various cultures, nationalities, and ethnicities, as well as mainstream Americans. Tariq, a fifth grader, attended the school. His family had immigrated from North Africa and settled in the United States. His father worked as a civil engineer while his mom stayed home taking care of Tariq's little brother and sister. Both parents spoke English as a second language, and Tariq was an English learner. Tariq's teacher was in her third year of teaching. She was a White female who grew up in Chicago and had moved to Arizona after completing her education to become a teacher.

One day, Tariq's father approached me after school. He wanted to complain about his child's fifth-grade teacher. I sat with the dad and listened to his story based on what Tariq had told his parents when he went home after school that day. Tariq told his parents that he was scared because of the way the teacher talked to him when he asked a question about his homework as the class was leaving the room for recess. Tariq felt the teacher was angry with him and asked him to stay in his seat while she was talking to him. He also claimed that the teacher was rude because of the way she was talking to him in a loud voice and kept staring at him during the entire conversation while staying behind her desk. The parent also told me that the teacher threatened Tariq at the end of the conversation by waiving the okay sign using her right hand.

Soon after listening to Tariq's dad, I realized that there was a huge misunderstanding given my knowledge of the teacher and her firm professional standing, her passion, and her genuine interest in students' success. I asked the parent if he talked to the teacher about the issue. He said, "No." So I told him that he needed to first have a conversation with the teacher, who could explain what happened, and that if I needed to intervene afterward, I would be available to assist in reconciling the issue.

Then, Tariq's dad sat with the teacher, who was shocked by what the parents heard. She clarified how she was trying to help his child understand what was expected for the homework when he asked her. Tariq's dad also developed a clearer understanding of the teacher's communication style and the formal posture dictated by her professional role to undertake her duties. He also got a sense during his interaction with her about the nature of discourse. When asked about threatening Tariq using the hand gesture (the okay sign), it was very striking to the teacher to learn that the okay sign she used to ensure that Tariq understood her explanations at the end of the conversation was misinterpreted as a sign of threat and intimidation in his language and culture.

Consequently, the misunderstanding was cleared as both the teacher and Tariq's dad apologized to each other. For the teacher, acting professionally seemed to have fallen short and lost in the translation of cross-cultural discourse. She became a lot more conscious of her vocal inflections and nonverbal cues and of establishing a rapport prior to attempting to get her students to accomplish their academic goals. On the other hand, Tariq and his parents learned about how to better communicate and not misjudge the *professional behavior of the teacher. For them, they learned that they had missed the teacher's point, albeit the seemingly rude behavior, of her attempt to promote Tariq's academic success. Finally, for the teacher, Tariq, and his parents, they all realized that one should seek to understand first before expecting to be understood.*

Establishing Rapport: Professional Interactions

Professional behaviors are manifested in many ways in various settings. Apart from appearance, dress, and other visible forms, the most important aspect involves how we interact, communicate, and conduct ourselves when engaging in various forms of discourse. We interact constantly as part of our human nature. We communicate with everyone around us and on a daily basis through speech, writing, and other media. We interact with family members, friends, acquaintances, strangers, colleagues, and many others. We engage in various forms of discourse: linguistic, social, cognitive, professional, emotional, and other forms and modes to accomplish our needs and wants, build connections, and make sense of everything around us. Nonetheless, one aspect we benignly fail to notice is *how* we do all these interactions simply because we just do them to fulfill our social needs. In the same manner, we move from one place to another, physically walking and using other tools available to us to get from one point to the next. Often, we do not even think about how these physical activities occur. In short, we talk and walk without thinking about how the process takes place because we take all of these for granted unless interruptions and obstacles hamper efforts and outcomes.

Think about it! Have you ever thought about *how* you were talking to a friend about an issue of mutual concern? Have you reflected on a conversation with your boss trying to reconcile a problem? Or have you thought about an interaction with a stranger you met at a social gathering? At the same time, have you considered how you came across to the person in any of these situations? These questions and others can help in reflecting on how we interact rather than what the subject of the interaction is. Of course, our interactions do not take place in a vacuum; they are context-bound and multidimensional and are largely dictated by responding to the *who, when, where, why,* and *what* questions.

Gladwell (2007) cautioned against the dangers of listening with our eyes especially when unconscious bias and implicit prejudice are used as lenses when interactions take place. Similarly, Gladwell (2019) calls for a deeper understanding of the interaction and communicative process that can guard against formulating hasty snap judgments, making unnecessary assumptions without a sound understanding of the underlying premise of invisible aspects when interacting with those are different from us.

In educational settings, perhaps one of the most often ignored aspects involves language complexity and its vital role in the interaction and discourse processes. Apart from being a vital tool to communicate, language has multiple functions and roles that facilitate discourse is various settings; it is a loaded construct that is frequently underused and abused (Bolinger, 1980, 1981; Labov, 2013). The holistic process involves cognitive, social, cultural, affective, and other dimensions deeply rooted in each learner's sociocultural prior knowledge and experience.

In fact, language is a construct that has a special place in everyone's life. It is a dynamic tool that has fascinated philosophers, linguists, and educators throughout history (Suleiman, 2013). It has also been studied and investigated as a unique social phenomenon given its role, impact, and value for humans and their complex wants and needs. Studying language can be a fascinating process that involves discovery and unraveling of the collective human experience (Chomsky, 1986; Suleiman, 1995a, 1995b). Because linguistic tools and patterns shed light on unique aspects of interaction among individuals and groups, language has occupied a central role in schools. Instructional and curricular activities have always integrated language as a basis for any effective learning and teaching.

Language is very central in educating all children early on in their lives, especially in diverse settings. Language is the currency of multiple forms of literacy, including cultural proficiency. Because acquiring language is an ever-changing, lifelong process, schools have always tried to place a great emphasis on language learning as a prerequisite for any study of other content areas and subjects. Language provides the foundation for thought processes, inquiry, interaction, and learning regardless of the context in which it is used (Bolinger, 1981; Chomsky, 1986). Students' and teachers' success can largely depend on their linguistic abilities and other language-related tools to solve problems and meaningfully interact with one another and with the world around them.

Although language is a key social capital (Bourdieu, 1998; Viniti, Gopinathan, & Yongbing, 2007), it is also an educational and professional capital given its vital place in the school's curriculum and instruction processes. Of course, this concept is not new. More than 40 years ago, for example, Bullock's (1975) report, *A Language for Life*, formed the impetus of language across content and curricular activities that shaped teachers' professional roles and skills. Originally based on this notion, the Language Across Curriculum (LAC) (see Thaiss, 1986) approaches have evolved. The premise that underlies these approaches is twofold: First, language transcends content and academic areas of the curriculum regardless of what the subject matter may be. The second aspect involves the role of teachers generally regardless of the subject they teach; that is, every teacher is a language teacher. Thus, teachers should be cognizant of this fact and that their metalinguistic awareness is equally important to their professional expertise in the content they teach. Additionally, the way teachers communicate and interact using language is critical in maintaining effective rapport with learners and their families, as well as others around them, especially in cross-cultural settings.

In culturally and linguistically diverse classrooms, establishing effective rapport has become more necessary than ever before. Studying language traits, aspects, and functions has become the basis for understanding language and academic development of all students. Thus, teachers are expected to become linguistic detectives to understand how students learn and, more important, to draw implications for curriculum planning and delivery to enhance learning outcomes. This need is imperative, especially when working with diverse student populations who bring unique linguistic experiences and cultural schemata that should be cultivated.

Language is one of the most formidable tools for cultural and academic and cultural brokerage in schools. It does exert a huge power on professional interaction, learning, teaching, and cross-cultural communication. Consider the following underlying assumptions:

- Language *speaks us* (i.e., it tells a lot about the speaker) as much as we speak it.
- Language is a window on the mind, heart, and soul.
- Language mirrors culture and vice versa.
- Language helps cultural unpacking.
- Language and culture are universal human phenomena.
- Language is a dynamic tool for cultural proficiency.
- Language matters in every aspect of interaction.

For native speakers of any language, interaction is a natural process when engaging in any speech or communicative event. In other words, it is a spontaneous, automatic, subconscious, and systematic process that is frequently taken for granted. For example, we do not think about how we talk the way we do not think about how we walk. We tend not to be conscious of the dynamics of walking or talking unless something breaks down.

Yet complex underlying factors could determine the ease or difficulty in the communication process. The deeper level of interaction involves a balanced juggling act that requires the subconscious application of multiple rules and principles. It is also dictated and governed by certain conditions, factors, elements, and certainly professional demands. All these are determined by a given context that frames the bulk of linguistic elements to give language use social and individual utility and value. The context also sets the parameters of "doing language" as to, for example, what to say, when, to whom, where, why, and how. In other words, a wide range of functions and purposes are accomplished simultaneously when professional interaction occurs in a given context.

Anatomy of Language Use: Multifunctional Dynamics

To unravel this process, a Russian-born American philosopher, Roman Jakobson, provided a model that dissects the discourse process and explains the underlying premise of various elements involved. Jakobson's (1960) classic piece, *Linguistics and Poetics*, outlined several functions of language that illustrate hidden elements of discourse during any speech event or communicative task. This landmark account has gained little attention among linguists and educators. Nonetheless, the model proposed by Jakobson has provided the impetus for many developments in linguistic theories and subfields of language study, such as semiotics, kinesics, pragmatics, proxemics, psycholinguistics, and sociolinguistics.

According to Jakobson (1960), any speech or communicative event involves six elements or factors. These include the following:

1. **Context:** The social and physical aspects in which the messages interchangeably take place
2. **Message:** The subject or topic of the conversational event
3. **Addresser:** The person involved in sending the verbal message (sender/enunciator)
4. **Addressee:** The person on the receiving end of the event (a receiver/enunciatee of the message)
5. **Contact:** The link and connection between sender/addresser and receiver/addressee through which the message is channeled
6. **Code:** Common language or agreed-on code of communication between participants

In fact, when engaging in any communicative acts or speech events with others around us, we employ multiple functions and strategies as we seek to accomplish our communicative needs and wants. This involves relaying not only the messages we are trying to communicate but also a wide range of variables that include engaging the receiver of the message, appealing to their cultural intelligences, being sensitive to their emotions and feelings, and meeting their social and others' expectations. For example, we should be able to adjust our speech and communication style to ensure that we are engaging the listener in meaningful and culturally sensitive ways. In other words, variations in communication require us to effectively utilize the language functions based on the contextual demands, nature of the message, traits of participants (personality, mood, gender, age, etc.), and a whole host of other intervening variables and conditions including acting professionally. This also includes our nonlinguistic behaviors, known as paralanguage, and nonverbal cues, during the communicative process. Despite the primacy of speech, language can take nonverbal and kinesthetic forms. In fact, very early in their life, children display this property by their verbal and nonverbal behaviors. Although oral discourse is the pathway to developing other language skills, nonverbal discourse is a major part of the process as well. The value of nonverbal cues lies in their role of enhancing the verbal messages to ensure effective communication; the reverse can be true as well.

It is worth noting that language nuances and nonverbal cues are culturally bound and may cause communication barriers in the diverse settings. For example, although the okay sign might connote approval and praise in one culture, it can be interpreted as a sign of threat and warning in other cultures (such as the case in some Semitic languages, such as Arabic). Likewise, rising pitch and intonation contours in one's speech, although appropriate and acceptable by speakers of a given region, might be interpreted as evasive and rude by members of other regions.

Paying closer attention to the dynamics of the speech events and the way we utilize them in everyday life has been a focus for many educators and scholars (Halliday, 1973, 1975, 1989, 2004). Educational implications from research and experience in the dynamics of the communication and discourse analysis have been drawn to help teachers undertake their roles meaningfully as cultural brokers as well as facilitators of learning (Gumperz, 1982,1986; Osoba & Sobola, 2014). As such, teachers can enhance their cross-cultural and global understanding when interacting with others in a culturally responsive way (Orelus, 2017; Sirbu, 2015). Students' literacy and academic skills in diverse settings can be promoted (Alsoraihi, 2019; Philomina, 2015) when teachers are seeking to improve their professional communication sensitivity and use flexible multicultural communication styles (Olshtain & Celce-Murcia, 2001; Suleiman, 1997; Suleiman & Hashem, 1995; Tang, 2008). Unless we take into account the multiple cultural variables that affect the communicative process, we will continue seeing communication breakdowns and barriers that hamper our efforts to connect with learners and engage them at various emotional, social, and cultural levels.

Parameters for Differentiated Communication

Despite the universal elements of the communicative process, variations exist within a language and across languages. Language uniformity seems to be a theoretical impossibility because language is utilized in creative ways based on multiple factors and dynamics within the same linguistic and cultural community. In addition, individuals have their idiosyncrasies and styles that shape their ways of interacting with others.

Having this in mind, Joos (1960) outlined in his book, *The Five Clocks*, five forms of language use based on the contextual demands of the speech event. These registers can be manifested by the level of formality in the style one uses to communicate in a particular situation. Joos (1960) labeled context-bound register variations as *frozen* (e.g., an urgent building evacuation announcement on a loudspeaker), *formal* (e.g., a report presentation to an education board), *consultative* (e.g., a conversation between a merchant and customer, a physician and a patient), *casual* (e.g., conversation between friends), and *intimate* (e.g., a conversation between a mom and her child; a conversation between lovers), styles that describe how language users engage in given spoken or written discourse events. Although these constructs are descriptive in nature, they should not be prescriptive under the circumstances. Still, they can be helpful lenses to understand what goes on in the minds and lives of language users.

Payne (1996) capitalized on the work of Joos (1960) to understand poverty and its impact on students and their families and their interactional styles. Her work sparked criticism and resistance. On one hand, the complexity of the sociocultural dimensions of poverty is deeply rooted in economic, racial, and cross-cultural gaps rather than academic or literacy deficiencies (Evans-Winters & Cowie, 2009). On the other hand, more empirical data and research are needed to combat stereotypes and prejudice against the racially and culturally different and the way they communicate and use their intelligence (Valencia, 2010).

Manifestations of these differentiated communication styles caught the attention of researchers and educators who sought to understand how cross-linguistic and cross-cultural connections are made among participants in diverse schools, including teachers, students, parents, and others. Labov's (1972, 2012) work in sociolinguistics shed light on the unique ways social registers are utilized in the communicative process within linguistically diverse American communities. In particular, his study of Black English, known as Ebonics, provided insight into language discourse in cross-cultural settings. Sociolinguistic research affirmed the premise that all forms of register are equally important in meeting the communicative needs of participants. By the same token, all languages are equally valuable in maintaining humans' social, affective, cognitive, and universal needs. At the same time, educators are cautioned against making hasty judgments and false assumptions about individuals or groups based on the language or form of language they use when interacting with others. The key is to understand the complexity of the speech event and the context in which language functions are utilized.

For professionals, this underscores the need to suspend judgment based on how one communicates and abstain from stigmatizing them given their unique differentiated communication styles. For example, teachers should be sensitive to the forms of language children bring to school. Children say certain things in certain ways based on their social milieu and cultural makeup; their language may be a reflection of how communication occurs in meaningful ways to them and their community. Thus, they should not be stigmatized because they are different. Rather, they should be cultivated and valued. At the same time, teachers should not only differentiate their communication styles but also expose children to various forms of interaction and communication modes. The following are some strategies teachers can use:

1. **Modeling Differentiated Styles.** Teachers can model each communication style based on the situations at hand. For example, they can illustrate how formal communication dictates certain words and structures to fit formal situations vis-à-vis communicating in other contexts in which slang with a lax form of style is used. In addition, teachers can make connections to interactions beyond the school and ask their students to observe divergent communication styles in different social settings such as watching a newscast, watching a movie, observing how their parents communicate with guests at their home, and the like. These authentic and rich experiences can provide learning opportunities and explore multiples ways of interaction.

2. **Contextual Variation Prompts.** Because contexts often drive the nature of the communicative style used in a given setting, teachers can provide contextual scenarios that reflect how communication occurs in unique ways according to various aspects of the task at hand. To do so, teachers can illustrate how various conversations should revolve around meeting the communicative needs in terms of *what, who, whom, how, when, where,* and *why* questions. A teacher may provide a context for students to converse using relevant communication patterns and styles based on the demands of the context in which the discourse occurs. For example, the task of working in small groups to solve a math problem will be determined by the context of the interaction that requires an academic discourse different from conversations among friends in the playground. Thus, students are expected to engage in math talk as conversations will be shaped by the academic language and reasoning skills needed for learning math concepts and functions.

3. **Style Transformation Frames.** Most teachers provided sentence frames for their students to promote grammatical competence in academic discourse—both written and oral. In the same manner, teachers can help learners develop an awareness about style shifts within contextual demands. For example, they can set criteria to guide discourse and interaction by providing structure and guidance about diction choices and the manner in which the communicative task (oral or written) should be carried out. This requires teachers to provide rich vocabulary and high utility words as well as structural frames that will guide the discourse activity and style choices. Another way of using transformation frames is engaging students in style shifts; for instance, after conducting a casual conversation between two students, the same students can be asked to conduct the same conversation in a less casual and more formal style.

4. **Role-Play Scenarios.** Scenarios are widely used in many learning and teaching situations. They are most effective in developing communicative competence and literacy skills. Teachers can assign and define roles for students to conduct a communicative event or task and monitor their performance accordingly. Examples include two students conducting a conversation as close friends using a casual style, another student delivering a formal speech on civics in front of the class while another student presents a formal report on a social science project focusing on missions, and two students acting out a conversation based on different roles, such as conversations emulating a teacher–student dialogue, a boss–employee formal conversation, and the like.

5. **Paralanguage Interaction Demonstrations.** The premise of nonverbal behaviors in communication cannot be undermined. Teachers can illustrate how paralanguage can be used and may vary considerably from one culture to another. This includes interpreting gestures, body language, contact, facial expressions, and other kinesthetic phenomena during an interaction. It also includes suprasegmental features focusing on pitch, tone, register, intonation, voice inflections, and the like—all of which are not only meaning-bearing but also culturally bound.

These strategies and others can help narrow the cross-cultural communicative gaps and enhance literacy and academic development in all learners. Apart from exposing learners to multiple ways of expression, such techniques can provide students choices and give them ownership for learning based on their unique talents and new ways of interacting with others and the world around them.

Because students in diverse classrooms bring unique linguistic repertoires and communication frames, teachers should have a global conceptual awareness and professional skills to build on learners' sociolinguistic capital. Thus, students should not be penalized for using their own style of communication that is socially grounded in the way they interact. In fact, they should be valued and encouraged to build on their own meaningful ways of communicating given the social, cultural, and linguistic capital they bring to schools. At the same time, they should be able to engage in style- and code-switching based on their communicative needs and contextual demands. This can be viewed as a product of their linguistic intelligence and cognitive and cultural flexibilities that also should be the basis for teachers' professional communication strategies.

Dimensions of Differentiated Cross-Cultural Communication

The discourse engagement is neither rigid nor static; it is rather a dynamic and flexible process. It allows participants in the speech event to use fixations and repairs to maintain the communion, focus, flow, clarity, emphasis, and meaningful professional communication. This can be illustrated by many shifts in tone, mood, roles, style, verbal and nonverbal cues, and paralanguage. Culture takes a central role in the dynamic.

Hall's (1959) classic work *The Silent Language* provided an anthropological account of how communication occurs in terms of a dichotomy he referred to as "high context" and "low context" settings, which are bound by sociocultural norms and patterns. Subsequently, Hall (1969, 1976, 1983) illuminated such a dichotomy in light of hidden cultural dimensions and social norms that account for the underlying premise of how messages are sent and deciphered in various discourse situations. High-context cultures reflect implicit communication styles with a great deal of nonverbal and paralanguage aspects used in communicative discourse. Examples of high-context patterns are manifested in Asian, Middle Eastern, Central European, African, Native American, and Latin American cultures, among many others. On the other hand, low-context cultures reflect a goal-focused, explicit, and rapid communicative process largely without any nonverbal cues. Such patterns are manifested in mainstream American, Western European, Australian, and other cultures.

Researchers such as Halverson and Trmizi (2008) capitalized on Hall's work and developed professional training instruments in various fields geared toward narrowing cultural gaps and promoting mutual understanding during the communicative process in particular settings. Table 12.1, a widely cited table, delineates Hall's dichotomy and illustrates varying culturally bound dimensions that govern interactions in cross-cultural contexts.

TABLE 12.1

HALL'S HIGH CONTEXT AND LOW CONTEXT DICHOTOMY

High Context (HC)	Low Context (LC)
Association	**Association**
• Relationships depend on trust, build up slowly, are stable. One distinguishes between people inside and people outside one's circle. • How things get done depends on relationships with people and attention to group process. • One's identity is rooted in groups (family, culture, work). • Social structure and authority are centralized; responsibility is at the top. Person at top works for the good of the group.	• Relationships begin and end quickly. Many people can be inside one's circle; circle's boundary is not clear. • Things get done by following procedures and paying attention to the goal. • One's identity is rooted in oneself and one's accomplishments. • Social structure is decentralized; responsibility goes further down (is not concentrated at the top).
Interaction	**Interaction**
• High use of nonverbal elements; voice tone, facial expression, gestures, and eye movement carry significant parts of conversation. • Verbal message is implicit; context (situation, people, nonverbal elements) is more important than words. • Verbal message is indirect; one talks around the point and embellishes it. • Communication is seen as an art form—a way of engaging someone. • Disagreement is personalized. One is sensitive to conflict expressed in another's nonverbal communication. Conflict either must be solved before work can progress or must be avoided because it is personally threatening.	• Low use of nonverbal elements. Message is carried more by words than by nonverbal means. • Verbal message is explicit. Context is less important than words. • Verbal message is direct; one spells things out exactly. • Communication is seen as a way of exchanging information, ideas, and opinions. • Disagreement is depersonalized. One withdraws from conflict with another and gets on with the task. Focus is on rational solutions, not personal ones. One can be explicit about another's bothersome behavior.
Territoriality	**Territoriality**
• Space is communal; people stand close to each other, share the same space.	• Space is compartmentalized and privately owned; privacy is important, so people are farther apart.
Temporality	**Temporality**
• Everything has its own time. Time is not easily scheduled; needs of people may interfere with keeping to a set time. What is important is that activity gets done. • Change is slow. Things are rooted in the past, slow to change, and stable. • Time is a process; it belongs to others and to nature.	• Things are scheduled to be done at particular times, one thing at a time. What is important is that activity is done efficiently. • Change is fast. One can make change and see immediate results. • Time is a commodity to be spent or saved. One's time is one's own.

High Context (HC)	Low Context (LC)
Learning	**Learning**
• Knowledge is embedded in the situation; things are connected, synthesized, and global. Multiple sources of information are used. Thinking is deductive, proceeds from general to specific. • Learning occurs by first observing others as they model or demonstrate and then practicing. • Groups are preferred for learning and problem solving. • Accuracy is valued. How well something is learned is important.	• Reality is fragmented and compartmentalized. One source of information is used to develop knowledge. Thinking is inductive, proceeds from specific to general. Focus is on detail. • Learning occurs by following explicit directions and explanations of others. • An individual orientation is preferred for learning and problem solving. • Speed is valued. How efficiently something is learned is important.

Source: J. W. Pfeiffer, *The 1993 Annual: Developing Human Resources*, San Diego, CA: Pfeiffer & Company. Retrieved from https://www2.pacific.edu/sis/culture/pub/Context_Cultures_High_and_Lo.htm

One can imagine how professional interactions can play out between individuals from diverse cultural backgrounds, especially when they are at odds with each other in their contextual variation and cultural orientation as outlined in the dichotomy. At the same time, participants in the interaction process are challenged to revisit their ways of professional communication to reconcile cultural barriers.

Having this mind, researchers and educators have focused on trying to understand how communication occurs when cultures meet in educational and social institutions. Recognizing the values Americans live by, Kohls (1988) illustrates how such cultural differences can be overcome and professional communication can be enhanced in diverse settings. His extensive research in the field has direct implications for promoting multicultural literacy in students and teachers. Kohls and Knight (1994) provide a practical approach to overcome cultural barriers that can be explained in terms of the following principles of the Intercultural Hypothesis, which include the following:

1. Humans are creators of culture.
2. Each group developed its own culture, thousands of years ago, in isolation.

3. Each group found its own ways to solve humankind's 10 basic problems:
   - Food
   - Clothing
   - Shelter
   - Family Organization
   - Social Organization
   - Government
   - War/Protection
   - Arts/Crafts
   - Knowledge/Science
   - Religion

4. It is inevitable that different groups would develop different solutions to these 10 problems.

5. There are no absolutely "right" responses—only "right" or "wrong" responses within any given culture. One culture is not "better" or "worse"—only different from another.

6. However, each culture thinks its ways are superior (= ethnocentricity).

7. All children raised into a particular culture are enculturated into that culture's "right" ways.

8. There is no problem of cross-cultural nature when a person stays in his or her own culture.

9. Problems of an intercultural nature occur when a person who has been enculturated into one culture is suddenly dumped into another very different culture or when a person of one culture tries to communicate with a person of another culture.

Although some may consider these to be problematic, others may see them as virtues necessary for developing a higher level of learning and more dynamic communication styles necessary for cross-cultural understanding in diverse and global settings. At the same time, professional discourse can be enriched when both teachers and students are challenged to examine the realm of their culture in relation to the culture of their peers as manifested in their differentiated communication styles. Teachers can lead the instructional professional process effectively when they possess the global cultural literacy that shapes their philosophy and belief system. As they seek to create a safe interactional environment and engage students emotionally, socially, and academically (Kapanadze, 2018; Trujillo, 2017), they should differentiate professional interactions in response to culturally relevant contexts. To do so, there are several key aspects to enhancing the communicative process in diverse settings.

Key Aspects for Professional Communication in Cross-Cultural Settings

For teachers to fulfill their professional role effectively, they should develop adequate conceptual awareness about the various aspects of the communicative process in cross-cultural settings. Their knowledge and professional skills should guide them about what to do and not do because their professional role and position define them rather than vice versa. The following keys should be the basis of professional mindsets for teachers:

1. **Having empathy, not sympathy.** Empathy makes one person walk in the shoes of another. In other words, empathizers wear game shoes rather than play the role of spectators. As far as communication is concerned, one should be conscious of the magnitude of this task across language variation and cultural differences. To engage students meaningfully, teachers should have empathy and active listening skills that would put them in the place of the learner, which will have a profound impact on everyone they interact with.

2. **Being flexible, not rigid.** This stems from the fact that communication should be a flexible process because there are multiple ways and dimensions of getting messages across. In fact, the creative aspect of language use has been a cornerstone of critical literacy and metacognitive processing. Teachers should be flexible and receptive to new ways of reasoning, communicating, and interacting manifested in diverse students' behaviors and their families, as well as others who differ from the teachers' cultural schemata.

3. **Showing humility, not hubris.** Pride and prejudice often creep into the interaction process. Subconscious bias, albeit subtle at times, can easily be deciphered by the participants

on the other end of the communicative spectrum. Diverse student populations can easily tell when teachers and peers have the humility and respect for them during interactions; they also can tell if they are being respected or looked at as inferiors vis-à-vis their mainstream peers. Although everyone should have pride in their identity, heritage, language, race, gender, and so on, no one should be made to feel inferior or disrespected. In other words, one's pride should not be fostered at the expense of another so much so that when one belongs to privileged (supreme) group, they should be cautioned against being condescending in their interactions that reflect their mindset that the grass is browner on the other side.

4. **Suspending unnecessary judgments, not showing prejudice.** It has been assumed that there is no room for wisdom when one is full of judgment. This is especially true when interacting with others who are different from us. Language overtones and nuances should not convey false judgments, negative attitudes, and offensive perceptions throughout any interactions. Stereotypes and perceptions can shape opinions and feelings in many ways. As far as professional interactions are concerned, they should be carried out free from prejudice, bias, or stereotyping. Rather, they should revolve around humane aspects that would promote mutual respect among participants regardless of the visible and invisible aspects of differences.

5. **Inviting trust, not hostility.** Focusing on the underlying similarities among diverse populations should be the basis for promoting cross-cultural understanding and mutual trust. Doing so requires proactive, rather than reactive, communication styles throughout which respect can be maintained. For many, difference creates hostility and mistrust and fear of the unknown. To break the cycle of ignorance and achieve trust, common grounds should be established as a basis for effective interaction. Professionals should inculcate such values and dispositions within the universal human expectations

regardless of the racial, ethnic, cultural, and linguistic differences. To bridge cross-cultural gaps, trust, compassion, acceptance, tolerance, and sensitivity should drive any active engagement process in schools and beyond. This also requires providing constructive criticism when needed and proactive outlook focusing on the common goals and interests rather than taking a passive stance driven by hostility toward differences in others.

In conclusion, professional and culturally responsive communication is key in everything we do especially when working with diverse student populations. As teachers seek to play their professional roles effectively, they should make connections with their students and their families by revisiting their approach to become responsive and relevant to students' expectations and cultural orientation. Teachers, for the most part, should not take language and its complex roles and functions for granted during speech events because it is a subconscious, automatic activity. Once communication breaks down due to a "malfunction" of one or more elements under certain conditions, users of language become more conscious and engage in "repairing" strategies to continue carrying on the discourse task at hand. Consequently, our language use involves an exchange of multiple domains that transcend the purely linguistic ones and embrace professional conduct. This underscores the need to cultivate students' assets by engaging them emotionally, culturally, cognitively, as well as academically; all of which can be determined by how we communicate with them and how they communicate with us.

Reflective Questions and Activities

1. *Examine Hall's high-context/low-context dichotomy and describe your communication style providing specific examples.*

2. *Based on your understanding of the multifunctionality of the speech event and communicative discourse, share a personal*

*experience about how communication broke down between you
and someone else. What went wrong? How did you reconcile the
issue?*

3. *As a professional, what are the strategies you would use to differ-
    entiate your communication styles with diverse students, parents,
    and colleagues?*

4. *Given the importance of paralanguage aspects in the communi-
    cative process, describe how you use nonverbal cues (e.g., contact,
    body language, gestures, etc.) and suprasegmental features (e.g.,
    voice inflections, pitch, register, intonation, etc.) when you interact
    with others.*

References

Alsoraihi, M. H. (2019). Bridging the gap between discourse analysis and language
    classroom practice. *English Language Teaching, 12*(8), 79–88.
Bolinger, D. (1980). *Language, the loaded weapon: The use and abuse of language today.*
    White Plains, NY: Longman.
Bolinger, D. (1981). *Aspects of language.* Fort Worth, TX: Harcourt Brace.
Bourdieu, P. (1998). *Practical reason.* Stanford, CA: Stanford University Press.
Bullock, A. (1975). *Language for life* (Bullock Committee Report). London: Crown.
Chomsky, N. (1986). *Knowledge of language: Its nature, origin and use.* New York,
    NY: Prager.
Evans-Winters, V., & Cowie, B. (2009). Cross-cultural communication: Implications
    for social work practice and a departure from Payne. *Journal of Educational
    Controversy, 4*(1), 1–12.
Gladwell, M. (2007). *Blink: The power of thinking without thinking.* New York, NY:
    Little, Brown and Company.
Gladwell, M. (2019). *Talking to strangers: What we should know about the people we
    don't know.* New York, NY: Little, Brown and Company.
Gumperz, J. (1982). *Discourse strategies.* London, England: Cambridge University
    Press.
Gumperz, J. (1986). Interactive sociolinguistics in the study of schooling. In J.
    Cook-Gumperz (Ed.), *The social construction of literacy* (pp. 45–68). London,
    England: Cambridge University Press.
Hall, E. T. (1959). *The silent language.* New York, NY: Doubleday.

Hall, E. T. (1969). *The hidden dimension*. New York, NY: Doubleday.

Hall, E. T. (1976). *Beyond culture*. New York, NY: Doubleday.

Hall, E. T. (1983). *The dance of life*. New York: Doubleday.

Halliday, M. A. K. (1973). *Explorations in the functions of language*. London, England: Edward Arnold.

Halliday M. A. K. (1975). *Learning how to mean*. London, England: Edward Arnold.

Halliday, M. A. K. (1989). *Spoken and written language*. New York, NY: Oxford University Press.

Halliday, M. A. K. (2004). The place of dialogue in children's construction of meaning. In R. Ruddell & N. Unrau (Eds.), *Theoretical models and processes of reading* (pp. 133–145). Newark, DE: International Reading Association.

Halverson, C. B., & Trmizi, A. (Eds.). (2008). *Effective multicultural teams: Theory and practice*. Rotterdam, The Netherlands: Springer.

Joos, M. (1960). *The five clocks*. New York, NY: Harcourt, Brace and World.

Jakobson, R. (1960). Linguistics and poetics. In T. Sebeok (Ed.), *Style in language* (pp. 350–377). Cambridge, MA: MIT Press.

Kapanadze, D. U. (2018). The effect of using discourse analysis method on improving cognitive and affective skills in language and literature teaching. *European Journal of Education Studies, 4*(5), 92–107.

Kohls, R. (1988). *Values Americans live by*. Duncanville, TX: Adult Learning Systems.

Kohls, R., & Knight, J. (1994). *Developing intercultural awareness: A cross-cultural training handbook*. Yarmouth, ME: Intercultural Press.

Labov, W. (1972). *Sociolinguistic patterns*. Philadelphia: University of Pennsylvania Press.

Labov, W. (2012). *Linguistic diversity in America: The politics of language change*. Charlottesville: University of Virginia Press.

Labov, W. (2013). *The language of life and death*. Cambridge, England: University of Cambridge Press.

Olshtain, E., & Celce-Murcia, M. (2001). Discourse analysis and language teaching. In D. Schiffrin, D. Tannen, & H. E. Hamilton (Eds.), *The handbook of discourse analysis* (pp. 707–724). Malden, MA: Blackwell Handbooks. Doi.: https://doi.org/10.1002/9780470753460.ch37

Orelus, P. W. (2017). *Language, race, and power in schools: A critical discourse analysis*. New York, NY: Routledge.

Osoba, S., & Sobola, E. (2014). Introduction to discourse analysis. In E. A. Adedun, & Yaw Sekyi-Baidoo (Eds.), *English studies in focus: Readings in language and literature* (pp. 200–219). Winneba, Ghana: Faculty of Languages, University of Education.

Payne, R. (1996). *A framework for understanding poverty*. Highlands, TX: Aha! Process.

Philomina, M. J. (2015). Diagnosis of reading and writing skills in primary school students. *International Journal of English Language Teaching, 3*(7), 1–7.

Sirbu, A. (2015). The significance of language as a tool of communication. *Naval Academy Scientific Bulletin, 18*, 405–406.

Suleiman, M. (1995a). The art of communicating multiculturally: Implications for teachers. Available ERIC Clearinghouse on Language and Linguistics. (ED391870). https://eric.ed.gov/?q=mahmoud+suleiman&pg=2&id=ED391870

Suleiman, M., & Moore, R. (1995b). Figures of speech, symbolism and the communicative process in the multilingual classroom. ERIC Clearinghouse on Language and Linguistics. (ED393960). https://eric.ed.gov/?q=mahmoud suleiman&pg=2&id=ED393960

Suleiman, M. (1997). Multicultural communication strategies for the diverse classroom. *Kansas Speech Journal, 57*(2), 18–25.

Suleiman, M. (2013). Communicative discourse in second language classrooms: From building skills to becoming skillful. Retrieved from ERIC database. (ED545715). https://eric.ed.gov/?q=mahmoud+suleiman&ffi=dtySince_2011&id=ED545715

Suleiman, M., & Hashem, M. (1995). Cultural factors influencing the communicative process in culturally diverse classrooms. ERIC Clearinghouse on Urban Education. (ED404381). https://eric.ed.gov/?q=mahmoud+suleiman&pg=2&id=ED404381

Tang, R. (2008). Studying discourse analysis: Does it have an impact on trainee English language teachers? *ELTED, 11*, 27–32.

Thaiss, C. (1986). Language across the curriculum in the elementary grades. Urbana, Ill: ERIC Clearinghouse on Reading and Communication Skills and the National Council of Teachers of English. https://eric.ed.gov/?q=Christopher+Thaiss&id=ED266467

Trujillo, K. R. (2017). The learner, the teacher, and the classroom community: Building safe spaces for emotional sharing. In P. W. Orelus (Ed.), *Language, race, and power in schools: A critical discourse analysis* (pp. 92–103). New York, NY: Routledge.

Valencia, R. (2010). *Dismantling contemporary deficit thinking: Educational thought and practice.* New York: Routledge.

Viniti, V., Gopinathan, & Yongbing, L. (Eds.). (2007). *Language, capital, culture: Critical studies and education in Singapore* (Transgressions: Cultural Studies and Education, Vol. 10). Boston, MA: Sense Publishers.

CHAPTER THIRTEEN

DRESSING FOR SUCCESS: VISUAL APPEARANCE MAKES A DIFFERENCE

Bre Evans-Santiago

Have you ever worked at a school where the air-conditioning is nonexistent? Have you ever depended highly on fans and any air or breeze from the windows? If you have not, that is great! Do not think it will not happen, however; everyone is considered equal when it comes to bad air-conditioning in buildings! I worked in a middle school without air-conditioning, and my classroom did not have a window that connected to the outside air, so we were not only hot; we often also felt like we were suffocating from the lack of air circulation.

The charter school had a very strict dress policy in place, and the number of days we were in school lasted longer than a typical academic school year. We did not finish until the middle of June, and we were all required to wear layers of clothing. One day I decided that I was tired of dripping sweat, so I planned an outfit that required the fewest pieces of clothing possible while still adhering to the dress code. I chose to wear a flowy dress that went almost to my ankles, and it was bright and colorful. The conflict of wearing this dress is that it was strapless and was held up with two thin strips of fabric that tied around my neck. Thinking it was just the right amount of minimal clothing, I wore a black thin cardigan that covered my shoulders and bra straps to adhere to the dress code.

This outfit went well for half of the day, and I stayed pretty cool. The one dreadful period where the outfit plan went downhill just happened to be filled with female students only. Thank goodness, because you can only imagine what happened next! I was teaching about story structure and really getting into it. "A climax makes you wanna slap yo mama!" was a phrase we liked to use. So we were laughing and really discussing how the climax impacts a story. Then lo and behold, my sweet, quiet Deja, her eyes wide, points to the lower part of my chest. "What's up, sweetie?" I ask her, and she begins to point rapidly without saying a word. I look down, and boom! My fluorescent pink bra was fully exposed all the way to the bottom of the cups! They could not see it was my bra, so I tried to cover it up by saying, "Oh thank goodness, I wore a tank top with this! Can you imagine?!" I tied the dress back up extremely tight, swallowed a little nervousness puke, and continued to teach. I do not know if they believed me, but they were pretty respectful and quiet about it. I never heard about it again, but if I ended up acquiring a nickname like "pink boobs," I would understand.

You Are What You Wear

Teachers cannot always afford to purchase outfits that match each day's weather and coordinate with the temperature inside of the classroom. Dress policies vary from district to district and school to school. There are varied gender restrictions or expectations for both men and women. Ladies may be required to wear closed-back or closed-toe shoes at all times, or there might be a sleeve-, skirt-, or dress-length requirement. Men may have to wear suits or khakis daily with dress shoes. Dressing as a teacher is not always comfortable, but something I have noticed about myself as well as my students: dress definitely affects a person's attitude.

Think back to picture day, or class picture day, with students. Elementary children wear their best outfits: ties for boys and fluffy white dresses from last

Easter for girls, right? Reflect on how children act on picture day; they eat neater, run slower, and sit straighter in their chairs. What about us as adults? When we wear a nice outfit, we walk taller and sometimes even speak or act more formally. We sit differently in our chairs, and we cover up our fabric with a napkin when we eat. When we wear clothes for the job, we act like that profession. If I wear my football gear, I turn into a tough <u>football offensive linewoman</u>[1] (Women's National Football Conference, 2018). If I wear my heels and skirt, I turn into a business professional. Rutherford, Conway, and Murphey (2014) state, "The very physical experience of walking into a school, staffroom, classroom and embodying teacher identity is powerful and memorable" (p. 326). We as teachers need to think about it—Are our attitudes on Friday, when we are in jeans and T-shirts, the same when we wear more professional clothes throughout the week? Probably not. We tend to sit more, lean on a desk, act more relaxed, and so forth. To be clear, "dressing down" does have positive effects. When I wore jeans to work, I was jumping rope with students and sitting with them wherever and not worrying about my clothes. But that was on Fridays. The other 4 days in the week, I dressed professionally, and after that experience at the middle school, I made sure I always had underclothes on as well.

    Looking at this from an equity lens, the discussion of affordability and being a role model comes to mind. As mentioned earlier, dress clothes can be quite expensive. Teacher candidates are full-time students without a consistent or steady income, and new teachers live up to 4 months without their first paycheck. This may hinder shopping sprees or various clothing options. On average, beginning teacher salaries range from $35,000 to $45,000 nationwide (National Education Association, 2018). According to the <u>2017 Consumer Expenditures</u>[2] (U.S. Department of Labor, 2017), more than $1,000 per household is spent on clothing each year.

    The quality of clothing will affect the amount of money spent per year based on the wear and tear, and more often than not, inexpensive brands of clothing or apparel from bargain stores do not last as long. Another factor that affects cost is the size of the clothing item. Sizes bigger than a large, such as an extra-large or double extra-large, cost more than do small, medium, or large

---

1   See Women's National Football Conference in the Online Sources section at the end of the chapter.
2   See U.S. Department of Labor in the Online Sources section at the end of the chapter.

sizes. The average size of American women[3] is size 16 (Fratello, 2017), and for men,[4] it is a size 38 (Painter, 2014), which is an extra-large for both, and therefore, more women and men are spending extra money on clothing because of the cost differences in size.

Another important factor that needs to be considered is the position of a teacher. Teachers are automatically viewed as a role model. Most important, teachers of color are often under a societal microscope because of surplus visibility (Patai, 1992), and at the same time, students who may have the skin complexion or relatable cultural backgrounds are often automatically drawn to them by representative bureaucracy (Atkins, Fertig, & Wilkins, 2014). There is a lack of teachers of color in the classroom (Rogers-Ard, Knaus, Epstein, & Mayfield, 2013), and therefore, the few in schools stand out. Because of the implicit role-model expectations, the outfits chosen for the professional look have more than one purpose: It is no longer to demonstrate professionalism for individuality; it is also to model what a professional should look like for students.

Contemplating the Professional Look

Understanding the challenges of affordability and the role-model responsibilities, planning ahead for professional dress[5] (Cox, 2019) is pertinent to job security and success. Several ideas can help with a teacher's professional look:

1. Arm-raise test: Before leaving the house, raise an arm high. This is a motion that might take place while writing on the board or pulling down a projector screen. If air is felt as that hand is raised, then there are options for covering that skin. Find a longer shirt, or add another layer underneath (usually a T-shirt or thin undershirt) that can be tucked into the bottoms being worn. This "raising-hand check" will help for checking whether the stomach, back, top of the bottom, or waist sides are showing with a shirt.

---

3 See *Today* in the Online Sources section at the end of the chapter.
4 See *USA Today* in the Online Sources section at the end of the chapter.
5 See Teach Hub in the Online Sources section at the end of the chapter.

2. Bend-over test: Another check for anyone is to bend over and pick something up. When bent over, is air felt from behind? Or, if bent over, is the front of the shirt exposing undergarments? Undergarments and/or body exposure could be a distraction for students and for the teacher.

3. Clothing[6] (Rosier, 2019) should be a statement of identity or expression, but it should not bring unwanted attention from the teacher or students.

4. Wear layers: There are uncontrollable temperature issues throughout a school site. One room may be freezing while the next is extremely hot. Come prepared to handle these temperature changes. Undershirts will probably be the first layer to either hide skin, catch sweat, or cover undergarments. After this layer, the main shirt, blouse, or dress that will be worn. Next, add another layer for warmth that can be removed and not interrupt the look. This layer can be a blazer, a thin professional jacket, a sweater, a cardigan, a dress scarf, or a poncho. The layers can be added or removed while walking throughout the school building. View scarf looks for men[7] and women[8] or poncho ideas[9] on Pinterest.

5. Hairstyles: Hair designs and jewelry are visual displays of personality and fashion. Hair length, texture, and color play a major part of our identities. There might be a person of habit that keeps a hairstyle consistent for years, or that changes it as often as possible. Hair is a defining visual of personality, and for many, it is a visual display of cultural beliefs. But, unfortunately, there are underrepresented minorities in schools (teachers, staff, administrators, and students) who, because of hair expression[10] (ABC 7, 2016), have been frowned on or have even suffered consequences.

---

6   See WikiHow in the Online Sources at the end of the chapter.
7   See Pinterest: Scarf Looks Men in the Online Sources at the end of the chapter.
8   See Pinterest: Scarf Looks Women in the Online Sources at the end of the chapter.
9   See Pinterest: Poncho Looks Women in the Online Sources at the end of the chapter.
10   See ABC 7 in the Online Sources section at the end of the chapter.

The controversy over "distractions" of hair color versus afros and <u>dreadlocks</u>[11] (Gandy, 2018) or hair extensions is a very necessary topic that is currently in the <u>limelight</u>[12] (Perry, 2019). The fear of conforming students into Whiteness instead of allowing them to wear their hairstyles has a negative effect on students' ability to socially interact and academically perform at fullest potential due to emotional stress and fear of <u>consequences</u>[13] (Ortiz, 2019) or ridicule. Learn what the school policies are and adhere to them, but also find ways of expression of hair within the boundaries. Learn various styles that can help self-expression because one's identity is valid. Research the history of various hairstyles that may seem different or that will turn heads. Are teachers ready to defend their styles? Do they know where it comes from, and why it is important? Hair is visible to students, so decide what it should look like. Also, think, "Does my hair affect my teaching?" This means that during lectures, blowing hair strands out of one's face or swiping hair one way or another is annoying. In this case, hair has become a distraction.

6. Accessories and body art: Necklaces, bow ties, neckties, scarves, and other accessories help accentuate outfits. Decide which accessories display personality while minimizing distraction during instruction. Age differences may be a deciding factor here. Do your students get easily distracted? Are they old enough to redirect themselves if they lose focus? These questions should be considered when deciding upon accents of choice. Although it may be a fun choice, it may not always fit the setting in which the teacher wears it, so be cautious.

Piercings vary from none to too many to count. The dress code as it pertains to piercings will depend on school sites. Some schools will allow various sized earrings and many ear

---

11 See Rewire News in the Online Sources section at the end of the chapter.
12 See the Hechinger Report in the Online Sources section at the end of the chapter.
13 See NBC News in the Online Sources section at the end of the chapter.

piercings, while others limit the size of the earring and the number of earrings allowable at school. Tongue rings and nose rings may vary based on location as well. Usually, tongue rings need to be clear or minimal in color, and nose rings need to be small and close to the nose for safety reasons. If unsure, start small and discreet with the tongue, nose, and lip piercings. Usually, other facial piercings are tiny or smaller in size, so they are not as obvious, but when starting, the gauges and gem size should be smaller, rather than larger, so that first impressions are not based on jewelry versus the whole look accompanied by personality.

Think about future tattoos and placements of those permanent art pieces. The words and pictures on tattoos will be a part of an everyday look. If there were tattoos prior to the teaching career, make sure they are appropriate[14] (Craig, 2016) for display. If not, clothing may become more limited to ensure that tattoos are covered or displayed in an appropriate manner (e.g., long-sleeved shirts in 100-degree weather). Tattoos and piercings come and go as trends, so it is important to think about the placement and the impact that the art will have on others when viewed.

7. Develop an identity: As a set style is created through clothing, favorite colors, accessories, and body, an identity will develop. This is important because dress will increase confidence and reflect personality. As a role model and a professional, people will begin to know teachers based on their visual appearances. Also, students may resonate with the teacher's style, thus creating opportunities for them to test out their own look. Some students may feel more connected to a teacher when they see them with tattoos, especially if they are used to seeing their family members with tattoos.

Another important component of identity is whether a teacher identifies as binary or nonbinary. Do you specifically

14   See the Northern Light in the Online Sources section at the end of the chapter.

identify as a male or female, or do you feel that you are neither male nor female? This may affect which dress code policy you tend to follow since the expectations are usually separated by gender. However you identify, ensure that you still follow the dress code.

For instance, if someone identifies as a <u>cis female</u>[15] (Trans Student Educational Resources, 2019) and chooses to wear khaki pants, she still needs to follow the dress code for pants that may be under the male expectations in the dress code policy. A nonbinary male may wear a blouse with his pants, but he will need to follow the female shirt policy. It is hoped that the expectations for teachers would be written in a format of clothing expectations versus gender expectations. Until then, remember that your visual appearance is the first impression and a lasting impression, so make it count (Stone, 2008). See Table 13.1 for an example of binary dress code expectations.

TABLE 13.1

EXAMPLE OF STRICT PROFESSIONAL DRESS CODE

*Men	*Women	All or Any Gender
Shirt and tie must be worn daily	Skirts and dresses • must be 3 inches above the knee or longer • cannot be too tight to hinder walking • slits must be no higher than 3 inches above knee	Shorts • only the P.E. teacher is allowed to wear shorts
P.E. teachers will wear golf shirts or collar polo shirts	Capris • must be below the knee	No jeans or jean color of any kind allowed
Slacks and casual dress pants are acceptable	Shirts • no T-shirts • no halter, tank or midriff tops • no see-through shirts • sleeveless shirts must cover undergarments	No hats worn inside

---

15   See Trans Student Educational Resources in the Online Section at the end of the chapter.

*Men	*Women	All or Any Gender
Facial hair must be kept neat and clean and hair should not impair vision		Shoes • must have a backstrap • cannot wear flip flops • only P.E. teachers may wear athletic sneakers
Shirts • No tank tops or T-shirts		Tattoos that are considered vulgar, racist, offensive, scenes of violence, drug or gang related must not be visible.
		Earrings are the only visible piercings allowed.

Source: Lakewood Dress Code (n.d.).
Note: P.E. = Physical Education.
* The gender labels used in the table are referencing policies that have been researched to create this table. We are fully aware of nonbinary individuals who may adhere to the dress code based on their own identities.

Clothing, piercings, tattoos, and hairstyles are a big part of everyday looks that help visibly represent individuality. School district policies will have specific enforced dress codes to follow. Various districts have different rules, so choose a school that supports your look or choose a look that supports your school. Teachers must take charge of individualized "space," and as teaching identities develop, teachers' visual appearance will reflect that. Teachers are role models and have high expectations for our students. Therefore, holding oneself to the same standards will demonstrate strength and empowerment through visible individuality.

Reflection Questions and Activities

1. *Review your dress code policy at your school site. What are the expectations for males and females? What do you agree with or disagree with? How might you address the dress codes that you may not agree with?*

2. *How do you identify? Take a few different gender identity tests (A Real Me,*[16] *What's Your Gender Identity?*[17]*). Did you measure out the way you thought you identify? What do you think about tests such as these? Explain.*

3. *Do you consider yourself a role model for students? If so, how might you alter or adjust your look to obtain the most professional look as a role model? If no, what makes you feel as though you are not?*

Online Resources

ABC 7: https://abc7.com/news/student-of-the-year-barred-from-walking-at-graduation-due-to-facial-hair/1350901/

The Hechinger Report: https://hechingerreport.org/stay-out-of-my-hair/

My Mental Gender Test: https://www.arealme.com/what-is-my-true-gender-quiz/en/

NBC News: https://www.nbcnews.com/news/nbcblk/n-j-wrestler-forced-cut-dreadlocks-still-targeted-over-hair-n957116

The Northern Light: http://www.thenorthernlight.org/appearance-versus-professionalism-tattoos-in-the-workplace/

Pinterest: Poncho Looks Women: https://www.pinterest.com/search/pins/?q= scarf%20looks%20women&rs=typed&term_meta%5B%5D=scarf%7Ctyped& term_meta%5B%5D=looks%7Ctyped&term_meta%5B%5D=women%7Ctyped

Pinterest: Scarf Looks Men: https://www.pinterest.com/search/pins/?q=scarf%20 looks%20men&rs=guide&term_meta%5B%5D=scarf%7Ctyped&term_meta%5 B%5D=looks%7Ctyped&add_refine=men%7Cguide%7Cword%7C7

Pinterest: Scarf Looks Women: https://www.pinterest.com/search/pins/?q=scarf %20looks%20women&rs=typed&term_meta%5B%5D=scarf%7Ctyped&term_ meta%5B%5D=looks%7Ctyped&term_meta%5B%5D=women%7Ctyped

Rewire News: https://rewire.news/ablc/2018/05/16/u-s-supreme-court-ignoring-black-hair-discrimination/

Teach Hub: https://www.teachhub.com/teacher-clothes-and-what-wear

Today: https://www.today.com/style/what-s-average-size-16-new-normal-us-women-t103315

Trans Student Educational Resources: http://www.transstudent.org/definitions

U.S. Department of Labor: https://www.bls.gov/news.release/pdf/cesan.pdf

---

16   See My Mental Gender Test in the Online Sources section at the end of the chapter.
17   See What's Your Gender Identity? in the Online Sources section at the end of the chapter.

USA Today: https://www.usatoday.com/story/news/nation/2014/09/16/waist-sizes-expanding-study/15723771/

What's Your Gender Identity?: https://www.allthetests.com/quiz32/quiz/1434941902/Whats-Your-Gender-Identity

WikiHow: https://www.wikihow.com/Dress-when-You%27re-a-Teacher

Women's National Football Conference: https://www.wnfcfootball.com/

References

ABC 7. (2016, May 26). *Student of the year barred from walking at graduation due to facial hair.* ABC 7. Retrieved from https://abc7.com/news/student-of-the-year-barred-from-walking-at-graduation-due-to-facial-hair/1350901/

Atkins, D. N., Fertig, A. R., & Wilkins, V. M. (2014). Connectedness and expectations: How minority teachers can improve educational outcomes for minority students. *Public Management Review, 16*, 503–526.

Craig, B. (2016, November 6). *Appearance versus professionalism: Tattoos in the workplace* [Blog post]. The Northern Light. Retrieved from http://www.thenorthernlight.org/appearance-versus-professionalism-tattoos-in-the-workplace/

Cox, J. (2019). Teacher clothes and what to wear [Blog post]. Teachhub. Retrieved from https://www.teachhub.com/teacher-clothes-and-what-wear

Fratello, J. (2016, September 29). *What's "average"? Size 16 is the new normal for US women. Today.* Retrieved from https://www.today.com/style/what-s-average-size-16-new-normal-us-women-t103315

Gandy, I. (2018, May 16). *The U.S. Supreme Court decided to ignore Black hair discrimination.* rewire. Retrieved from https://rewire.news/ablc/2018/05/16/u-s-supreme-court-ignoring-black-hair-discrimination/

Lakewood Dress Code Policy. (n.d.) Retrieved from https://www.lakewoodpiners.org/cms/lib/NJ01001845/Centricity/Domain/4/Staff%20Dress%20Code%20Policy.pdf

National Education Association. (2018). *Average starting teacher salaries by state.* Retrieved from http://www.nea.org/home/2017-2018-average-starting-teacher-salary.html

Ortiz, E. (2019, January 10). *N.J. wrestler forced to cut dreadlocks still targeted over hair, lawyer says.* nbcnews. Retrieved from https://www.nbcnews.com/news/nbcblk/n-j-wrestler-forced-cut-dreadlocks-still-targeted-over-hair-n957116

Painter, K. (2014, September 16). *Loosen your belts: U.S. waist size keeps expanding. USA Today.* Retrieved from https://www.usatoday.com/story/news/nation/2014/09/16/waist-sizes-expanding-study/15723771/

Patai, D. (1992). Minority status and the stigma of "surplus visibility." *Education Digest, 57*(5), 35–38.

Perry, A. (2019, March 5). "Stay out of my hair!" [Blog post]. Hechinger report. Retrieved from https://hechingerreport.org/stay-out-of-my-hair/

Rogers-Ard, R., Knaus, C. B., Epstein, K. K., & Mayfield, K. (2013). Racial diversity sounds nice; systems transformation? Not so much: Developing urban teachers of color. *Urban Education, 48,* 451–479. https://doi.org/10.1177/0042085912454441

Rosier, S. (2019). *How to dress when you are a teacher.* Retrieved from https://www.wikihow.com/Dress-when-You%27re-a-Teacher

Rutherford, V., Conway, P. F., & Murphy, R. (2015). Looking Like a Teacher: Fashioning an embodied identity through "dressage." *Teaching Education, 26,* 325–339.

Stone, E. (2008). *The dynamics of fashion* (3rd ed.). New York, NY: Fairchild.

Trans Student Educational Resources. (2019). LGBTQ+definitions. Retrieved from https://www.transstudent.org/definitions/

U.S. Department of Labor. (2018). *Consumer expenditures 2017.* Retrieved from https://www.bls.gov/news.release/pdf/cesan.pdf

Women's National Football Conference. (2018). Retrieved from https://www.wnfcfootball.com/

CHAPTER FOURTEEN

CO-TEACHING IN YOUR FIRST YEAR: PROFESSIONAL MARRIAGES RESULTING IN SUCCESS OR DIVORCE?

Kira A. Hamann

Brand new to the field, I walked into my first year of teaching dual-language public prekindergarten in Chicago excited to put all my preparatory beliefs and ideas into practice, and I had spent hours considering how my classroom would look and feel—literally down to the brightly colored displays on the walls and the kinds of songs I would sing and books I would read aloud. Although I knew I would have a teaching assistant because of state-issued teacher–child ratio guidelines in prekindergarten, my teaching preparation glossed over the fact that my classmates and I would most likely be in co-teaching scenarios due to the nature of staffing in the early childhood years. Because of this, I had imagined/ idealized/ forgotten the fact that I would be "living" with another adult in my classroom space in my first year.

Thus, I was ready to launch my idyllic vision of my prekindergarten classroom when I realized a massive roadblock to executing this vision in the co-teacher whom I had been assigned to work. Flor, the teaching assistant assigned to this prekindergarten classroom, had been a licensed and practicing social worker in Peru before immigrating 6 years before. Unfortunately, her credentials did not transfer when she moved to the United States, so she had found work as a prekindergarten assistant teacher at our school, even though she was skilled enough to practice social work anywhere! She was twice my age, with two sons who could have been my peers. Her English was limited; my Spanish, the same. She had been assigned to work with three different lead teachers in 3 years because our dictator of a principal (another story) thought it was best practice to test newly hired teachers in the prekindergarten classrooms and then move them up to other grade levels when they had proved themselves.

In this classroom of equal English-speaking and Spanish-speaking students and for the previous 3 years, Flor had been forced to co-teach with three different teachers (a formidable task!), and her guard was definitely up when I walked in bright-eyed and bushy-tailed. She felt that the ways in which her prior co-teachers had set up the classroom and facilitated classroom learning were the best ways, and what I planned to do did not align with these ideas. My attitude was that I had been hired to be the lead teacher, not her! It seemed that every time that I said, "Up," Flor said, "Down." When I said, "Colorful walls [with emphasis!]," Flor said, "Neutral is best." Where I was loud and passionate, Flor was soft-spoken and subdued. Needless to say, we had so many cultural differences, including language, age, manners, experiences, and norms, and these were outside of our classroom setting! Layer on the fact that we were spending more hours together than apart with children where these differences were magnified. Due to our language limitations, we struggled with understanding each other's meanings and intentions. Although we were respectful of each other in front of the children and families, I was unnerved by the fact that she could communicate with them in ways that I could not, and I am betting she felt similarly. Knowing her background as a social worker, as well as having worked in this classroom for 3 years, I knew she was knowledgeable about early childhood education—yet she did not share the same understanding that I was bringing from my teacher preparation. Although I constantly worried that she would disapprove of my *teaching ideas, I was also indignant that it did not matter if she did because I was the lead teacher!*

Being stuck in what seemed like a hopeless marriage, I was very unhappy— not with my young students or their families, the content, or my instruction but with the other adult with whom I was cohabiting this classroom. Many nights I went home feeling frustrated, disappointed, and hurt by Flor's words or lack thereof. I do not imagine that she felt any differently. Being so underprepared for this relationship, I was clueless about the benefits that having both of us in the classroom offered for providing access and equity for my young students. Although, in hindsight, I like to believe that our issues did not affect our young students or their families—this is wishful thinking. There is no possible way that it did not. Yet it did not have to be this way in my first year—nor does it have to be for any new teacher!

My first-year experiences with the educational practice of co-teaching are not singular to me. In this chapter, I hope to outline the dilemma—nay, the gift—of two (or more!) adults cohabiting classrooms, discuss how this practice intersects with philosophies of inclusion and social justice, describe the pros and cons of co-teaching, and then walk you, as the reader, through the three main steps of every co-teaching relationship. My hope is that by sharing everything I should have learned in my teacher preparation about co-teaching, you can avoid the first year struggles I had with this educational practice and can feel rewarded by every co-teaching relationship you encounter!

Flor was my first co-teaching partner but not my last! In my work as an educator, I have encountered many of these co-teaching relationships, and each one has offered possibilities for equity and access for my students and opportunities for strife and conflict for me as an educator. These co-teaching relationships have taken on many shapes—not only in my first year with Flor but also in multiple preservice field experiences leading up to graduation, and in countless lead teacher–assistant teacher relationships in subsequent years, and then with a total of five other adults and "semi-adults" (i.e., an eighth-grade volunteer) in my final year of classroom teaching. My final year of classroom teaching, my team included two assistant teachers (who were both licensed teachers), a one-on-one aide for a student with autism, an undergraduate teaching assistant who joined us in the afternoons, and an occasional eighth-grade volunteer who loved helping out in our classroom—not including family volunteers across the year. That was a lot of adults working together! Since reentering the world of higher education, I have co-taught courses with other faculty members as well. When I write that I have grown a lot from my first year of work with Flor, it has been by leaps and bounds! First, recognizing that co-teaching takes place anytime two or more adults share responsibility in the classroom is a first step to understanding this dynamic practice and how it can be used to provide equity and access for your students.

What Is Co-Teaching, and What About This Metaphor?

Although pinpointing one definition for the practice of co-teaching is difficult (Beninghof, 2011; Cook & Friend, 1995; Friend & Cook, 2013; Murawski, 2019; Van Garderen, Stormont, & Goel, 2012), this practice, sometimes referred to as collaborative teaching, refers to more than one educator jointly sharing in the responsibility of teaching. Originally referring to a general education teacher and a special education teacher or another specialist teaching together for the purpose of jointly delivering instruction to all learners in a general education classroom with a focus on supporting students with special needs (Cook & Friend, 1995), this phrase has taken on new meanings and relevance in the last 20-plus years. In the field of early childhood education where I have taught, due to state licensing standards and best practices related to teacher-to-child ratios, a team approach and the practice of co-teaching have been around much longer and are very prevalent (Shim, Hestenes, & Cassidy, 2004; Whitebook, Gomby, Bellm, Sakai, & Kipnis, 2009).

Yet, this has not been the case for elementary, middle, or high school education. Historically, general education teachers have been teaching on their own. Traditionally, students with special needs of all kinds were segregated into separate special education classrooms taught by special educators (Nierengarten & Hughes, 2010). At times, these separate classrooms were housed within the same attendance school; however, in many cases, these classrooms were not in the same school, and students were bussed to buildings that could support their needs. With the authorization of the Education for all

Handicapped Children Act in 1975, later known as the Individuals with Disabilities Education Act (IDEA, 1997), a move toward social justice for children with special needs surfaced in that the least restrictive environment (LRE) provision required that students with disabilities be educated in mainstream general education classrooms with their peers to the maximum extent possible (Hoppey, 2016). Subsequent reauthorizations of this law (IDEA, 2004; ESSA, 2015) and components of the No Child Left Behind Act (NCLB, 2001) have each strengthened this mandate and have included support for best practices in supporting inclusive practices, such as co-teaching (National Center for Education Statistics, 2008).

The U.S. Department of Health & Human Services and U.S. Department of Education (2015) state, "First, equal opportunity is one of America's most cherished ideals. Being meaningfully included as a member of society is the first step to equal opportunity and is every person's right—a right supported by our laws" (p. 2). Although there are many definitions for *inclusion,* two leading researchers on co-teaching, Murawski and Dieker (2008), provide a cohesive definition: "Inclusion is a philosophy that states that students with disabilities have the right to receive their education in a general education classroom" (p. 40). Thus, instead of creating silos for special education students separate from general education settings or pulling special education students out from general education classes to provide services, nationally, there has been a move towards keeping general education and special education students together and providing support for inclusion to take place. This approach provides access for learners in ways that were unheard of before the passing of IDEA. Educators with the Committee for Action on Social Justice wrote that "access is the gateway to inclusion and participation" (British Columbia Teacher Federation Committee for Action on Social Justice, 2019, p. 1). Making education open and available for all is one of the four pillars of this organization's social justice lens, and this pillar outlines foundational tenets that resonate within the foundations of co-teaching, including a practice built on a welcoming and inclusive approach for all learners equally, practice models that value multiple perspectives, an approach built on cooperation and a sense of community, and, inherent within the model, a responsivity to all learners. See this model on the first page of the *Social Justice Lens: A Teacher Resource Guide* (British Columbia Teacher Federation Committee for Action on Social Justice, 2019).

Because of the move towards more inclusive practices such as co-teaching, over the past 20 years and into today, the number of students with special needs being served primarily in general education classrooms has risen significantly, and more co-teaching is taking place at elementary, middle school, and high school levels today than ever before (Howard & Potts, 2009; Hurd & Weilbacher, 2017; Nierengarten & Hughes, 2010; Strieker, Gillis, & Zong, 2013). Traditionally, the term *co-teaching* has referred to general education and special education teachers working together (Cook & Friend, 1995), and the workload related to this relationship and the fact that one may spend more waking hours in a week with their co-teacher than a spouse resulted in the metaphor of the professional marriage for co-teaching (Murawksi, 2019; Murawski & Dieker, 2008).

Co-Teaching Today

For a new teacher, considering the number of ways one can be in a co-teaching-like relationship, the benefits these relationships can offer can be beneficial. Often, the workload in various pairings mirrors that of a lead teacher and a specialist or a general and special educator. However, in today's classrooms, the co-teaching relationship can take many forms such as a lead teacher and someone in a paraprofessional role as I shared in my first-year experience. This can also look like an English-language learner (ELL) resource educator, or another resource teacher (Peery, 2017) or specialist (U.S. Department of Health and Human Services & U.S. Department of Education, 2015), pushing in to support students while a general education teacher teaches or two general education teachers grouping students up to teach together or teaming in the middle school years (Hurd & Weilbacher, 2017; Strieker et al., 2013) or two teacher candidates in a partner field placement in teacher preparation (Baker & Milner, 2006) or an early childhood floater in a childcare center (Russell, 2016) or having volunteers, such as parents, family members, or others, teaching alongside or working in a supportive role with classroom educators. This can also look like relationships you most likely were in during your teacher preparatory experiences! Teacher candidates working with cooperating or mentor educators or being co-placed in a field experience creates a preservice co-teaching relationship. As a first year teacher, you have more experience with this practice than you may think! You may also have strong feelings either for or against this practice because of these preliminary relationships.

Although you may not feel fully prepared for this aspect of your first years of teaching, this relates to the fact that you may have only scratched the surface of co-teaching (if addressed at all) in your teacher preparation program. Problematically, similar to my experiences, most teacher graduates, whether or not they are special educators or general educators, are underprepared or not prepared at all for this critical dimension of teaching (Faraclas, 2018; McKenzie, 2009). In their recent study of 77 teachers (67% general education and 33% special education) in classrooms ranging from elementary to high school-level inclusive settings, Chitiyo and Brinda (2018) found that only 44% of teachers had received any sort of preparation for co-teaching in their teacher preparation programs. This finding mirrors that of others in the last twenty years including Kamens (2007); Griffin, Jones, and Kilgore (2006); and Schwartz (2018). These researchers argue that because the practice of inclusion is so common and necessary now, the fact that so few graduates are learning about co-teaching is very problematic and leads to settings in which teachers do not take advantage of the benefits of this practice. This is even though national (CCSSO's Interstate Teacher Assessment and Support Consortium, 2013) and state standards may require that teacher candidates learn about and practice co-teaching and co-planning in teacher preparation, as they do in my home state of Illinois (Illinois State Board of Education, 2013).

The Pros and the Cons

With more new teachers walking into more inclusive settings across all grade levels, the likelihood that you will be working closely with one or more educators is high. Because of a lack of preparation, the possibility of realizing the negative outcomes of poor co-teaching relationships is very real—as I realized in my first year of teaching. Cons to this practice include cost, time, power concerns, the possibility for personality, style, and the content clashes—the list goes on and on. Imagine the metaphor of too many cooks in the kitchen—this can definitely be the feeling within certain co-teaching relationships. More research-backed concerns with co-teaching include (a) a lack of training for co-teachers, (b) a lack of time for collaboration and co-planning, (c) a lack of fidelity in co-teaching methods, (d) a lack of special education services actually provided to students with special needs in co-taught classes, and (e) grave concerns regarding parity between co-teachers (Keefe & Moore, 2004; Magiera & Zigmond, 2005; Murawski, 2009; Rivera, McMahon, & Keys, 2014). Cobb and Sharma (2015) outline issues with co-teaching including problems with finding time to plan and dialogue, concerns of power dynamics, the need to establish and balance roles, and issues with negotiating differences in personality and teaching style. Each of these concerns can derail co-teaching relationships! Issues of hurt feelings, the lack of a warm and cuddly relationship, a real lack of awesome opportunities for learners and teachers alike, and concerns with lack of access, equity, and social justice abound in co-teaching relationships.

Yet, with teachers' proper training and support, these concerns can be quickly transformed into benefits with this dynamic practice, and the possibilities related to co-teaching are endless. In inclusive classrooms using co-teaching, the focus is on a true sense of community—a place of learning that is *welcoming to all*. In co-teaching settings, all students' learning needs can be addressed or accommodated (Chitiyo & Brinda, 2018). Campbell and Jeter-Iles (2017) outline that the benefits of co-teaching have great potential for fostering inclusion at the just-right social and academic levels for many students with special needs. They identify three major benefits of inclusion including that fact that inclusive settings foster "dignity and respect for diversity," the opportunity to reduce stigma around labels and segregation of learners, and increased access to the general education curriculum and even the student body at large (Campbell & Jeter-Iles, 2017, p. 157). These benefits aid in transitioning learners into future educational experiences and future roles in society, providing access to those who have not been privy to this in the past. One reason is because in a co-teaching model, two educators have the potential to provide more opportunities, services, and support for learners than a solo teacher can. With educators collaborating, the likelihood is greater for the delivery of more individualized instruction, possibly meaning that more students' needs are being met (Hurd & Weilbacher, 2017).

Cobb and Sharma (2015) describe a term they label "holistic co-teaching," which involves ongoing collaboration in developing and implementing engaging learning experiences and assessments, and then reflecting upon them afterward through critical dialogue, and they argue that this collaboration is a perfect format in which to practice social justice–informed co-teaching (p. 42). Co-teaching can promote divergent thinking by bringing together more than one perspective. I found this in every co-teaching relationship I was in! Seeking out the unique perspectives my co-teachers had on the direction the learning in our classroom could go, noticing the different lenses through which each was viewing challenging behavior, and playing off each other's strengths, for example, when my co-teacher led a monthlong yoga-for-10-minutes series because she was studying to become a yoga instructor or when another who had earned a minor degree in dance in her undergraduate experience led mini-dance units across the winter months when we could not outside due to weather. Ultimately, this kind of divergent thinking, planning, and teaching can allow for more learning opportunities in the classroom and can provide more than one impact on students growing understanding of the world.

One example in my fourth year of teaching was when my teaching assistant that year spearheaded a project on what it is like to live in the country of Bolivia because she has family there. For the majority of my class, this project provided a window into what it could be like to grow up in a different country, but for my students from other countries and/or with family outside the United States, my co-teacher and her experiences provided a much needed mirror for them in which they saw themselves in her lived experiences. Because I was born in the United States and have no family abroad, I cannot share this perspective. When the strengths that each co-teacher brings are respected and celebrated, your co-teaching pushes back against traditional views and practices. Typically, the general education teacher has been viewed as having expertise in content, and the special educator as having this in research-based strategies and techniques (Campbell & Jeter-Iles, 2017). However, differences in expertise can lead to "greater instructional delivery" (Friend & Barron, 2016, p. 4). Additionally, differences in background knowledge, life experiences, views, attitudes, and practices can lead to more diverse and ultimately supportive opportunities for learners.

The potential for a healthy classroom climate in which social-emotional skills are modeled daily, such as conflict resolution, respect, and parity between two adults makes co-teaching unique and a wonderful platform for life learning.

With two adults, there are more opportunities for students to bond and connect with at least one educator in the room and form strong relationships (Nierengarten & Hughes, 2010). Being able to see when adults are frustrated and find a resolution, when adults care and have positive relationships with each other, and when adults can collaborate with respect are all powerful examples for students to experience—whether or not they also see adult relationship models such as this in their homes.

Additionally, this model can provide support for educators in ways that solo teaching cannot. With a co-teacher, I can take breaks (this is huge!) and share in the overall workload. Yes, it takes time to co-plan, but sharing in the planning work, as well as daily practice, can lead to less fatigue and burnout. I found that when co-teaching, my teaching stamina was higher because I was less strained during the day, and I found excitement for my teaching in collaborating with my co-teachers. The possibilities for shared humor—not at learners' expense but instead in private between you and your co-teacher—are endless. Thinking about this benefit of having a co-teacher makes me smile as I reflect on all the shared, humorous experiences I had with my co-teachers. We were the only ones that knew of our students' funny behaviors or the wacky events across a day, and no amount of trying to explain a funny story to my mother at day's end could compare to the easy looks my co-teachers and I would trade across the room when we were internally dying of laughter! The camaraderie and respect that can come through living together in a classroom space can help to remove barriers and can push back against traditional modes of one authority in the classroom and lead to even more mutual camaraderie and respect (Cobb & Sharma, 2015; Nierengarten & Hughes, 2010), and can ultimately contribute to a more positive classroom and school environment.

Acknowledging that, although anecdotally, these benefits can be realized is critical, as I have shared from my personal experiences, in the research, findings related to the outcomes of co-teaching are mixed (Kauffman, Schumaker, Badar, & Hallenbeck, 2019; Van Garderen et al., 2012). As a result, several researchers argue for more research related to co-teaching to fully understand the benefits and costs of this dynamic practice (Strieker et al., 2013; Van Garderen et al., 2012). Regardless, the potential to realize these positive outcomes exists if you have the chance to be in a co-teaching relationship in your first few years of teaching.

Co-Teaching Through the Lens of Social Justice— Your Marriage Can Be Successful!

Approaching this relationship from the stance that you are seeking the benefits of this inclusive practice is a place to begin. Create your pros and work at it, new educator! Although some researchers believe that "while we have exemplars of what is and is not co-teaching, the process of co-teaching itself is natural, unfolding, and difficult to pin down" (Hurd & Weilbacher, 2017, p. 1), others believe that if you follow certain steps, you are more likely to find success with living within a co-teaching marriage in the classroom (Cook & Friend, 1995; Sileo, 2011). The metaphor of a professional marriage is realized through thinking through the stages that a natural marriage takes and finding similarities within the relationships of co-teachers. Every time you enter a new co-teaching relationship, you begin at Stage 1, the "Relationship-Building Stage," and hopefully make your way to Stage 3, the "Ongoing Relationship Stage." The more you know about these stages and where you are within them as a co-teaching team can be enlightening and allow you to strengthen what you bring to the relationship and how well your team ultimately functions for learners in your classroom.

The first stage in any marriage is getting to the point where you say, "I do," and decide to spend the rest of your lives (or at least this school year) together, that is, the "Relationship-Building Stage." In this stage, you and your co-teacher have to get to know each other. The more that you do this up front, the less likely you are to have fires that flare up later at inopportune moments due to a lack of understanding between you two. In my first co-teaching relationship with Flor, I did not know to first self-assess what I was bringing to the relationship related to my educational beliefs and values, and as a result, she and I were often at odds when our philosophies clashed. Do as I say, not as I did, and instead, enter this relationship with proper dating under your belt! Although this may sound silly, the more that you approach the relationship from a getting-to-know-you perspective, the more likely you are to find commonalities, consensus, and mutual respect. Within this stage, some specific steps will help lay this positive foundation:

- First, recognize that you each walk in with your own teaching identities—no matter how long or short your time in the field, this is who you are as an educator. Your co-teacher has his or her own identity. Starting from this understanding respects that you are each a dynamic individual with assets that run deep related to your background, your culture, your language, your upbringing, your experiences as a student growing up, your career preparation, and every other aspect that helps to make you each distinct.

- Enter this relationship knowing yourself—or least owning where you stand on beliefs, values, and practices that relate to your classroom and context. Cook and Friend (1995) have identified nine domains related to teaching and the co-teaching relationship that are a great place to begin, including analyzing your instructional beliefs, your beliefs related specifically to instructional planning, confidentiality in the classroom and school, parity signals between co-teachers, classroom noise levels, classroom routines, discipline, feedback, and your overarching pet peeves. Cook and Friend's seminal article about co-teaching from 1995 includes great probes for reflecting on these nine domains. Additionally, other educators have provided blog posts that can provide you with great probing questions to discuss as an individual and with your co-teacher. The Inclusion Lab at Brookes Publishing Company (2019) has a fantastic list of 25 questions[1] and details related to these, all packaged in a helpful handout that guides co-teachers through the possibly awkward phase of dating. Elizabeth Stein (2012) at MiddleWeb: A CoTeaching Blog outlines four key conversations[2] you should be having in your co-teaching relationship too.

- Then chat about these beliefs, attitudes, and perspectives with your co-teacher! Find a coffee shop, a library, a virtual platform, your classroom—somewhere where you can get

1   See Inclusion Lab in the Online Sources section at the end of the chapter.
2   See MiddleWeb: A CoTeaching Blog in the Online Sources section at the end of the chapter.

comfortable and share more about yourself. With every belief, attitude, and perspective you two share, you are building
understanding, trust, respect and camaraderie with your co-
teacher. Through conversations, you get to know each other,
and cultural competence, mutual respect, genuine care, and
respect for each other can grow. This will set a foundation for
a wonderful relationship and strong co-teaching!

Once you've worked through the Relationship-Building Stage, you are living the day-to-day with your co-teacher. This stage of the relationship is what
Sileo (2011) calls the "Marriage/ Co-Teaching Stage." During this stage, you
are working together daily, supporting learners, and hopefully supporting each
other in the process! After working through the nitty-gritty of what makes you
each tick in the first stage, in this stage of the relationship, you are getting down
to the logistics of teaching together. Figuring out when it works best to co-plan
and what this format looks like, identifying instructional areas of strength and
growth, having a common developmental understanding of the learners in your
classroom, and mapping out your teaching together is the focus in this stage.
Think about the following specifically:

- Consider your model of instruction. With two educators able
  to teach and teaching together, there are wonderful options
  for the shape that your instructional delivery takes, maximizing the instructional potential for all learners. Variety
  can keep a marriage fresh and exciting and exploring different models of co-teaching can be just what your team needs
  to better serve your students' and content needs, and keep
  you refreshed. These different models include (a) One Teach,
  One Observe, in which one teacher takes on the instructional
  responsibility and the other conducts observations either to
  identify targeted supports in the classroom or document
  learning or behaviors, and so on; (b) One Teach, One Assist,
  in which one teacher takes on the instructional responsibility and the other provides individual support; (c) Station

Teaching, where teachers establish different learning stations and provide support for students when they rotate to that station in the classroom; (d) Parallel Teaching, in which two teachers teach the same content simultaneously, each with one half of the class; (e) Alternative Teaching, in which one teacher takes responsibility for a large group of students and the other teacher works with a smaller group of the classroom who needs specific support; and (f) Team Teaching, where both teachers co-lead the whole class.

- There are pros and cons to using each model. When deciding which model to use and when, consider the student and content needs in your classroom (Friend & Bursuck, 2012), along with each of your teaching styles, and choose a model accordingly. The beauty of co-teaching is that you have options! Throughout the day, an opportunity for each of the models may surface in your co-teaching, which provides the likelihood for all learners to be better supported versus spending the day pulled out of the classroom or only supported off to the side of the room.
- The only way that Stage 2 progresses is through logistics and setting structures in place for co-planning and co-teaching. Utilizing protocols for co-planning meetings can be very helpful for holding team members accountable. Consider this tool created by the William and Mary College Training and Technical Assistance Center[3] (2015) that provides guidelines for how to prepare for, engage in, and reflect upon co-planning sessions to maximize the benefits of your co-teaching practice.

The final stage of co-teaching, like within a real marriage, is the "Ongoing Relationship Stage." To live successfully in this stage, predictability and consistency within your co-teaching relationship are required. The need for common planning time is essential, but teachers have become creative through the use of

---

3   See William & Mary Training & Technical Assistance Center in the Online Sources section at the end of the chapter.

cloud-based collaborative sites, such as Google Drive and Dropbox, and online communication tools, such as Skype, text messaging, and e-mail, to collaborate in and out of school with co-teachers (Campbell & Jeter-Iles, 2017). This stage requires the ability to troubleshoot and manage the ebb and flow of the school year with minimal hiccups or disruptions. Living in this stage offers benefits for learners, you, and your co-teacher, and your instruction, as well.

- Decide what your system for communication, shared resources, and co-planning will be. Staying organized can help, so determining whether an internal shared site or a cloud-based platform, such as Dropbox or Google Drive, will be the best way for you and your co-teacher to collaboratively plan and work together. Explore possibilities within your school and district and find out if any district policies require you to co-plan in a specific way or with a specific platform.
- Consider what your troubleshooting plan will be when issues surface. Will you first address the problem in class and then follow up right after school over the phone, considering options, and deciding an appropriate solution? No matter what direction your plan takes, in this stage, the goal is to identify issues quickly, develop alternative plans of action while analyzing the risks and benefits, then choose your course of action and take it. Then finally, evaluate the results and assume responsibility. This will require clear communication within your relationship. This way, no matter whether a child is vomiting, a parent is upset, a student is acting out, or your pants rip down the inside seam (this really happened to me!), you and your co-teacher will be able to roll with the hit and keep moving. When communication issues or troubleshooting have not been addressed, cracks within your relationship will impact everything from your well-being to your students' learning.
- When issues are quickly mitigated, and you feel comfortable within this relationship, you can get to the real work of critically reflecting on your teaching practices and whether they

are as socially just and inclusive as you believe them to be. Educators with the Committee for Action on Social Justice within the British Columbia Teachers' Federation (2019) have created a helpful social justice checklist within this booklet[4] to walk educators through critically reflecting upon their teaching practice. Conducting this introspection as a team can provide insights into different beliefs about the teaching in your classroom and provide an opportunity to support each other in growing and learning together to provide the best instruction for all learners.

Conclusion

Although I do not believe I ever truly made it to this final stage with Flor, my first co-teacher, because we never found a comfortable and easy consistency in our practice together, within a few years, by being conscious of the stages and keeping all my students and my desire to provide access to them at the forefront, I definitely moved much more smoothly through the three stages and was so in sync with my co-teachers that we had few issues and our teaching was the strongest it had been for each of us! Ultimately, for inclusion to work and social justice to be realized for all learners in classrooms, students must see inclusion modeled by their co-teachers. Seeing their co-teachers as equal and contributing members of the classroom is critical to offset power differentials and status. What makes this relationship work and truly benefit all learners is when both educators enter the relationship willingly, create mutual goals, share resources, work towards parity, share responsibility for key decisions, and share accountability. Many more resources are readily available for today's educators to support them in living in co-teaching relationships than when I became a first-year teacher, such as this quick blog post[5] by an elementary education teacher and posted on the National Educators Association website (Marston, n.d.) or the great infographic in this blog post[6] on the *Cult of Pedagogy* website

---

4   See British Columbia Teacher Federation in the Online Sources at the end of the chapter.
5   See National Educators Association in the Online Sources section at the end of the chapter.
6   See Cult of Pedagogy in the Online Sources section at the end of the chapter.

covering the author's tips for how to make the most of a co-teaching relationship (Peery, 2017). There is no reason that any new educator should live through the "don'ts" of my first few years with Flor. Embury and Kroeger (2012) state it best: "Teacher behavior toward one another can create a visible 'us versus them' mentality among students or it can create a community of inclusive learners and teachers" (p. 110). Keeping a focus on inclusion and working to make this relationship work can do much to enhance your teaching and professional work and provide access—such an integral feature of social justice for our learners and society.

Reflection Questions and Activities

1. *Reflect on past co-teaching experiences you have been in either as a teacher candidate or first-year teacher. Did your experiences mirror my first ones with Flor where they were challenging and disappointing? Or were they the opposite—invigorating and enlightening? Consider what made these relationships work or not work and how this connected with the aspects presented in this chapter about the professional marriage stages of co-teaching.*

2. *Have you experienced co-teaching as a learner before? From a student perspective, what did you think about the relationship you observed your two educators having? What impact did having more than one educator have on you? What impact did this have on your class as a whole?*

3. *If you did not experience co-teaching as a student growing up, what impact do you think having two educators could or would have had on you?*

4. *As you consider your co-teaching relationship or one that you will be beginning in your first few years of teaching, remember to start with your attitudes and beliefs that you carry with you into the relationship. Consider using a helpful tool such as S.H.A.R.E. (Murawski & Dieker, 2013) to reflect and come from a place of honesty and ask your teaching partner to also complete a tool like*

this so that you can discuss your results: https://gatewayimpact.
org/student-agency/resources/share-co-teaching-collaboration

5. *Consider the British-Columbia Teachers Federation's full Social
   Justice Teaching Lens Teacher Resource Guide at* https://bctf.ca/
   uploadedFiles/Public/SocialJustice/Publications/SJLens.pdf.
   *Reflect on each of the four aspects presented in this social justice
   framework of access, agency, advocacy, and solidarity in action.
   This chapter has made the case that the practice of co-teaching
   supports the pillar of access. Do you see any other aspects of social
   justice at play in co-teaching relationships and co-taught classrooms? Make the case for one of the other critical aspects identified
   in this resource guide and how co-teaching works to support that
   aspect of social justice.*

Online Sources

British Columbia Teacher Federation: https://bctf.ca/uploadedFiles/Public/Social
   Justice/Publications/SJLens.pdf
Cult of Pedagogy: https://www.cultofpedagogy.com/co-teaching-push-in/
Inclusion Lab: https://blog.brookespublishing.com/25-questions-for-new-co-
   teachers-to-answer-together/
MiddleWeb: A CoTeaching Blog: https://www.middleweb.com/3905/4-critical-co-
   teacher-conversations/
National Educators Association: http://www.nea.org/tools/6-steps-to-successful-
   co-teaching.html
William & Mary Training & Technical Assistance Center: https://www.middleweb.
   com/3905/4-critical-co-teacher-conversations/

References

Baker, S., & Milner, J. (2006). Complexities of collaboration: Intensity of mentors'
   responses to paired and single student teachers. *Action in Teacher Education,*
   28(3), 61–72.
Beninghof, A. M. (2011). *Co-teaching that works: Effective strategies for working together in today's inclusive classrooms.* Hoboken, NJ: John Wiley & Sons.

British Columbia Teacher Federation Committee for Action on Social Justice. (2019). *A social justice lens: A teaching resource guide.* Retrieved from https://bctf.ca/uploadedFiles/Public/SocialJustice/Publications/SJLens.pdf

Brookes Publishing Company. (2019). 25 questions for NEW co-teachers to answer together [Blog post]. Brookes Publishing Company. Retrieved from https://blog.brookespublishing.com/25-questions-for-new-co-teachers-to-answer-together/

Campbell, D. B. Jr., & Jeter-Iles, P. (2017). Educator perceptions on co-teaching more than a decade later. *Journal of Behavioral and Social Sciences, 4*, 156–163.

CCSSO's Interstate Teacher Assessment and Support Consortium. (2013, April). InTASC model core teaching standards and learning progressions for teachers 1.0. Retrieved from https://ccsso.org/sites/default/files/2017-12/2013_INTASC_Learning_Progressions_for_Teachers.pdf

Chitiyo, J., & Brinda, W. (2018). Teacher preparedness in the use of co-teaching in inclusive classrooms. *Support for Learning, 33*(1), 38–51.

Cobb, C. & Sharma, M. (2015). I've got you covered: Adventures in social justice-informed co-teaching. *Journal of the Scholarship of Teaching and Learning, 15*(4), 41–57.

Cook, L., & Friend, M. (1995). Co-teaching: Guidelines for creating effective practices. *Focus on Exceptional Children, 28*(3), 1–16.

Education for all Handicapped Children Act. (1975). Retrieved from https://www.govinfo.gov/content/pkg/STATUTE-89/pdf/STATUTE-89-Pg773.pdf

Embury, D. C., & Kroeger, S. D. (2012). Let's ask the kids: Consumer constructions of co-teaching. *International Journal of Special Education, 27*, 102–112.

Every Student Succeeds Act [ESSA]. (2015). Retrieved from https://www.congress.gov/114/plaws/publ95/PLAW-114publ95.pdf

Faraclas, K. L. (2018). A professional development training model for improving co-teaching performance. *International Journal of Special Education, 33*, 524–540.

Friend, M., & Barron, T. (2016). Co-teaching as a special education service: Is classroom collaboration a sustainable practice? *Educational Practice and Reform, 1*, 1–12.

Friend, M., & Bursuck, W. D. (2012). *Including students with special needs: A practical guide for classroom teachers* (6th ed.). Upper Saddle River, NJ: Pearson.

Friend, M., & Cook, L. (2013). *Interactions: Collaboration skills for school professionals* (7th ed.). Boston, MA: Pearson Education, Inc.

Griffin, C. C., Jones, H. A., & Kilgore, K. L., (2006). A qualitative study of student teachers' experiences with collaborative problem solving. *Teacher Education & Special Education, 29*, 44–55.

Hoppey, D. (2016). Developing educators for inclusive classrooms through a rural school-university partnership. *Rural Special Education Quarterly, 35*(1), 13–22.

Howard, L., & Potts, E. A. (2009). Using co-planning time: Strategies for a successful co-teaching marriage. *Teaching Exceptional Children Plus, 5*(4), 1–12.

Hurd, E., & Weilbacher, G. (2017). "You want me to do what?" The benefits of co-teaching in the middle level. *Middle Grades Review, 3*(1), article 4. Retrieved from https://eric.ed.gov/?id=EJ1154829

Illinois State Board of Education. (2013). Illinois professional teaching standards. Retrieved from https://www.isbe.net/Documents/IL_prof_teaching_stds.pdf

Individuals with Disability Education Act Amendments of 1997 [IDEA]. (1997). Retrieved from https://www.congress.gov/105/plaws/publ17/PLAW-105publ17.pdf

Individuals with Disability Education Act Amendments of 2004 [IDEA]. (2004). Retrieved from https://www.congress.gov/108/plaws/publ446/PLAW-108publ446.pdf

Kamens, M. W. (2007). Learning about co-teaching: A collaborative student teaching experience for pre-service teachers. *Teacher Education & Special Education, 30,* 155–166.

Kauffman, J. M., Schumaker, J. B., Badar, J., & Hallenbeck, B. A. (2019). Where special education goes to die. *Exceptionality, 27,* 149–166.

Keefe, E. B., & Moore, V. (2004). The challenge of co-teaching in inclusive classrooms at the high school level: What the teachers told us. *American Secondary Education, 32*(3), 77–88.

Magiera, K., & Zigmond, N. (2005). Co-teaching in middle school classrooms under routine conditions: Does the instructional experience differ for students with disabilities in co-taught and solo-taught classes? *Learning Disabilities Research and Practice, 20*(2), 79–85.

Marston, N. (n.d.). 6 steps to successful co-teaching: Helping special education and regular education teachers work together. NEA. Retrieved from http://www.nea.org/tools/6-steps-to-successful-co-teaching.html.

McKenzie, R. (2009). A national survey of pre-service preparation for collaboration. *Teacher Education & Special Education, 32,* 379–393.

Murawski, W. (2019). Successful co-teaching. Special Education Today. Retrieved from CEC Today: https://www.cec.sped.org/News/Special-Education-Today/Need-to-Know/Need-to-Know-CoTeaching

Murawski, W. W., & Dieker, L. A. (2008). 50 ways to keep your co-teacher: Strategies for before, during, and after co-teaching. *Teaching Exceptional Children, 40*(4), 40–48.

Murawski, W. W., & Dieker, L. A. (2013). *Leading the co-teaching dance: Leadership strategies to enhance team outcomes.* Arlington, VA: Council for Exceptional Children.

National Center for Education Statistics. (2008). The nation's report card. Retrieved from http://nces.ed.gov/nationsreportcard

Nierengarten, G. M., & Hughes, T. (2010). What teachers wish administrators knew about co-teaching in high schools. *Electronic Journal for Teacher Education, 2*(6), 1–20.

No Child Left Behind Act [NCLB]. (2001). Retrieved from https://www2.ed.gov/policy/elsec/leg/esea02/107-110.pdf

Peery, A. (2017, February 5). Co-teaching: How to make it work. [web log post]. Cult of Pedagogy. Retrieved from https://www.cultofpedagogy.com/co-teaching-push-in/

Rivera, E. A., McMahon, S. D., & Keys, C. B. (2014). Collaborative teaching: School implementation and connections with outcomes among students with disabilities. *Journal of Prevention & Intervention in the Community, 42*(1), 72–85.

Russell, E. (2016). The teacher floater: Let's define best practices. *Texas Child Care Quarterly, 40*(1), 1–7.

Schwartz, S. (2018, December 5). What it takes to make co-teaching work. *Education Week*. Retrieved online from https://www.edweek.org/ew/articles/2018/12/05/what-it-takes-to-make-co-teaching-work.html

Shim, J., Hestenes, L., & Cassidy, D. (2004). Teacher structure and child care quality in preschool classrooms. *Journal of Research in Childhood Education, 19*, 143–157.

Sileo, J. M. (2011). Co-teaching: Getting to know your partner. *Teaching Exceptional Children, 43*(5), 32–38.

Stein, E. (2012, October 28). 4 key co-teacher conversations [Blog post]. Middle Web. Retrieved from https://www.middleweb.com/3905/4-critical-co-teacher-conversations/

Strieker, T., Gillis, B., & Zong, G. (2013, Fall). Improving pre-service middle-school teachers' confidence, competence, and commitment to co-teaching in inclusive classrooms. *Teacher Education Quarterly, 40*(4), 159–180.

William & Mary Training & Technical Assistance Center. (2015, February 20). *Co-planning for student success consideration packet*. Retrieved from https://education.wm.edu/centers/ttac/documents/packets/coplanning.pdf

U.S. Department of Health and Human Services & U.S. Department of Education. (2015, September 14). Policy statement on inclusion of children with disabilities in early childhood programs. Retrieved from https://www2.ed.gov/policy/speced/guid/earlylearning/joint-statement-full-text.pdf

Van Garderen, D., Stormont, M., & Goel, N. (2012). Collaboration between general and special educators and student outcomes: A need for more research. *Psychology in the Schools, 49*, 483–497.

Whitebook, M., Gomby, D., Bellm, D., Sakai, L., & Kipnis, F. (2009). *Preparing Teachers of Young Children: The Current State of Knowledge, and a Blueprint for the Future. Part 2: Effective teacher preparation in early care and education:*

Toward a comprehensive research agenda. Berkeley, CA: Center for the Study of Child Care Employment, Institute for Research on Labor and Employment, University of California at Berkeley.

Contributor Bios

DR. JEANNETTE D. ALARCÓN is a teacher educator who works with both pre-service and practicing teachers to understand culturally relevant pedagogy, social studies education, and critical awareness as key tools for promoting access and equity in elementary education. She has worked in the field of education for 20 years and the field of teacher education for almost a decade. Her research investigates the ways in which teachers work through moments of dissonance in order to become more equitable and inclusive in their teaching.

DR. BRITTNEY L. BECK is an Assistant Professor of Teacher Education at California State University, Bakersfield. Her body of work resides at the intersection of democratic education, teacher and student activism, the history of education, and university-school-community partnerships. At these intersections, she explores how school systems can best engage the material and ideological realities of the community to inform and reform curricula, pedagogy, and school climate initiatives in ways that engage teachers and students as active citizens. She has published her work in the *American Educational Research Journal, Perspectives on Urban Education*, and the *Journal of Critical Thought and Praxis*.

DR. BRE EVANS-SANTIAGO is an Assistant Professor in the Teacher Education Department at California State University, Bakersfield. Her research focuses on culturally-sustaining pedagogy and practices in TK–8 schools. Dr. Evans-Santiago also has research experience in improvement science as it relates to educational programs. Her current research projects include, but are not limited to, lesbian, gay, bisexual, transgender, and queer issues in education and supporting minority males. She has published work in *Young Children, New Teacher Advocate* and *Quality Approaches in Higher Education*.

DR. KIRA A. HAMANN is an Instructional Assistant Professor of Early Childhood and Elementary Education at Illinois State University and serves as a consultant on several Illinois early childhood teacher preparation initiatives for the Governor's Office of Early Childhood, the Illinois Network for Child-care Resource and Referral Network, and the Illinois State Board of Education, among others. Her bachelor's (Illinois State University) and master's (Erikson Institute) are both in early childhood education, and her doctorate from Illinois State University is in curriculum and instruction. Prior to her current roles, she was an early childhood educator in the Chicago Public Schools. As a certified Positive Discipline Parent and Teacher Educator, she leads professional development for parents and teachers in the areas of teaching social-emotional skills, problem solving, and building family and classroom communities. Her research focuses on teacher preparation, classroom management and community building, professional development, and new teacher mentorship.

DR. JAY C. PERCELL, after spending a decade as a high school English teacher, now teaches literacy and technology curriculum courses for undergraduate secondary education teacher candidates. He focuses on utilizing 21st-century skills to teach a diverse population of students. He has redesigned several of his course sections with a focus on urban education, embedding opportunities for candidates to participate in clinical experiences within Chicago Public School District.

DR. ANNI K. REINKING is currently an Assistant Professor in the Department of Teaching and Learning at Southern Illinois University Edwardsville. She is also the co-president of the Illinois Division of Early Childhood, the president of the Illinois Association of Early Childhood Teacher Educators, the co-chair of the Sharing A Vision conference, and a faculty lead on a statewide committee working on competency-based, technology-embedded assessments. She has degrees in psychology, early childhood education, and curriculum and instruction.

DR. DAVID SANDLES, a longtime K–12 teacher and restorative classroom specialist, is currently a full-time lecturer in the Teacher Education Department at California State University, Bakersfield. He is a Western Association Schools and Colleges (WASC) evaluator dedicated to improving schools and instructional practices that directly impact students. A passionate early literacy proponent, he worked in the Reading Across the Disciplines program, tutored with the Kern Adult Literacy Council, and is the president of the Friends of the Library for a local library branch. His research interests include the development and strengthening of all Black men educators, the academic achievement of underserved populations, Black superheroes, and early establishment of foundational reading skills.

DR. ADAM SAWYER is an Assistant Professor of Teacher Education and Director of the Liberal Studies Program at California State University, Bakersfield. His work examines the theorization, design, and impact of innovative teacher professional development programs and pedagogies responsive to the cultural and linguistic needs of immigrants, language minorities, and other historically marginalized populations. He is also a specialist on the topics of global migration, transnationalism, and displacement and their intersection with schooling. His work has been published by such outlets *Teacher Education Quarterly*, the *Journal of Latinos and Education*, and *International Migration Review*, and he is the co-editor of the 2013 Teachers College Press volume *Regarding Educación: Mexican American Schooling, Immigration, and Binational Solutions*. Previous to his academic career, Adam served as a Spanish bilingual elementary school teacher in California and as an academic consultant to the Mexican Ministry of Education.

DR. MIRNA TRONCOSO SAWYER is an Assistant Professor of Public Health in the Department of Health Sciences at California State University Northridge. Her research is focused on addressing overweight, obesity, and related chronic diseases among Latinos, an underresearched population. In her research on food decisions, she has aimed to understand how the dinnertime routine is shaped by food preferences, beliefs, and the community food environment. She is also currently developing an intervention to understand how Latinos with prediabetes respond to genomic risk information. She has more than 10 years' experience as a health educator and now trains future health educators. Her research has been published in journals such as the *Diabetes Educator* and the *California Journal of Health Promotion*.

DR. SARA SCHWERDTFEGER is an Assistant Professor in the Elementary Education/Early Childhood/Special Education department and Director of the

Professional Development Schools (PDS) program at Emporia State University, Emporia, Kansas. She currently teaches math and science methods courses for undergraduate students, leads the PDS program, and teaches graduate courses in the Instructional Specialist: STEM program. Dr. Schwerdtfeger has been in education for 22 years, including 16 years of elementary school teaching in Grades 1 through 6. She has a master's degree in elementary education, graduate endorsements in teacher leadership and building leadership/administration from Emporia State University, a graduate endorsement in English as a Second Language, and a PhD in Curriculum and Instruction in Mathematics Education from Kansas State University, Manhattan, Kansas.

Laura Shelton is in her fourth year of teaching and is currently a fifth and sixth-grade teacher at The Experiential School of Greensboro (TESG), a new grassroots charter school in downtown Greensboro, North Carolina, that focuses on social justice, experiential education, and arts integration. In her current position, Laura teaches all subjects in a multiage classroom, and prior to teaching at TESG, she taught fourth and fifth grades in other districts in central North Carolina. She has a Master of Arts in Teaching from the University of North Carolina at Greensboro and a Bachelor of Arts in Theatre Performance from Greensboro College.

Dr. Mahmoud Suleiman is a Professor of Teacher Education at California State University, Bakersfield (CSUB). He earned his PhD from Arizona State University in 1993. He previously taught at the Maricopa Community College District, Arizona; Arizona State University, Tempe; and Fort Hays State University, Kansas. He joined CSUB in 1999 and has taught a variety of credential and graduate courses in the areas of multiculturalism, reading/literacy, action research, instructional leadership, and second-language acquisition, among others. During his tenure at CSUB, he served as Director of the Multiple Subject Credential Program and as Chair of the Teacher Education Department, as well as Chair of the Advanced Educational Studies. He is a Fulbright Scholar (2009/2010) and completed his residency at the Bahrain Teachers College, University of Bahrain, Bahrain, and was a Fulbright Scholar (2016/2017) at the Faculty of Educational Sciences and Teachers' Training, An-Najah National University, Nablus, Palestine.

Index